ORTHOGRAPHY IN SHAKESPEARE AND ELIZABETHAN DRAMA

ORTHOGRAPHY IN SHAKESPEARE AND ELIZABETHAN DRAMA

A Study of Colloquial Contractions, Elision, Prosody and Punctuation

by

A. C. PARTRIDGE

UNIVERSITY OF NEBRASKA PRESS · Lincoln

Publishers on the Plains

UNP

© A. C. Partridge 1964

Library of Congress Catalog card number 64–17222

Manufactured in the United States of America

Published by arrangement with Edward Arnold (Publishers) Ltd.

Preface

In these studies language questions bearing on Shakespearian textual scholarship are tentatively raised. The trend of recent investigations has not deterred me from offering theories which I have based upon a close study of original texts.

Much that has been written stems from discussions with scholars in England during 1948, 1950 and 1953, when I was honoured with a fellowship from the Leverhulme Trust. My indebtedness to the advice of scholars no longer with us, Sir Walter Greg, Sir William Craigie, Professor D. Nichol Smith, Professor F. P. Wilson and Mr. John Munro, is inestimable; and I owe no less to Professors J. Dover Wilson, Peter Alexander, Allardyce Nicoll and Dr. Percy Simpson.

In 1950 a Dominion Fellowship at St. John's College, Cambridge, made it possible for me to renew the investigations begun two years earlier with Shakespeare's *Henry VIII*. The courtesy and solicitude of the late Masters, Mr. E. A. Benians and Sir James Wordie, the privileges I enjoyed in the use of the Bodleian Library in 1948, and the criticism of friends at the Shakespeare Institute, Stratford-on-Avon, in 1953, among them Professor R. A. Foakes, all contributed to whatever merit this work may have.

I should like to thank Messrs. Bowes and Bowes Ltd. for permission to reprint, with improvements, my essay, *The Problem of Henry VIII Re-opened*, published in 1949, but now out of print; the Cambridge University Press and Professor Allardyce Nicoll for allowing me to use much of my article on 'Shakespeare's Orthography in *Venus and Adonis* and Some Early Quartos', from *Shakespeare Survey* 7 of 1954; and the Editor of *Shakespeare Quarterly*, Dr. McManaway, for permitting the use of some paragraphs from a review of the new Arden Edition of *Othello*, published in the Winter 1959 issue of his Journal.

University of the Witwatersrand,   A. C. Partridge
   Johannesburg.
     28th April, 1963

Contents

APPENDICES

Abbreviations

Chapter 1

The Meaning of 'Orthography', and its use in Shakespearian Textual Criticism

THE object of this study is to submit Elizabethan dramatic language, as nearly as it can be ascertained to be the product of a playwright's hand, to detailed graphic analysis, and so to add to our knowledge of the textual history of the plays. A study of Elizabethan and Jacobean plays in general, and the language of Shakespeare and Ben Jonson in particular, persuade me that pointers to habits of expression of any dramatist of the time are to be found in his use of colloquial contractions and weakenings, marks of elision, and certain grammatical forms. When in 1948 I began with what was probably Shakespeare's last play, viz. *Henry VIII*, I was conscious that no finality on the subject of authorship could be reached from conclusions based on a single and late text. Chronological examination of the whole canon, beginning with the earliest of the good quartos, seemed necessary.

Shakespearian orthography has not been placed in relation to its historical background, nor is such work as has been done systematic or thorough. What follows is itself only a sketch and a location of some of the landmarks.

As the term 'orthography' occurs frequently in these pages, it is necessary to justify and define its use. When the word came into English via French in the late Middle Ages, it meant 'right writing'. As late as 1640 Simon Daines in *Orthoepia Anglicana* so defined it, and distinguished it from *orthoepie*, or 'right speaking'.[1] Most of Daines's section on Orthography deals with capital letters, punctuation and elision. Grammarians of an earlier generation, such as Hart and Bullokar, seemed to give to orthography a more restricted meaning (one favoured by the *Oxford English Dictionary*), viz. 'that part of grammar

[1] *Orthoepia Anglicana*, ed. M. Rösler and R. Brotanek, Halle, 1908, p. 75, lines 5–12.

that determines the value of letters, individually or in combination, in making sounds or words'. This was nothing more nor less than spelling, which Hart and Bullokar realized as needing reform and regularity. They failed in their proposals because writers and printers ignored the suggested improvements as figments of pedants.[1] Eventually the practical considerations of haste during the polemic activity of the Civil War in the seventeenth century compelled the printers to systematize.

Along with developments in spelling went changes in pointing or *distinction*. In sixteenth-century England punctuation was lacking in the subtleties of Western European practice. In ephemeral English works, such as plays then were, punctuation was at first almost entirely impressionistic. When piracy or economic pressure compelled theatre-companies to part with the rights of their plays, speed in getting their wares to market was, for the publishers, a primary consideration; there was neither time nor much reason for the printer to revise punctuation. It was only in subsequent editions, of such plays as *Richard II*, that the dramatic punctuation which Percy Simpson and Dover Wilson attribute to Shakespeare, was gradually superseded. Printers of the last quarter of the sixteenth century had, in fact, learnt much from Continental preceptors, especially from editions of the classics and the works of Latin grammarians; they acquired a logical system of punctuation, founded largely on the grammarian Ramus (Pierre de la Ramée) and the printer Aldus Manutius, whose *Interpungendi Ratio* appeared in 1566. At the beginning of the seventeenth century English writers who were also classical scholars, such as Bacon and Jonson, followed this lead; so did educated scribes like Ralph Crane, who made privately commissioned copies of works. Independently, the techniques of punctuation were often carried to extremes of fussiness; for example, the use of the co-ordinating comma in Ben Jonson, and the varieties of elision and parenthesis found in Ralph Crane's manuscripts. While the editing of the plays was poor in textual accuracy, a more sophisticated orthography became a general feature of all published works intended for the new generation of readers.

Except in a technical or historical sense, the term orthography is now little used; spelling and punctuation are separate conventions. But in the sixteenth and seventeenth centuries their functions to some extent overlapped. For instance, elided letters or syllables could be indicated equally by a modification of spelling or by punctuation. Before 1600

[1] See Sir Philip Sidney's remarks on English Grammar in 'An Apology for Poetry', *Elizabethan Critical Essays*, ed. Gregory Smith, Vol. II, p. 204, lines 9–14.

the apostrophe to mark elisions and contractions was used mainly by those printers and scribes who wanted their works to reach a scholarly or aristocratic circle. Plays, when Shakespeare became associated with the drama, were non-literary works; they employed many contractions, which were achieved at first by the simple omission of letters. But at the turn of the century plays had begun to acquire prestige as poetry. Then metrical accuracy was deemed important, marks of elision began to predominate, where before they had been numerically inconspicuous, being simply taken for granted. Jonson was a stickler for the carefully pointed elision; after 1600 the dramatic orthography of his plays was remarkable for its range of colloquial and contracted forms of all kinds.

A study of orthography in the thirty years 1593–1623, the period of earliest publication of Shakespeare's works, should account for all aspects of the graphic representation of words, both in verse and prose. It is unsatisfactory to think of the orthography of that period implying spelling or other conventions, which did not exist. There was, perhaps, a *sensus communis* or common denominator of correct usage visible in the writings of this age; but it is small and obvious. If, on the other hand, orthography is seen as external grammatical authority, a system comparable to Bullokar's or Hart's, English never submitted kindly to it. It is preferable, therefore, to convert a rather vague term to preciser use by defining *ORTHOGRAPHY* as 'that part of writing, peculiar to author, scribe, editor or printing-house, which is concerned with accidentals such as spelling, punctuation, elision, syncope and contractions generally'. This definition has the merit of dealing with actualities, viz. literary works, the product of an individual or a house, often of both.

Because the printing-house has undoubtedly tampered with Shakespeare's manuscript orthography, a reconstruction of his writing has been generally regarded as impossible. Recovery cannot, indeed, be reduced to scientific method, like the reconstruction of a dinosaur from a few fossil bones. The evolution of a Shakespearian text from the pen of the author to its earliest printed form must, therefore, remain largely a matter of conjecture. Although Heminge and Condell declared that they had 'scarce received from him a blot in his papers', *prima facie* the inference must be that Shakespeare endeavoured to supply his Company with fair copy. The extent to which foul papers needed to be made legible may not, however, have been considerable; the compact emotional power of the major speeches, as well as their syntax, confirms that the mind and hand of the author did indeed go together.

The success of the Chamberlain's Men may have been mainly due to their team-work; they were a band of friends united in their art, not merely a theatrical syndicate. If parts of the earlier plays had to be re-copied before submission for licensing, as likely as not the work would have been done by a fellow-actor. In the more prosperous later days, which took the Company into the seventeenth century, Shakespeare would probably have had the help of a professional amanuensis. The copy for *Richard II* (Q_1) seems to have been the work either of Shake-speare's own hand or a careful transcription by a competent assistant. Though the book-holder usually prepared plays for production, Shakespeare's direction of his own plays is more than a possibility; he would then be likely to submit his draft in more or less final form. The Company probably had a manuscript copy of every play in its present or past repertory, and these would be either (a) an author's foul papers, or (b) an author's fair copy, or (c) a version wholly or in part another person's transcript. According to the exigencies of the Company, any one of these types of copy could be sent to the printer; but publication did not voluntarily happen until a play had lost its immediate appeal with the public. An endeavour would always be made to retain the prompt copy, bearing the precious licence. Use of the latter would usually have been made when the plays were assembled for the First Folio. Piracy seems to have been checked after 1603, owing to royal protection of the Company; probably no play then went to the printer, except by the back-door.

Characteristic evidence of Shakespeare's autograph in parts of the canon is found in the scarcity of marks of elision, the nature and scope of the colloquial contractions, individual and archaic spellings, and a preference for certain grammatical forms. Many intended contractions and elisions are not indicated in the earlier quartos, as they are in later texts, when the orthography of the plays came steadily under the influence of Ben Jonson and the orthoepists. Consequently the lines have internal extra syllables, and it is a matter of conjecture whether they are intentional or oversights of the printer. The use of initial capitals, more considerable in First Folio texts, is a less soluble problem, especially in relation to dramatic emphasis. There was both a scribal and printing convention to begin certain classes of substantives with capital letters; but these capitals may well have been absent in the author's manuscript. Generally, nouns are the parts of speech that call for most emphasis; but I think that Shakespeare himself (along with other dramatists) capitalized few substantives, and those without regard to their dramatic significance. There is a suggestion in *Venus and Adonis* and elsewhere that he employed *unusual stops* before words, in certain situations, to secure poetic, dramatic or rhetorical effect; and there seems no reason why he should have employed two techniques simultaneously.

In the absence of any authenticated Shakespearian manuscripts, certainty about his spelling is impossible; one may only suggest from the evidence a degree of probability regarding his practice, and allowance must be made for error or inconsistency. Uniformity, as we have seen, was as yet an unfulfilled grammarian's dream; but although a writer was under no compulsion to spell words in the same way in the same text, his own habits and ease might be supposed to restrict excessive variation. In regard to Shakespearian orthography, I should be disposed only to suggest the following:

If a certain spelling of a particular word (or a certain graphic rendering of a particular sound) occurs with reasonable regularity in texts that good bibliographical or other evidence leads us to believe are based directly on autograph copy, then the spelling in question may be assumed to derive from Shakespeare himself.

Regularity, however, can never be absolute, since there is the ever-present possibility that original spellings were subsequently altered by the compositor or some other agent. For instance, characteristically Shakespearian full spellings (e.g. *sonne* for *son*) were frequently dispensed with in the verse of the First Folio because the compositor was limited by the width of the column. A check on printing-house practice is fruitfully made, however, by examining the spelling of other published plays from the same printer, dated as nearly as possible to the Shakespearian text.

That dramatists did not consistently represent sounds by certain spellings, was partly due to there being approved alternative methods of representing the same sound. Shakespeare, an individualistic West-countryman who came to London at a time when there were few rules of spelling and no real English dictionaries, might be expected, when in doubt, to favour pronunciation spellings. His orthography may even, on occasion, represent a peculiar Warwickshire pronunciation of some types of words, in such spellings, for instance, as *spleet* (split), *cleffe* (cliff), *week* (wick); the memorable pun on *ships* and *sheeps* (Warwickshire plural) in *Love's Labour's Lost* springs to mind. But I am inclined to believe that, if this longer vowel was a Western peculiarity, it had by 1600 also reached London (cf. *creeple* for *cripple* twice in Acts XIV of the *Authorised Version*). The converse was certainly in London usage;

the spellings *ee* and *i* (e.g. in the variants *been* and *bin*) must have been recognized alternatives in the city for a sound whose length and quality were indeterminate for the untrained Elizabethan phonetic ear.

If we allow it to be derived from Shakespearian manuscript, the earliest quarto to reproduce the author's spelling and elision is *Richard II* (1597). From this it appears that Shakespeare was a more painstaking orthographer than is sometimes supposed; indeed, his capacity for taking pains may also explain the reputation he enjoyed among his fellows of producing immaculate papers. If, in the printed pages, there are lapses, they can be explained by the printers' probable difficulty with his hand, or with his line arrangement. But printers and scribes, in general, though they were sometimes careful to preserve Shakespeare's text, had no more scruple in the matter of spelling and punctuation than had editors of the eighteenth century, because Shakespeare's own practice was considered arbitrary.

The greatest reliance cannot, therefore, be placed on spelling and punctuation, in the transmission of which there is an element of chance, and almost always the possibility of scribal or compositor interference. There is less ground for suspecting interference in accidence and contracted forms, and practically none in the idiosyncrasies of syntax. To these some attention will therefore be directed. The standard work on Shakespeare's grammar is W. Franz's *Shakespeare Grammatik*; but the book makes little attempt to separate material gleaned from quartos, folios or modern editions, nor to apply orthographical or grammatical tests to textual problems.

When this has been done, and more attention paid to seemingly trivial elements of morphology, some new light will be thrown on Shakespeare's text, of which an old spelling edition has still to be prepared comparable to that of Herford and Simpson for Ben Jonson. It has been said that the English, in their methods of scholarship, have a passion for details. If this is true, it is to the English themselves, and not to the Continental scholars that we should look for deeper knowledge of Shakespeare's mastery of language and of the secrets which go to its making.

The facts of the new bibliography, which have revolutionized Shakespeare textual studies, need supplementing; but it is difficult to see how textual knowledge can be advanced without closer analysis of Shakespeare's methods of composition.

Chapter 2

The Rise of Clipped Forms of Speech in the Fifteenth and Sixteenth Centuries; their Importation into Printed Drama

HISTORIES of the English language, with few exceptions, give inadequate notice to the remarkable development of colloquial and poetical contractions in the sixteenth and early seventeenth centuries. There was considerable appreciation of their usefulness in dramatic dialogue in the last quarter of the sixteenth century, which was elaborated in the first quarter of the seventeenth century. In the years which followed the Restoration, colloquial weakening, slurring and curtailment reached their apogee, declining again under the fire of eighteenth-century Augustan correctness, and the satirical discredit which Swift, in particular, poured upon them.

Historical dates for the rise of contractions in speech can only be conjecturally assigned, since contractions in colloquial parlance certainly antedated their appearance in literature. Contractions are as old as language itself, and represent phonetic facility, organic laziness or bucolic peculiarity. Notable curtailments in Anglo-Saxon were, for instance, syncope of the inflexion of the second and third person singular present indicative e.g. *hilpst*, *hilpð*, and the combination of the negative particle *ne* with auxiliary and some of the commoner notional verbs beginning with *h* or *w*, e.g. *næfde* and *nyste*. Syncope is, however, only one of the forms of contraction for which Verner's Law seems to have been originally responsible; and it was often followed in Germanic speech by assimilation or the simplification of double consonants, especially at the end of monosyllabic verbal forms, e.g. set(t), third pers. sing. pres. indic. of O.E. *settan*. In the earliest English a fruitful source of contraction was the vocalic nature of *h* or *w*; especially the first, *h* disappearing between two vowels, which were then coalesced, with a reduction of the syllables of the word by one.

The processes of contraction continued in the Middle English period, and were aided by many factors, e.g. (a) the general weakening and loss of inflexions, (b) the vocalization of certain consonants, such as *g* and *v*, (c) the gradual change of the character of the hybrid Middle English language from a synthetic to an analytic type, resulting in the greater use of curtailable prepositions and articles in unstressed positions, (d) the development of subtler tense expressions, and the consequent increased employment of unstressed auxiliaries in the composite verbal forms, (e) the emergence of London English, with its admixture of bordering dialect forms, as the literary language adopted by Caxton and succeeding printers, and (f) the triumph in the fourteenth century of syllabic verse measures in the hands of Chaucer and his followers. The last produced a more elaborate system of elision than has been necessary in alliterative verse, and also in the freer narrative measures which Coleridge revived and improved in *The Ancient Mariner* and *Christabel*. The principles of elision in strict syllabic or accentual verse were influenced by French, resembling those of other rising vernacular languages of Western Europe. The most probable explanation is that they represent the conventional acceptance, for metrical reasons, of colloquial practice, since the basic reason for elision is the contiguity of two vowels normally merged in the animation of speech.

With Chaucer a common form of elision is the telescoping of an insignificant word, such as *to* or *the*, with the important notional word following it. Coalescence, with loss of a syllable, is deemed permissible only where two vowels are juxtaposed; e.g.

Knight's Tale (*C.T.* 1944) *Th*enchauntementz of Medea and Circes
Nun's Priest's Tale (*C.T.* 4478) I am not come your conseil for *te*spye.

Chaucer's elisions are the technical licences of a poet, with no probable intention of reflecting popular usage. But that syncope and contraction were a feature of everyday speech is to be noted earlier in dialect writers such as Layamon and Ormin, and later in private correspondence such as the *Paston Letters* (1456) e.g.

Letter from Thomas Bourchier, Archibishop of Canterbury, to Sir John Fastolf: ye shall find me hertly welwillid to doo that I can or may for *th*accomplishment of youre desire.

The contraction *th* for *the* continued in use, both in verse and prose, throughout the fifteenth and sixteenth centuries; it is found in Medwall's verse interlude *Fulgens and Lucres* (acted 1497), is the only contraction used in the verse interlude *Gentleness and Nobility* (*c.* 1529) and in *The Book of Common Prayer* (1549), and is common in the loosely versified mid-century comedies *Ralph Roister Doister* and *Gammer Gurton's Needle*.

The homely *Paston Letters*, with their often naive orthography, are not as rich in colloquial contractions as might have been expected. Using Gairdener's edition, I found the following:

Vol. I.69 he wold *a* and *a* sett to morgage all that he hath (*a* = have).
Vol. I.140 I shuld my self *a be* with his Lordship (*be* = been).
Vol. III.177 For Gods sake, *a* pity on hym (*a* = have, imperative).

In familiar literature of the fifteenth and sixteenth centuries, *a* is the most rudimentary form of *have*, and that it is a relic of earlier dialect usage is clear from its use in the fourteenth century in *William of Palerne* and Mandeville's *Travels*. So are the aspirateless forms *affe* and *ad* of *The Cely Papers* (1473–88). Under the influence of French pronunciation, the uncertain quality of initial *h* continued until the late seventeenth century.

Another interesting occurrence in both *The Paston Letters* and Caxton's *Book of Curtesye* (C.U.P. reprint) is the Old English form *hem* alongside of Scandinavian *them*; e.g.

Paston Letters. II. 191 I auwnsweryd *hem*
　　　　　　　 II. 359 to know of *hem*
B of C 158–161 Saynt austyn amonessheth with besy cure
　　　　　　　 How men atte table / shold *hem* assure (emphatic)
　　　　　　　 That there escape *them* / no suche langage (unemphatic)
　　　　　　　 As myght other folke hurte to disparage

The *O.E.D.* says that 'In the fifteenth century *theym* and *hem* are both used by Caxton, as more and less emphatic.' The reverse is here the case. It is possible that *hem* is what Caxton found in the scribe's copy, and that *them* is an editorial improvement. Wynkyn de Worde in *Sermo die Lune* (C.U.P. reprint) has *them* or *theym* throughout. Up to about the close of the fifteenth century, *them* and *hem* were apparently literary forms; but later *hem* became a colloquialism. However, except for a single use of *um* by Scroop in *Thomas of Woodstock* (M.S.R. 1786) of *am* in line 1630 of *Sir Thomas More* (M.S.R. p. 54) and of *em* in line 27 of Addition IV of the same play (M.S.R. p. 80), I have found no colloquial weakenings of *them* (such as *hem* or *em*) until the plays of Jonson at the turn of the century. The same gap (1485–1600) is notice-

B

able in the citations in the *O.E.D.*, except for an archaic use of *hem* by Spenser in *The Shepherd's Calendar*, May 27.

By 1500 the nature of colloquial contraction and weakening in literature was somewhat limited; but the principle of restricting it in the main to insignificant words, particles or prefixes, was clearly operative in Medwall's *Fulgens and Lucres* (1497) and in the sixteenth-century plays that followed. The unstressed words suitable for clipping were articles, prepositions (reduced very early in oaths), pronouns, and later auxiliary verbs.

Fulgens and Lucres

Articles:	70 *th*empire, 75 *th*author, 110 *th*effect
Prepositions:	1261 *i*faith (The contraction *i* was commonly found before consonants in Southern texts from the twelfth century.)
Pronouns:	897 quoth*a* (*a* may stand for almost any reduced personal pronoun, and is cited first in *O.E.D.* from Layamon *c.* 1205. The expression *quotha* became a conventional interjection, *O.E.D.*'s first example, in the form *quod a*, being from Rastell's interlude *The Four Elements* 1519.)
	24 cal*t* (= call it. The aphetic form of *it* began to appear in texts such as the *Ormulum c.* 1200; earliest citation 3e*t* (= ye it) see *O.E.D.* under *Ye* A.b.)
	50, 418 etc. *ye*. (In the nom. sing. and oblique cases after about 1500.) This can be regarded in many positions as an unemphatic weakening of *you* by then in general use, except in religious literature. Jespersen, *Progress in Language*, Section 198, regards *ye* in the sixteenth century as frequently a phonetic weakening of *you*, especially after verbs; but it was so earlier, e.g. Pecock, *Repressor* (*c.* 1449), I.XVI. 86 y preie, *ye* seie *ye* to me. It survives in dialect in the form *ee*.

Contractions of the auxiliary verb *will* have not been ascertained until the middle of the sixteenth century, the first example in the *O.E.D.* (shee*le*) being from the undated ballad of *King Estmere* in F. J. Child's *English and Scottish Popular Ballads*, and the second (*wyll* = wee'll) from Whetstone's *Promos and Cassandra* (1578).

Among the notional verbs, *gan* (= began), the familiar metrical and temporal expletive of Chaucer, was still in occasional use, but was largely superseded by the periphrastic auxiliary *do*, *did*. This, too, provided an extra metrical syllable when occasion demanded, its syntactical function being mildly or wholly emphatic, e.g.

Fulgens 754 Would not take that way that I *do* intend.

Discussing the rise of poetic forms and contractions in §242 of *The Growth and Structure of the English Language*, Jespersen says that the later English poets often wrote *'tis* for *it's*, *whate'er* for *whatever*, *taketh* for *takes*, *movèd* for *moved*, *o'er* for *over* and *morn* for *morning*. 'The history of some of the poetical forms,' he continues, 'is rather curious: *howe'er*, *e'er*, *e'en* were at first vulgar or familiar forms, used in daily talk. Then poets began to spell these words in the abbreviated fashion whenever they wanted their readers to pronounce them in that way, while prose writers, unconcerned about the pronunciation given to their words, retained the full forms in spelling. The next step was that the short forms were branded as vulgar by schoolmasters with so great a success that they disappeared from ordinary conversation while they were still retained in poetry. And now they are distinctly poetic and as such above the reach of common mortals.'

This generalization is a fairly accurate account of what began to take place in the latter half of the sixteenth century. By about the middle of that century the drama had been emancipated as a secular form of entertainment, and the significance of colloquial contractions, as part of the representation of everyday speech, began to be felt, especially in realistic comedy. The verse of the pioneering comedies was extremely free, and made greater play with these contractions than did contemporary prose, even when used in drama. This is apparent from a comparison of the verse comedies *Ralph Roister Doister* and *Gammer Gurton's Needle*, which belong to the period 1550–70, with the prose comedy *Supposes*, translated by Gascoygne from the Italian of Ariosto in 1566. Udall in *Ralph Roister Doister*, an academic play in loose Alexandrines, written about 1553, uses: 291 *een*, 289 *ere*, 145 *nere*, 437 *Tis*, 449 *ist*, 361 *Ill* (= I will), 478 *thother*, 1198 *ientman* (= gentleman) 1641 *bie* (= abide), 361 *chieve*, 542 *lowe* (= allow), 1662 *ray* (= array), 1746 *scape*, 425 *vise* (= advise), 919 *ko* (= quoth), as well as some bucolic forms such as 362 *ch* for *ich* (= I), and 363 *bore* for *born*.[1] *Gammer Gurton's Needle*, by a Cambridge don (either William Stevenson or John Bridges), is in rhyming fourteeners, and fully divided in Acts and Scenes; it is also more prolific in colloquial shortenings than any play until *Thomas of Woodstock* (c. 1594—see Chap. V),

---

[1] Citations are from M.S.R. Earliest uses noted in O.E.D. are: *een* (1553, this play), *ere* (fourteenth century, no citation), *ner* (c. 1205, Layamon's *Brut*), *Tis* (1598 Haydocke's trans. of Lomazzo's *Arts of Curious Painting*), *ist* (c. 1250 *Genesis and Exodus*), *Ile* (1591 Shakes. *Two Gentlemen*, 11.6.29), *th* for *the* (1470–85, Malory, *Arthur, thold*), *ch.* for *ich* (1528, More, *Heresies* IV).

though probably written thirty years earlier. But in Gascoyne's *Supposes*, although the prose dialogue is flexible and natural, there is no use of colloquial contractions whatever.

Gammer Gurton's Needle, which cannot have been written later than 1563, is a comedy of low life, and is so important a document for the study of Tudor colloquial forms that it is worthy of more detailed analysis. There seems to be a direct line of descent from it to the domestic comedy of Porter's *Two Angry Women of Abington* and of the earlier Acts of Shakespeare's *Romeo and Juliet* (for these plays have affinities not confined to the date of their appearance); and we may pass thence to the Cheapside scenes of *Henry IV*. Diccon, an ex-Bedlam beggar like Poor Tom in *King Lear*, living by his wits, makes game of a group of village rustics, whose racy speech is realistically depicted by an expert observer. But there is no hint of any specific dialect, except the South-Western aphetic first-personal pronoun *ch*, prefixed to both auxiliary and notional verbs, e.g. *cham* or *chym* (= I am), *chad* (= I had), *chil* (= I will), *chot* (I wot), *chard* (= I heard). Apart from *fixen* (III.2.8), there is no indication of South-Western speech;[1] and Dr. H. Bradley, who edited the play for Gayley's *Representative English Comedies*, found only one East Anglian word, viz. *pes* (= a hassock). From this and other plays with rustic characters, it appears that aphetic combinations of *ich* + verb were a conventional Elizabethan attempt to indicate bucolic speech of no particular area.

The bulk of the colloquialisms, however, though they must have been of mixed dialect origin, and often of pre-Chaucerian stock, represented the impact of regional dialects on the Standard English spoken by educated people within a radius of sixty miles from London, and was already in literary acceptance. The best evidence of the provincial origin of colloquial contractions is, perhaps, the language of the Ballads. But it is a notable fact that the contractions occur chiefly where the transmitted form of the poems is of comparatively late date (e.g. sixteenth and seventeenth centuries), when they had received the sophisticating touch of the printers. In the ballads either in print or in manuscript as early as the fifteenth century, the orthography of contraction is strictly limited, and is found largely in nouns and notional verbs.

The varied range of colloquial contractions and weakenings in *Gammer Gurton's Needle* appears from the following table. Most of the forms survived in the comedies of the next generation, but surprisingly few in the dramas of the University Wits, even such folk-plays as

---

[1] I have used the Percy Reprint, ed. H. F. B. Brett-Smith, 1920.

George a Green and *The Old Wive's Tale*. Though most plays between 1575 and 1600 contain the limited and conventional contractions found in *Ralph Roister Doister* (see above), few extend to the range of the author of *Thomas of Woodstock*, or of Henry Porter and Ben Jonson. The priority of *Woodstock* or the *Henry VI* trilogy is an unsolved problem of dating; but probably the unknown author of the first must be given the credit of extending the use of contractions, in some abundance, to Chronicle History, and thence to Elizabethan tragedy.

The forms cited below are in their original orthography. It is noteworthy that the apostrophe is not used to indicate omitted letters; indeed there are only sporadic examples of its use even in the last decade of the sixteenth century. That scribes were casual, and printers hardly less indifferent, appears from manuscript plays such as *Sir Thomas More* and *Woodstock*, and from the early printed quartos of Porter and Shakespeare, which are amongst the most valuable for the student of orthography. In the fifteen-nineties the apostrophe was used with moderate freedom, but inconsistently enough to justify the complaint of Ben Jonson that 'it many times, through the negligence of Writers and Printers, is quite omitted'.[1] It was Jonson who set the example of correct writing in these matters (not without lapses) in the quartos which began to appear in 1600; more systematically in the folio of 1616.

Gammer Gurton's Needle

Articles:	*The:* I.4.9 *th*end, II.3.2 *th*oter (= thother)
	III.4.20 *t*oore (= tother, O.E. *pæt ōper* > M.E. *pet oper*, whence *t* of the article became attached to the open syllable of the indef. pronoun, before 1250. Later *the* was often dropped, but the first instance of *tother* alone, cited in *O.E.D.*, is in the phrase *my toder letter* (see under B.1.b.), from the *Cely Papers* (1482))
Prepositions:	*In:* III.3.44 *I* faith
	At: III.4.28 *a* do (= at, Northern equivalent of *to*. First citation of reduced form *a* in *O.E.D.* from Barbour's *Bruce* (1375))
Adverbs:	*Over:* I.5.2 *our* (= o'er. First citation in *O.E.D.* with this spelling from Douglas's *Aeneis* (1513); Hampole's *Psalter* (c. 1340) has *ouyr*)

[1] *English Grammar*, Bk. II, Ch. I, 9–10 (Herford and Simpson's *Ben Jonson*, Vol. VIII, p. 528).

Pronouns: *Ich:* (bucolic) I.2.14 *ch*em (= I am), I.5.11. *ch*ym I.2.34 *ch*ad, II.1.55 *ch*yll (= I will)

My: II.1.52 Be*m* vathers soule, III.3.40 bi*m*, IV.2.3 By*m* (= by my. Obviously a dialectạl weakening, but not noted in *O.E.D.* until 1712, Arbuthnot's *John Bull*, and there proclitic,[1] *m'*own)

Thou: I.2.19 *th*art, IV.2.81 *th*adst (*th*art is first noted in *O.E.D.* from Shoreham's *Poems, c.* 1315)

He: III.4.27 *h*ad (= he had. Sometimes regarded as an omission of the personal pronoun, but more probably intended for *h'ad*, representing weakened *he* + aspirateless form of *had* (see *shad* below). The combination *h'had* is first cited in *O.E.D.* from Butler's *Hudibras* (1663)).

She: III.4.8 *Sh*ase (= she has). This is the first example noted in *O.E.D.*)
IV.2.23 *Sh*ad. (= She had.)

It: I.2.19 *t*ys (The form history in *O.E.D.* shows this abbreviation as early as the twelfth century, but no example is given earlier than 1598, see p. 11 footnote 3.)
V.2.89 do*t* (= do it. Enclitic *t*,[1] according to *O.E.D.*, dates from the thirteenth century, see *calt* from *Fulgens and Lucres*, p. 10.[2] The earliest example noted is 3e*t* = ye it, in the *Ormulum, c.* 1200 (see under *Ye*))

Us: I.5.1 let*s* (*O.E.D.* regards *let's* as colloquial, but all other uses of *s* (= us) as dialectal. The first citation is from *Love's Labour's Lost*, date assigned 1588)

Our: I.3.19 By*r* Ladie (Regarded by *O.E.D.* as a dialect expression, and first cited from *Wit and Science*, 1570.)

You: I.4.45 (and frequently) *ye*, III.2.14 *ye*ad (modern *you'd*)

Auxiliary Verbs: *Have:* I.4.7 *ha* (Earliest citation in *O.E.D.* from *Cursor Mundi, c.* 1300.)
II.2.60 Goda*mercy* (Reduced form *a* apparently from thirteenth century.)

---

[1] The terms 'proclitic' and 'enclitic' are derived from Greek Grammar. *Proclitic* is applied to any combination of two words in which the *first* is so reduced as to have no independent accent, but in pronunciation is attached to the following stressed word, e.g. *'tis. Enclitic* is applied to the combination in which the *second* is so unemphatic as to be heard in pronunciation as part of the preceding word, e.g. *is't.*

[2] In 111.2.4 *leese it* rhymes *iest*, indicating the contracted form *t*, not printed.

I.2.34 she*ad* (= she'd. *O.E.D.* shows aspirateless form of *had* in thirteenth century only, but gives no examples. The modern vowelless contraction *'d* is not cited until eighteenth century)

Will: I.4.44 wee*le*, III.3.48 i*le*, V.2.81 hee*l*. (No definite early date can be assigned to these contractions, which must have come into literary use about the middle of sixteenth century.)

Shall: (bucolic) I.5.39 you*sh*, III.3.42 i*se* (= I shall), III.3.45 thou*se*, III.3.62 We*se* (No dates or citations in *O.E.D.*)

Verb 'to be':

Is: I.5.50 what*s* (First example in *O.E.D.* from Lyly's *Sappho*, 1584.)

Aphetic or contracted notional verbs:

II.1.34 *ga* (= gave), II.1.85 *fet* (= fetch, really a different verb), III.4.16 *ma* (= made), V.2.67 *have* (= behave) V.2.196 *scape*

Curtailed inflexions of verbs:

I.5.47 think*s* thou (for *thinkest;* originally a Northern dialect ending); III.2.15 Wa*s* not thou; so III.3.6 Intend*s*, V.2.50 telle*s*.

Nouns: Prol. 12 Ma*s* (= master), I.5.6 *neele* (= needle)

Uninflected genitive: III. 3.4 bim *father* soule

Omnibus words: V.2.115 *washical* (= what shall I call it)

The past participle of the verb 'to be' *bin* (I.1.2) has not been included, though it seems to have developed as an unstressed form of Northern *been* in the fifteenth century, and later to have passed into Standard English. It was then, not infrequently, used in stressed positions, and in estimable prose. There is, as I have pointed out in Chapter I, some doubt about the value of radical *i*, as there is warrant in other contemporary spellings for a sound usually represented by *ee*.

Chapter 3

Henry Porter and *The Two Angry Women of Abington*

OWING to the anonymity or loss of much of Henry Porter's work in comedy, a literary genre in which Francis Meres in 1598 regarded him as one of the notables, it has not been possible to estimate the full significance of his influence on Shakespeare, Ben Jonson and other comic dramatists of the last decade of the sixteenth century. Since 1940, however, Mr. J. M. Nosworthy, in three important articles,[1] has added to our knowledge. Little has been ascertained of Porter's life, except that he was constantly in debt, bound himself just before his death to sell all his plays to Henslowe (a novel transaction), wrote for the Admiral's Men (or Servants of the Earl of Nottingham), collaborated with Chettle in a lost play called *The Spencers*, and with Chettle and Jonson in *Hot Anger Soon Cold*, was mortally wounded by John Day in a brawl on 6th June, 1599, and died the following day. In the year of his death Joseph Hunt and William Ferbrand published his only extant independent work, *The Two Angry Women of Abington*, which was printed by Edward Allde. A second part of *The Two Angry Women* was written and performed, but has not survived. There is no doubt that the extant quarto represents the first part, as the closing lines promise a sequel; but the earlier version was possibly augmented for publication, since the quarto runs to 3037 lines.

When Porter commenced his dramatic career is uncertain; but it is now thought unlikely that he was the Henry Porter, born 1573, who matriculated at Brasenose College, Oxford, in 1589. From the following reference in Richard Harvey's *Plaine Percevall*, published in that year, *The Two Angry Women of Abington* appears to have been on the stage when Gayley supposed Porter to be entering Oxford:[2]

---

[1] See 'Notes on Henry Porter', *M.L.R.* XXXV (1940); 'The Case is Altered', *J.E.G.P.*, LI (1952); 'The Two Angry Families of Verona', *S.Q.*, III (1952).

[2] See *Representative English Comedies*, pp. 519–20.

yet I will nicke name no bodie: I am none of these traft mockado mak-a-
dooes: for 'Qui mochat, moccabitur' quoth the servingman of Abingdon

Cf. *Two Angry Women* (M.S.R. 888–90):

And it seemeth unto me, I it seems to me, that you maister Phillip mocke me
do you not know *qui mocat mocabitur*, mocke age and se how it will prosper?

For what it is worth, H. C. Hart in his Arden edition of 3 *Henry VI*
also compared the humorous use of proverbs made by Richard Duke
of Gloucester with that of Nicholas Proverbes, a character in Porter's
comedy.

By 1596 Porter's plays must have been highly esteemed, as is shown
by the nature of his transactions with Henslowe after that year, and the
sums expended on costumes for staging. If *The Two Angry Women*
was written before 1589, or even before 1596, it must be the earliest
known comedy of humours, since Chapman (born 1559) did not com-
mence his stage career until he was thirty-seven, and his *Humorous Day's
Mirth* (published 1599) was first performed in 1597. Not much later
Jonson was probably busy with *Every Man in His Humour*, which was
performed by Shakespeare's Company (apparently because of a difference with Henslowe and the Admiral's Men) in 1598. It is practically
certain that the realistic comedy of humours grew out of the association
of Porter, Chapman and Jonson, working for the Admiral's Men
between 1595 and 1597, and was conceived as a counterblast to
romantic comedy and chronicle history.

In *The Two Angry Women of Abington* Mistress Barnes, her daughter
Mall, Nicholas Proverbes and Dick Coomes, are in the best vein of
Jonsonian 'humour', and the last may be the predecessor of both
Bobadil and Pistol. What is important is not only that Porter appears
to have been the first in the field with a new comic genre, but that he
had a secure grasp of the atmosphere of village gossip and intrigue,
which he preserved in the colloquial tradition of *Gammer Gurton's
Needle*. If Porter was at Oxford, he walked abroad in the neighbouring
villages with eyes for local character, and ears for colourful dialect
speech, which he emphasised with some old and some new colloquial
contractions. But whereas the people in *Gammer Gurton's Needle*
remained villagers, Porter's protagonists, with the exception of the
bucolic Hodge, and the other servitors Proverbes, Coomes and the
Boy, are raised in social status to the dignity of estimable blank verse.

Porter's dramatic verse is forceful, flexible and even musical; but
prose suited him better for the babble of inconsequent praters, such as

Nicholas and Dick. It became the purpose of Chapman and Jonson to make verse sufficiently resilient for most occasions, and for conversation as flippant, racy and down-to-earth as any character could utter. But Porter effects transitions from verse to prose, without noticeable change of style. 'Of all Elizabethan dramatic styles,' writes Nosworthy,[1] 'Porter's is, with the exception of Marlowe's and Shakespeare's, the most personal, and if it exists in any of these plays (anonymous plays between 1-585–95) it should not be hard to identify. The main verse determinants are regular blank verse freely breaking into couplet, frequent use of identical rhyme, and sporadic use of tetrameter.'

Shakespeare, always ready to take advantage of a new fashion, and professionally well-placed to profit by the experience of other playwrights, produced his only homogeneous 'humour' comedy in *The Merry Wives of Windsor* (written *c.* 1600), though he had created individual characters in the mould of Porter earlier. The most interesting single group is in *Romeo and Juliet* (written *c.* 1595, published 1599), and consists of Capulet, Mercutio, the Nurse and the servant Peter, the last played by Will Kempe. These are lively Porterian figures, with a distinct idiom, marked by a vigorous influx of conventional oaths (such as *zounds* and *'sblood*), and colloquial weakenings and contractions (such as *ye* for *you*, *a* for *he*, *a* for the prepositions *of* and *on*; and prepositional or conjunctival combinations with *it* and *the*, the latter being curtailed, e.g. *toote*, *ont*, *ast*, *byth* etc). The comic style is that of *The Two Angry Women of Abington*, and specimens from both plays are appended, though they illustrate only one aspect of the manner, the headlong talk of less literate persons. A noticeable feature in the script of impetuous speech is the bareness of the punctuation, often reduced to commas.

(1) *Two Angry Women of Abingdon* (M.S.R. 2382–2397)
Dick Coomes: . . . I have seene the day, I could have daunst in my fight, one, two, three, foure, and five, on the head of him: six, seaven, eyght, nine and ten, on the sides of him, and if I went so far as fifteen, I warrant I shewd him a trick of one and twentie: but I have not fought this foure dayes, and I lacke a little practise of my warde, but I shall make a shift, ha close, are yee disposed sir? . . . Sbloud how pursey I am, well I see exercise is all, I must practise my weapons oftner, I must have a goale or two at Foote-ball, before I come to my right kinde. . . .

(2) *Romeo and Juliet* (S.Q.F. I.3.32–45)
Nurse: . . . Shake quoth the Dove-house, twas no need I trow to bid me trudge: and since that time it is a leven yeares, for then she could stand bylone,

[1] 'Notes on Henry Porter', *M.L.R.* XXXV (1940), p. 520.

nay byth roode she could have run and wadled all about: for even the day
before she broke her brow and then my husband, God be with his soule, a
was a merrie man, tooke up the child, yea quoth he, doest thou fall upon thy
face? thou wilt fall backward when thou hast more wit, wilt thou not Iule?
And by my holydam, the pretie wretch left crying, and said I . . .

It is true that Shakespeare had used some of the newer contractions,
though sparingly, in the speech of such characters as Moth and Dull in
Love's Labour's Lost (written *c.* 1593, published 1598); but the copy
sent to the printer, as the title-page shows, was about as late a revision
of the text as the 1599 quarto of *The Two Angry Women* appears to
have been of Porter's. In any case, if Porter was a practising dramatist
by 1589, the inference that he was the innovator is unshaken;[1] provided
that (a) by innovation is meant here a fusion of traditional elements
in the mind of an intelligent interpreter of life through language, and
(b) one does not accede to the belief of Peter Alexander that Shakespeare began his dramatic career as early as 1584.[2] If the evidence of the
good quartos is to be believed, colloquial contraction was not a pronounced feature of Shakespeare's dialogue before 1600; his use, as compared with that of Porter and Jonson, and the authors of *Thomas of
Woodstock*, and *Sir Thomas More*, was economical; and the further
inference ensues that patches of racy colloquialism as early as *Love's
Labour's Lost* and *Romeo and Juliet* are a tour de force of imitation.
Shakespeare's art, though original, is at the same time a mirror reflecting what pleases him most in his contemporaries; and he excels all in
the blend of comic realism and romantic illusion. *Romeo and Juliet* is,
however, a tragedy, though not a characteristically Shakespearian one,
being overloaded with domestic palaver and comic bickering in emulation of Porter. Despite the difference in dramatic aim, the parallel
between the plots of *The Two Angry Women* and *Romeo and Juliet* is
fairly close, since in each there is a family feud resolved by the marriage
of the son of one family to the daughter of the other.

[1] It is worth noting that a remark of Goursey's in *The Two Angry Women*,
'Here's adoe about a thing of nothing,' suggests the title of another Shakespeare
play: and that lines 1375–80 of Coomes's speech at the end of Sc. VI foreshadow
the 'conscience and the fiend' soliloquy of Lancelot Gobbo in *The Merchant of
Venice*, Act II Scene 2. Similarly, the rhymed dialogue and punning at the beginning of the hunting scene (VII) recall the self-same features in that kind of scene
(I), Act IV, of *Love's Labour's Lost*. Nosworthy cites interesting Porterian echoes
in *Romeo and Juliet*, e.g. *R and J.* (Q2) III.5.141. and *T.A.W.A.* 1628; *R and J.*
I.5.46 and *T.A.W.A.* 2022–28 etc.

[2] See *A Shakespeare Primer*, chronological summary, pp. VIII and IX.

The following are the more interesting of the colloquial contractions and weakenings in Porter's comedy, the citations being from the Malone Society reprint:

The Two Angry Women of Abington.

Articles: *The:* 386 *th*'house
                      661 *t*other, 2899 *t*one, the *t*other

Prepositions: *Of:* 740 Light *a*love, 1098 *a* yeere, 1482 *o* my friend
                      (The weakening of prepositional endings before con-
                      sonants began in eleventh century, and was similar
                      to loss of final *n* in the indef. article. The vowels
                      were later also weakened, producing spellings *a* or *e*.
                      The literary reduction of *of* and *on* adopted by
                      printers at the turn of the sixteenth century was *o*.)
                      On: 1213 *a* bed
                 Amongst: 263 *mongst* (earliest use of this aphetic form in
                      O.E.D. is from Marlowe's *Faustus*, date assigned
                      1590)
                 Betwixt: 1121 *twixt* (an aphetic poetical form found in
                      Cursor Mundi, but not again cited in O.E.D. until
                      1570)

Adverbs: *Over:* 278 *ore* (in 945 there is a prepositional use; this is the
                      normal orthography in Elizabethan plays)

Pronouns: *My:* 1433 *me* (a weakened form of *my* used by the
                      country squire Sir Ralph Smith)
                     Thou: 384 *th*'art
                      He: 902 *a* have (Proclitic. Used by Nicholas Proverbes,
                      Coomes and Mistress Barnes.)
                      It: 155 for'*t*, 1618 on'*t*, 1927 in'*t*, 1501 is*t*, 2571 wer'*t*,
                      877 ha'*te* (early instance of double contraction, both
                      parts of speech being reduced), 1273 hav'*te*, 161 *t*'is
                      erroneously placed apostrophe), 398 *t*'as (= it has),
                      609 '*t*would
                      You: 2000 quoth *a*

Auxiliary Verbs: *Have:* 810 Thaus*t* (cf. 163 you'*r*. Enclitic verb not pre-
                      viously found, proclitic pronoun being usual in
                      Elizabethan combination, e.g. *th*'hast), 877 *ha*'te
                     Will: 162 she'*l*, 201 they'*l*, 323 hee'*l*, 1351 wee*ll*, 1555
                      you'*l*, 1745 thou'*lt*

Verb 'to be':   *Is:* 117 ther'*s*, 155 wife'*s*, 164 that'*s*
                      Are: 163 you'*r* (I have not discovered an earlier use of the
                      second person pron. + *are* in which the verb is an

enclitic contraction, as in Modern English. The usual combination in Elizabethan English has proclitic pronoun, *y'*are, cf. 384 *th'*art); 881 you*'re*, 2085 ye*'re*

Contracted Notional Verbs:	2115 *tane* (This contraction of *taken* was apparently in use from fourteenth century.)
Past-Participle endings with apostrophe:	249 din'de, 638 fac'te, 2114 forc'st (erroneous *s*)
Bucolic forms of verbs:	1952 *do* (= doth, used by Mistress Barnes): 2130 *traine* (uninflected past participle. Used by Will, Sir Ralph Smith's man)
Uninflected Genitives:	1028 *heart* bloud (this is a common phrase in Chaucer)
Telescoped colloquialisms:	1185 God boye yee (= God be with you), 2142 God boye sir, 865 *Ber*ladie (= by our Lady), 1509 *Be*ladie, 1978 *by* Ladie
Oaths with proclitic s:	(= God's) 367 *S*wonds (Coomes), 871 *S*wounds (Phillip), 1500 *S*ownes (Frank), · 987 *s*bloud (Hodge)

The significant new features of the above citations are (a) reduced forms of the common prepositions *of* and *on*, (b) enclitic *t* (= it) after almost any preposition, (c) enclitic uses of the verbs *have* and *be* after personal pronouns e.g. you*'re*, (d) the introduction of double contractions, e.g. ha*'te*, (e) bucolic loss of inflexions of verbs, e.g. *do* for *doth*, and (f) the greatly increased use of contractions in oaths and near formulas, such as *God be with you*. There should be added the very frequent, though inconsistent, use of the apostrophe to indicate the suppressed portion of the word, or of two words in combination. It is hard to believe that these apostrophes originated with the author himself, as there is no hint of their use in the prose prologue (presumably from Porter's draft). Nor do holograph passages in manuscript plays of the nineties, e.g. *Sir Thomas More*, suggest that authors were much given to these niceties. The orthography (and stage directions) of the first quarto of *T.A.W.A.* indicate theatre-copy in the hand of a scrivener, who may have been responsible for the marks of elision, as well as erroneous contractions of expanded forms, which mar the metre of many lines. Alternatively, both apostrophes and carelessly printed text may be ascribed to the printer Edward Allde, who also produced the earliest extant quarto of Kyd's *Spanish Tragedy* (1592), the Malone

Society reprint of which indicates the sporadic use of elisional apostrophes at an earlier date.

The general character of the colloquial contractions cannot, however, be attributed to anyone but Porter, and their considerable number, variety and characteristic use substantiate my claim that the main lines of Elizabethan practice were laid by this lively comic dramatist before Jonson's plays were known or came into print in 1600.

It is relevant to note here the further indebtedness of others to Porter in some of their grammatical features. I do not claim that Porter was the originator, but only that a number of early grammatical practices are integrated in his comedy, and thence pass into the common stock of dramatic dialogue. Jonson seems to have acquired his fondness for the Western preterite *rid* (a form not found in Shakespeare) from Porter (e.g. *T.A.W.A.* 287, 291), as well as his use of *-eth* instead of *-s* endings (then well established) in the third person singular present indicative of notional verbs, when the stem ends in a sibilant or affricative consonant (e.g. *T.A.W.A.* 496 *graseth*, 2335 *useth*, 3023 *hisseth*). In other usages (all but one in prose by the proverb-monger Nicholas, 888) *-eth* is introduced only for metrical convenience. On the other hand, *hath* and *doth* are found throughout, which confirms an early date for the play, since the more colloquial *has* and *does* seem to have been in dramatic use by the end of the eighties, both occurring in Peele's *Old Wives Tale*, written about 1590, performed by the already declining Queen's Players, and printed by 1595. Another Jonsonian usage (helped by certain scribes and printers) is the orthographically correct *-t(e)* for *-d(e)* or *-ed* in the past tense or past participle of weak verbs ending in a voiceless consonant (see examples above), a convention far from consistently used by Allde in printing *The Spanish Tragedy*.

In conditional clauses Porter is addicted to the use of the original conjunction *and if* (e.g. *T.A.W.A.* 281, 308, 802), later simplified to *and* or *an* or *if*; and this may emphasize the rural character of the play, as does his use of the wrongly inflected second person singular subjunctive *beest* for *be* in the mouths of his rustics, such as Hodge (e.g. 979 and thou *beest* a man draw). Shakespeare, Jonson and other dramatists began to use *beest* extensively, whoever the speaker might be. Porter's inclination for the weakened form *ye* is excessive, greatly outnumbering his uses of *you*, and in this he had much influence on Fletcher (whose falling rhythms, especially at the line-end, he anticipates), less on Jonson and only spasmodically on Shakespeare. Not once, however, does Porter contract the pronoun *them*, though reduced forms must have been in dialect use; Jonson was the first dramatist to use *hem*, and Fletcher to use *em*, extensively after 1600. Yet another feature in Porter is his frequent failure to observe concord between subject and verb. Plural subjects with singular verbs mark the speeches of all characters, and though the *-s* endings of plural verbs are often explained as relics of the Northern inflexions, I am inclined to believe that they were universal in stage dialect, and are simply a sign of provincialism, if not of illiteracy. Shakespeare has many examples in the dialogue of his most courtly characters, but Jonson few that cannot be otherwise explained, which I take to be a mark of his superior learning.

In the second person singular preterite indicative of the verb 'to be', the regular form of Porter and Shakespeare is *wert* (from the subjunctive), and no usage has been found earlier than theirs. Jonson has the other anomalous sixteenth-century form *wast* almost as frequently as *wert*. As *wast* was generally substituted for *wert* in the Shakespeare First Folio, it looks as though the former was the accepted form by the first quarter of the seventeenth century. *Bin* for *been* is much more frequent in Porter and Jonson than Shakespeare. Porter I believe to be the first dramatist to popularize the use of colloquial *it*, without definite reference, as object of originally intransitive verbs, or nouns used as verbs, e.g. *T.A.W.A.* 324 *trips it*, 861 *phillip it*, 883 *proverbde it*, 1162 *wanton it*, 2260 *Spaniell it*. Finally, it is worth noting that no dramatist uses the periphrastic auxiliary verb *do*, as a non-emphatic expletive in affirmative sentences, as extensively as Porter. Shakespeare's number of such devices to eke out the metrical line is considerable, but Porter's is excessive, and probably represents the peak of the graph for this sixteenth-century licence, almost as popular in prose as in verse.

Chapter 4

Classification of Contraction Types and Summary of Conclusions

IT would be well to conclude this survey of colloquial contractions in drama before 1600 with (a) a classification of contraction types, according to their formation, and (b) a summary of conclusions.

(a) *Classification of Contraction Types*

1. Vowel-weakening, e.g. *you* to *ye*. This is an old phenomenon, and goes back at least to Old English.
2. Loss of aspirate, owing to dialectal or French influence e.g. *ave* for *have, em* for *hem* (O.E. *heom*). This probably dates back to Middle English.
3. Aphesis or Aphæresis. The first of these terms was invented by Sir James Murray, editor of the *O.E.D.*, in 1880, for the 'gradual and unintentional loss of a short unaccented vowel at the beginning of a word'; and further described in Vol. I, p. 384, as 'a special form of the phonetic process called Aphæresis, for which, from its frequency in the history of the English language, a distinctive name is useful'; e.g. *gainst* for *against, chieve* for *achieve, squire* for *esquire*. This appears to date at least from the fifteenth century.

   The term 'Aphæresis', used by the Latin grammarians and in 1611 by Cotgrave, is defined in *O.E.D.* as 'the taking away or suppression of a letter or syllable at the beginning of a word', e.g. *vise* for *advise*. A phenomenon of roughly the same date, fifteenth century.
4. Apocope (or end-curtailment), e.g. *ha* for *have, ko* for *quoth*. There are different dates for different forms, but the phenomenon must date from Late Old English or Early Middle English.
5. Syncope (or medial-curtailment), e.g. *nere* for *never, een* or *in* for *even, gentman* for *gentleman*. This undoubtedly goes back to Old English, e.g. *gefēon* for *gefehan*.
6. Synaloepha (or combined contraction), where two words are

coalesced in speech, with the obscuration or loss of one syllable. This involves one or more of the above types, e.g. *Single: th* end, *yare*, I*ll* or I*le*, i*st*, By*r* Ladie. Some of these date from Middle English. *Double: ith*, *oth*. This type is literary and Elizabethan, belonging to the last decade of the sixteenth century.

7. Initial assimilation, resulting from combined contraction, the proclitic word being reduced to the same letter as the beginning of the following word, and consequently assimilated to it, e.g. *'has* (or *h'as*) < *h'has* < *he has*. This is a novelty that seems to have been introduced in the last decade of the sixteenth century.

8. End assimilation, resulting from combined contraction, the enclitic word being reduced to the same letter as the end of the preceding word, and consequently assimilated to it, e.g. *this* < *this's* < *this is*. An innovation of the fifteen-nineties.

Of the above types 1, 2, 4 and 6 are the most significant for the study of Shakespearian texts. The point of interest in all is not their early date of origin, but their acceptance in standard literary English, if the language of the drama can be included under that title. Classes 1–5 are of pre-Caxton dialect origin; classes 6–8, i.e. nearly all of the combined contractions, are later sophistications. But my thesis is that contractions in the later categories were likewise suggested by popular parlance beyond the pale of the literary élite.

(b) *Summary of Conclusions*

In spite of the last observation, it would be wrong to suppose that types of colloquial contraction are confined to particular social strata. There are nevertheless recognizable conventions of use in the last decade of the sixteenth century, observed especially in the humour-group of comic writers, which deserve attention, because contractions serve to emphasize colloquial flavour. Oaths, in which the Deity is euphemistically disguised by contraction, are the prerogative of the young bloods about town, men of education and station with no great intellectual capacity. *A* for *he* is occasionally permitted in the unbuttoned moods of intellectuals like Hamlet—I suppose the play to have been first written by Shakespeare about the turn of the century. Combinations of preposition, conjunction or verb with curtailed *it* or *the*, such as *tot*, *ont*, *ast*, *byth*, *dot*, belong to the mercurial, nimble-witted types, persons given to animated speech and repartee, such as Mercutio on the one hand, and Moth, the tender Juvenal or pert page of *Love's Labour's Lost*, on the other. These contractions, indicative of speed and clipping,

c

in the course of time became fairly general in their use, as had already become *ha* for *have*, *-le* for *will*, the expletive *quotha*, the prepositional contractions *i* for *in*, *o* for *of* and *on*, and proclitic *th* for *the*, and *t* for *it*. Wholly bucolic remained *ch* for *I*, and *-se* for *shall*; and predominantly so the rudimentary word *a* which could be used for *he*, *have*, *on*, *of* etc. *Them* was nearly always written in full before 1600, except possibly by Jonson, whose early work was touched up later, and whose colloquial form in his first published play, *Every Man out of His Humour* (1600), was *'hem*. The vulgar *'em* comes later in Jonson's Masques, as the usage of illiterate or rustic types. Fletcher and some of his successors, however, employed *em* or *um* for all characters and on all occasions. *Ye*, later further reduced to *y'*, was in general use in racy dialogue, but sparingly by Shakespeare, who in *Romeo and Juliet* uses it for the bantering talk of the characters reminiscent of Porter. Following the latter, too, he permits the Nurse to use *a* for *he* when angered. Aphesis of notional words was a poetic licence, and so were the contractions *oft*, *een*, *eer*, *gainst*, *twixt* etc. *Tane* for *taken* was of Northern origin, and as much used in prose as verse. As a general rule, before the turn of the century, contraction in set verse speeches, especially those of people of high rank, was limited to metrically useful forms.

It has been suggested in the foregoing analysis that the rise of colloquial contractions in the sixteenth century was stimulated by popular comedy, especially where life in a country village is depicted with realistic appreciation of its characteristic 'humours'. That it was not, after 1590, confined to such types of drama must also be emphasized; that the orthography of the generally accepted forms was guided, if not fixed, by the theatrical scriveners will become apparent from later chapters. Two plays in manuscript, *Thomas of Woodstock* and *Sir Thomas More*, together with those discussed in the preceding pages, contain (with possibly a few exceptions) all the types of colloquial contractions found in Elizabethan literature (1557 to 1603)—so, at least, the considerable body of plays carefully reprinted by the Malone Society leads one to believe. Only a small percentage of the contractions then in use has passed into modern colloquial standard usage, other or modified forms having taken their place.

There are unluckily no manuscript plays of the University Wits, Lyly, Marlowe, Greene, Peele and Kyd, and few quartos of their dramatic work printed early enough to afford decisive evidence of their influence on Shakespeare. Their printed works do not abound in colloquial contractions, and it is unlikely that their manuscripts were different in this respect. For even if printers regarded the orthography of authors and scribes as within their power, they would hardly have introduced or expanded colloquial contractions that could affect the proprieties of metre. Their alterations were probably confined to spelling and punctuation (including capitalization). The choice of variant forms such as *bin* or *been*, *ye* or *you*, and the prepositions and adverbs with alternative -*s* endings, such as *toward*, *towards*, *beside*, *besides*, is unlikely to have been a matter in which printers would have exerted themselves. These variations were probably the work of the copyists, or such persons as were entrusted with the task of playhouse editing. To the labours of these important agents in the chain of dramatic evidence, some part of the next chapter is devoted, in the belief that variations between quarto and first-folio versions of Shakespeare's plays may be ascribed largely to them.

Chapter 5

The Contractions and other Characteristics of a Manuscript Play of the Fifteen-Nineties (*John a Kent*)

MANUSCRIPT plays are of two kinds, holograph and transcript. W. W. Greg's descriptive list of manuscript Elizabethan plays written for production on the public stage (pages 237 et seqq. of *Dramatic Documents from the Elizabethan Playhouses*), gives a full account of both types, and is particularly valuable because it indicates revisions in the theatre or arising out of censorship by the Master of the Revels, and provides a record of all significant stage directions. Of the four manuscript plays written before 1600, only one is holograph, *John a Kent* by Anthony Munday; two are transcripts, the anonymous plays *Thomas of Woodstock* (sometimes called *The First Part of Richard II*) and *Edmund Ironside*; and one, the much-discussed *Sir Thomas More*, is of a mixed type, containing a considerable number of lines that are indubitably holograph.

The object of this and the next two chapters is, briefly, to discover (a) the nature and orthography of colloquial contractions when a manuscript play is prepared for the theatre, (b) what differences there are between the practices of dramatic authors themselves and those who copy their work, and (c) in what respects contractions in print in the early quartos differ from contemporary authors' or scriveners' forms. In regard to (b), it may be possible from the analysis of selected plays to see the work of the authors that lies behind that of the scriveners. The plays most useful for this purpose are *John a Kent*, *Thomas of Woodstock* and *Sir Thomas More* (they are examined in the probable order of their dates of composition). As regards (c), inference can be the only guide, since no play in manuscript also exists in print, except Middleton's *A Game at Chess*, of which there are a holograph copy, four transcripts (c. 1624), and a quarto version of 1625. This date is too late to be of much service for a study of the orthography of Shakespeare's plays; and in any case, not one of the manuscripts of *A Game at Chess* is as full as the printed text.

John a Kent (1705 lines)

The thirteen folio leaves of this manuscript are in the carefully formed and almost wholly English hand of Anthony Munday, the last leaf bearing his autograph signature, as well as the date, December 1596, in a different hand. The very adequate stage directions are Munday's, but a few in the margin were added by the theatre scribe employed on the manuscript of *Sir Thomas More*, who also wrote the ornamental title of the vellum wrapper. For this wrapper the same mediaeval manuscript of Canon Law was used as that which contains the *More* play. Greg assigns the date *c.* 1590 to *John a Kent*; but it may even have been written earlier, and it is probable that the 1596 on the manuscript refers to the date of acquisition of the play by an individual or company. There is no record that the play was ever performed, and J. W. Ashton maintains that the manuscript is a fair copy made by Munday from another manuscript, possibly his own revision of an older play.[1] He bases his conclusion on the excision of speeches, particularly in the part of Evan, the shortness of the play, and the occurrence of hypermetrical lines, owing to the addition of words to make the dialogue more natural. *John a Kent* must have been Munday's own work, since he was a known writer of plays, and there is no evidence of stylistic variation. His only palaeographic contractions are *w^{th}* for *with* and the vowel with superimposed stroke (e.g. *ẽ*, M.S.R. 666) to indicate omitted nasal consonant *m* or *n*. His spelling is remarkably consistent and more modern than that of most contemporary playwrights. His punctuation is meticulous and often overdone, and is characterized by a colon frequently used at the end of the penultimate line of a speech—a peculiarity which recurs in his share of *Sir Thomas More*.

The use of colloquial contractions in *John a Kent* is not extensive; but there are a few notable features, commented upon in the appropriate place. The citations are from the Malone Society reprint, edited by Miss M. St. Clare Byrne.

Articles: *The:* 813 *t*hother (This is the only example in the play of
the common proclitic contraction of *the*.)

[1] Revision in Munday's *John a Kent* and *John a Cumber*, M.L.N. XLVIII, 1933, pp. 531–7.

Prepositions: *In:* This is not contracted, even in the expression *in faith*

Of and *on:* Contractions are rare, e.g. title John a Kent (= of), 799 *a* sunning (orig. = on)
Aphetic forms: All poetical uses, 801 *mongst*, 1444 *gaynst*, 1517 *bout*

Adverbs: 778 and 877 *ope*, 995 *oft* (Both obviously poetic uses.)

Pronouns: *It:* 1353 if*t* (= if it—this is the first observed enclitic use of *it* after the conditional conjunction *if*)
548 bee'*t*. Enclitic *t* occurs only three times in the play; but proclitic forms, as in *tis*, *t*were, are common

Us: 595 Let*s* (Only used after *let*.)

Our: 51 Bir Lady (Only used in this oath.)

You: The number of uses of unstressed *ye* after verbs, frequently at the line-end, is excessive, and therefore a feature of Munday's dramatic style. But stressed examples, or uses of *ye* in any other circumstances (e.g. 59), must be counted as rareties
There are no contractions of *my*, *thou*, *he*, *she*, *we*, *they*, *them*, though some sort of elision is implied in the following verses:
78 Thou shouldst be John a Kent, *thou art* so peremptorie
1008 *heere* is no getting in, *we are* fayre lockt out

Auxiliary verbs: *Will:* This is the only auxiliary verb contracted, the normal -*le* occurring with most pronouns, but only once preceded by an apostrophe, 706 wee'*le*; cf. also 1463 thou'*t*

Verb 'to be':   *Is:* 902 It'*s* Iohn a Kent (Nonce use. This is the earliest use of the combined contraction with modern enclitic '*s*, in place of the form *tis*, with proclitic pronoun. The earliest example noted in *O.E.D.* is dated 1625.)
In other combinations *s* occurs inconsistently with and without apostrophe, e.g. 251 wo*es* me, 306 The town's beset

Are: 1210 they'*r* (Nonce use. This, with Porter's *you'r* (see Ch. III), is the earliest example of the modern enclitic contraction of *are*, which thus precedes Jonson's combinations *Y'are*, *th'are*.)

Aphæresis or contraction of notional verbs: 308 *scape*, 1052 *vendge*, 366 *vaunce* (= advance—used by Turnop. All the bucolic characters tend to discard their prefixes); 1172 *tane* (*taken* does not appear; the alternative past participle is 1346 *tooke*); 1116 *turn* (past participle, not bucolic, and probably a slip of the pen for *turnd*)

Aphæresis or contraction of nouns: 341 *vise* (= *advice*), 342 *scression* (= discretion. Aphæresis is one of Munday's devices to mark the bucolic speech of the clowns); 483 *haviour*, 707 *sennight*, 827 *mends* (= amends), 1287 *poynting* (= appointing)

Uninflected genitives: 165 St Iohn *Baptist* day, 1115 for *Sidanen* sake, 1600 her *hart* cares

The conventional oaths are few in number, and there are none with initial *s* = God's.

Some noteworthy *orthographical features* of Munday's play are:

(a) Capitals are irregularly used at the beginning of verse lines, and *w* is practically always in the lower case, e.g. 18 England wales and Scotland, 260 Saint winifrides.

(b) After *w* in words like 200 *wunt*, 702 *wun*, 982 *wursse*, 1066 *wurst*, 1445 *wunder*, the graphic *u* of the mediaeval scribes is regular, where modern English has *o*.

(c) Elisional apostrophe occurs chiefly in relation to verbs: (i) in the second pers. sing. pres. indicative, e.g. 4 *dream'ste*; (ii) in the preterite and past participle of weak verbs, e.g. 866 *daunc'ste*,[1] 119 *beloov'de*; (iii) in combinations where the *verb to be* precedes, or is itself, an enclitic contraction, e.g. 548 *bee't*, 528 *Heer's*; (iv) in combinations where *will* is an enclitic contraction, e.g. 706 *wee'le*, 1463 *thoul't*. Even in these circumstances the use is sparse and inconsistent. There is one elision in the superlative, 625 *auncient'st*, but in 688 *powerfulst* there is none.

(d) Most important, because consistent, is the use of -*t*(*e*) instead of -*d*(*e*) or -*ed* in the preterite and past participle of weak verbs with an unvoiced stem-final. In 1456 *promisde*, the quality of *s* must have been [z], as in 9 *advisde*.

Idiosyncrasies of grammar are:

(e) *Dooth* is used throughout, and *hath* by all persons of education and standing. *Has* is used three times (355 (twice) and 565), but only

---

[1] In line 866 the preterite *daunc'ste* with intrusive *s* is to be compared with Porter's past partic. *forc'st* in line 2114 of *T.A.W.A.*, and Shakespeare's *sawc'st* (= sauced) at I.9.53 of *Coriolanus*. Cf. also *Woodstock* 317 *pronouncst*, 439 *gracst*. Some dramatists and scribes were apparently given to this trick of spelling.

by the clowns of bucolic origin. *Sayth* or *saith* (thrice) and *sayes* (twice) are used without much discrimination. The third pers. sing. pres. indicative of other notional verbs generally has inflexion -(*e*)*s*, with -(*e*)*th* reserved for metrical needs[1] and three stage directions (371, 1249, 1250), all apparently the author's. The -*th* ending in stage directions, much favoured by Jonson, was apparently theatrical convention (there is much of it in the 1592 edition of *The Spanish Tragedy*), and must have been introduced by the older scriveners, who were used to transcribing literary works. The inflexion -*s* is more common.

(f) *Dare* and *dares* are both used in the third pers. sing. pres. indic. of affirmative statements. Similarly, in the second sing. *wast* and *wert* both occur, as in Shakespeare, but the only use of *wast* (1303) is after the temporal conjunction *ere*, where the subjunctive would have been expected. *Wert*, the form presumably influenced by the subjunctive (e.g. 907), occurs also in the indicative (1275).

(g) The Western preterites *writ* (28, 454) and *sung* (598, 793, 866), and the biblical forms *sate* (799), *bare* (1178), are the only ones that appear, indicating Munday's preference for the same alternatives as Jonson favoured later.

(h) The provincialism, 1054 *there be that* (= there are *those* that), used by the rustic Turnop, is one of the commonplaces of Jonson. But persons of rank use the plural *be* for *are* in other circumstances, e.g. 1414 shaddowes they *be* not, 1598 the greefes wherein you *be*.

(i) There are a number of solecisms of concord, frequent in Elizabethan drama, in which plural nouns are in agreement with singular verbs. In all but one case (467) this seems to be occasioned by inversion e.g. 315 *Is* Moorton and Sydanen maryed?

> 587 *Is* Marian and Sydanen gon
> 597 *Is* fayre Sidanen and my Sister fled?
> 467 but your fayre starres *affoordes* ye better fortune
> 865 foure *was* there of them
> 924 now afreshe *beginnes* our woes.

(j) The demonstrative *yon* is twice used (1341, 1407), but not *yond* or *yonder*.

(k) The use of *self*-reflexives is so preponderant that Munday appeared

---

[1] There is an isolated prose use of -*eth* by Turnop, the rustic, in line 360. This is because he has assumed the lofty tone of the scholar and rhetorician. Cf. 'documentary' uses of -*eth* in lines 81, 85, 88 of Munday's contribution to *Sir Thomas More*, in which Lincoln reads a Bill of the wrongs of London citizens.

only to have used the alternative personal pronoun, then in common employment (e.g. I hurt *me*), in stereotyped phrases.

(l) Most important, because consistent, is the use of the adverbs *afterward* (114, 1596), *toward* (1005), *beside* (1356, 1422, 1581), and the prepositions *toward* (213, 235, 571, 1178, 1692) and *beside* (1551), without final -*s*. I can recall no other play of the fifteennineties in which the alternative *s* endings are wholly absent.

If *John a Kent* is a typical example of a careful author's draft, prepared for the theatre, as we have no reason to doubt, a few conclusions are inescapable, and indeed would at this date be expected. Elisions are perfunctory, and the rejection of an occasional extra syllable within the line is left to the intelligence of the actor. Munday's use of colloquial contractions happens to be sparing, and this would not probably be otherwise if the play were more provincial in flavour than it actually is. The contractions used are mainly of the kind useful in verse, and there are no new orthographies other than *It's* and *they'r*, which are very early uses of the modern forms. The rarity of our modern contractions in printed plays may be due to the printers' compositors following their own conventions, so long as no increase of syllables was involved. A sensible compositor, not being a skilled poet, would be likely to adhere to the latter principle. Generally, it may be inferred that the number of marks of elision was increased in the process of printing, but without any attempt at consistency or complete regularity. An author who himself provided the stage-business would be likely to ensure that the directions were carefully worded.

Chapter 6

The Manuscript Play *Thomas of Woodstock*

THIS anonymous play of twenty-five folio leaves (2989 lines) is actually without title, and forms part of the British Museum manuscript collection of fifteen play-books (Egerton 1994), supposed to have been assembled by William Cartwright, a King's Revels actor 1629-37, who during the Civil War became a bookseller and collector of plays. The manuscript is in the shapely English hand of a copyist, who makes an unskilled attempt at Italian script for the speakers' names. His spelling is old fashioned and unorthodox (see p. ix of Miss Wilhelmina Frylinck's introduction to the Malone Society reprint); but in his elisions, parentheses and use of the semicolon the copyist reveals that his punctuation has affinities with the work of the seventeenth century. This contradiction leads to the belief that the irregular and archaic spellings are attributable to the material which the copyist had before him. This, according to Miss Frylinck, was not the author's manuscript, but a rough draft, since speech-prefixes were added after the copy had been made (and are consequently sometimes wanting when passages have been deleted), line division is faulty, and stage-directions occasionally appear where they have no bearing on the text. But she does point to a few linguistic features that should be the author's (pp. IX–X), words that are unnoted or rare in the *Oxford English Dictionary*.

The manuscript was obviously prompt-copy, because of the number of prompt directions added in different hands and inks, which point to repeated revivals. The deletion of 'my god' in line 142 suggests a revision for performance after 1606, when the enactment prohibiting oaths on the stage came into force. But the internal evidence and end-stopped verse of the play indicate that the original composition belongs to the early nineties of the sixteenth century. In spirit and plot it belongs to the chronicle period of *Edward II* and the *Henry VI* trilogy. Most critics regard certain verbal parallels in *Richard II* as implying precedence for *Thomas of Woodstock*. The subject of the chronology of this group of plays has been ably handled by Mr. A. P. Rossiter in his *Woodstock, a Moral History* (1946), in which he urges consideration of the order 2 *Henry VI—Woodstock—Edward II* (followed, one assumes, by *Richard II*), and suggests the limits 1591–4 for the writing of *Thomas of Woodstock*.

If the above reasoning is correct, the extant manuscript of this play was made by the copyist (not a professional scribe) probably ten or more years later than the original date of composition. Additional evidence for placing the transcript in the early seventeenth century is (1) the high incidence of later contracted forms such as *th'are* for *they are* (the orthography of which suggests post-1600 theatrical revision—See Pronouns (g) below); (2) the sophisticated use of elision, particularly the Jonsonian type (e.g. 244 *we 'had*);[1] and (3) the occurrence of the combined contraction *shalls* (= shall we). The use of *us* for *we* is first cited in *O.E.D.* from Dekker and Webster's *Sir Thomas Wyatt* (1607). The contraction *s* is frequent in Shakespeare, but *shall's* only occurs in one quarto, the doubtful *Pericles* (1609), and in folio texts of late date such as *Coriolanus*, *The Winter's Tale* and *Cymbeline*, all of which must have been written between 1607 and 1610.

The more important instances of contraction are as follows:

Articles
  (a) Proclitic *th*: 496 *th'*unhoulsome, 2045 *th*important, 2440 *th*eternall, 2668 *th'*old
  (b)   ,,   *t*: 457 *t'*other, 454, 832 *t*other, 463 *t*oth'er (misplaced apostrophe).
  (c) Enclitic *th* after prepositions: 9 by*th*, blest Saints (= by the; the comma may be an apostrophe placed too low). The use of the contraction *th* before consonants is an innovation, much resorted to after 1600 by dramatists who favoured these new combined contractions. The earliest observed use of *byth* by another sixteenth-century dramatist occurs in *Romeo and Juliet* (Q_2), 1599. The usual spelling in *Woodstock* is *bith*, and it is found commonly in the oaths out of which this form of combined contraction seems to have arisen, e.g. 105 *bith rood*. The frequency and variety of this contraction-type in *Woodstock* make it almost certainly the author's.
  149 *i'th* grass, 159 *ith* country. (This is a double contraction, the usual

---

[1] The name for this type of elision was given by W. W. Greg (*The Library*, March 1942, XXII, pp. 213–15), Jonson using it frequently in *Sejanus* and later plays. He was not, however, the originator. The name applies to a combination of two words in which elision of a vowel is intended and indicated by an apostrophe, though graphic suppression does not actually take place. (See Chap. VIII.)

orthography being *eth* (1320, 1543, 1562 etc.), which may have been
the author's spelling.)
668 to*th* block, 2618 to'*th*, 1745 and 2392 *thoth* erroneously. Jonsonian
elision occurs at 1166 to '*the queene*, which is apparently the orthography of the copyist.
856 *oth* (generally a*th*)

Adverbs

949 *backeward* (but 1565 *towards*, 2467 *sometymes*. Before 1600
adverbial types, without final -*s*, were most commonly used; after
the turn of the century, there was considerable competition from the
-*s* forms).
1291 *nere*
1452 etc. *ene* (= even), 1567 *en*

Prepositions

The most important innovation is the double contraction combination of preposition and definite article, e.g. 149 *i'th* 856 *oth*. The
orthography is varied; but, as stated, the spelling *eth* of the first is
probably the author's, the more sophisticated *i'th* the copyist's.

In: 149 *i'*th, 1591 *ith*, 1320 etc. *eth*; 24, 1296 *ifaith*, 217 *e faith*, 382 *efaith*;
1413 *agodsname*. (This expression, with preposition reduced to *a*,
goes back to the early fourteenth century, and was used by Chaucer.)

Of: 801 *o'the* lower, 856 *oth* parlament, 1851 *ath* Realme, 2604 *ath*
sudden; 187 Anne *a* Beame (= Anne of Bohemia. So 359, 409 etc.).

On: 1727 sett you *a* worke, 1804 *a*making.

To: 982 *t'*abridg, 1257 *t*assist. (The earliest citation of the reduced form *t*
in O.E.D. is from Chaucer's *Romaunt of the Rose*.); 2595 *to'*excuse
(Jonsonian elision).

Poetic forms (*with aphesis or contraction*) 317 '*gainst*, 2019 *gainst*, 846 etc. *ore*

Pronouns

Though in Woodstock *ye* is much used as a weakened form of *you*, it is not
confined to the post-verb position, and is not as frequent as in *John a Kent*.

(a) Proclitic *it*: 86 *t*were, 262 *t*will etc. (This poetical combination is very
common.)
Enclitic *it*: (i) after conjunctions: 198 tho'*t*, 474 If*t*;
(ii) after prepositions: a'n*t* (= on it; apostrophe misplaced; *ant* (1145,
1452, 1540 etc.) must have been the author's form; *ont* (976) is less
frequent); 488, 1583 for*t*, 1269 too*t*, 1433 by*t*, 2269 in*t*;
(iii) after verbs: 146 is*t*, 1484 was*t*, 728 hear'*t*, 1664 sha*t* (= shall it),
1832 ha*t*e (= have it), 2855 sea*lt*.

(b) Proclitic *thou*: 139 etc. *t*hart, 2005 tha'st (apostrophe misplaced), 2270
*t*hast, 896 *t*hadst, 1137 *t*h'adst.

(c) Proclitic *ye* (singular): 164, 425, *y'*are, 1456 etc. *y*are, 377 *y'*ave.

(The contraction *y*', first cited in *O.E.D.* 1631, occurs erroneously at I.3.180 (*y'owe*) of *Richard II* (Q$_1$) 1597, but not again before 1600 in my investigations.)

(d) Proclitic *he*: 1441 *h*'as (= he has. See Chapter 2 and classification of contraction types (7), Chapter 4).

(e) Proclitic *we*: 486 *w*'ere. (Apostrophe probably misplaced; contraction of *are* (we're) intended.)

(f) Enclitic *us*: 101, 1207, lett*s*, 1623 lend*s* (= lend us), 999 shall*s*. (This is the earliest use of the contraction *s* (= we) after *shall*.)

(g) Proclitic *they*: 1210 *th*'are (and four identical uses up to line 1589); 1654, 1763, *tha*'re (apostrophe misplaced); 1674, 2092 *th*are; 1657 *th*'ar; 1902 *th*ar (*O.E.D.*'s first citation of the contraction *th* for *they* is from Weever's prose *Ancient Funeral Monuments*, dated assigned 1540, but not printed until 1631. Jonson used the contraction, always with apostrophe, for verse elision only, first in line 187 of the Induction of the quarto of *Every Man out of his Humour* (1600); he seems to have introduced it into verse drama. In *Woodstock* the contraction *th* is used also in prose; but however employed, it is confined to less than 900 lines (1210–2092) in the middle of the play, which may indicate a theatrical revision of this part after 1600).

(h) *them*: 1786 *um*. (Nonce form.) The earliest uses of this contraction in *O.E.D.* are from Chapman's *Gentleman Usher* (1606) and Beaumont and Fletcher's *Philaster* (*c.* 1610).

(i) Enclitic *his* after prepositions and verbs: 1418 an'*s* (= on his), 1814 at*s*, 2612 a bout*s*, 2395 cutt*s*. The first citation of enclitic *s* for *his* in *O.E.D.* is from Marlowe's *Jew of Malta* (*c.* 1592).

Auxiliary verbs

Will: 72 I*le*, 437 he*le*, 468 we'*le*, 487 w'e*le*, 722 we*le*, 165 you*le*, 602 thei*le*. (These are common, with and without apostrophe.)
1998 thou*t* (= thou wilt; nonce form).

Would: 1068 I*de*, 2855 I*d*, 1830 you*d*, 45 h'e*ed* and 48 h'e*d* (apostrophe misplaced), 204 we*de*. The contraction *d* for *would* is not cited earlier in *O.E.D.* than *Timon of Athens* (1607), in the form *thoud'st*.

Have: 591 *ha* done, 1832 *ha*te (= have it).

Had: The contraction *d* for *had* is not found, but Jonsonian elision is once used, 244 we'*had*.

Verb 'to be'

Am: 56 etc. I*me*, 307 etc. I'*me*. *O.E.D.* has no example of this contraction until Cowley's *Mistress*, 1647. The normal orthography before 1600 is found in *Woodstock* 282 'I am sweld more plump, than erst I was', the licence of elision or slurring being assumed by the actor.

Is: 137 tyme*s*, 189 that*s*, 379 etc. hee*s*, 383 h'ee*s* (apostrophe misplaced), 674 ther*s*, 695 treason*s*, 1572 what*s*.

Are: 315 you're, 486 w'ere (apostrophe misplaced), 2091 we'are (Jonsonian elision). Contraction of *are* is not common in this play, and its occurrence may be another mark of revision. Porter had used it, but there is no date in *O.E.D. Woodstock* generally has proclitic contraction of the pronoun ye (see Pronouns (c)), which is Jonson's convention and that of many Jacobean dramatists.

Aphæresis or contraction of notional verbs.

16, 237, 580 etc. *tayne.* (Always in this spelling, which was apparently the author's.)

1415 *light* (= alight)

Aphæresis of nouns.

2405 *havior* (= behaviour).

Interjections.

(a) *Aphesis:* 383 *las* (= alas).

(b) *Proclitic 's' or 'z'* (= *God's*) *in oaths:* 229 etc. *s*blud, 467 etc. *s*foote, 270 etc. *z*ounes.

Notable *grammatical features* of the play are concerned mainly with verbal inflexions:

1. Third pers. sing. pres. indic. of *have*: Except at 1722 where *hath* is affected as the legal phraseology, Nimble always uses *has*, and so do the country folk and tradespeople whom he is persecuting. Elsewhere the use of *hath* and *has* is indiscriminate, and more or less of equal incidence. The use of colloquial *has* in verse by king, queen and nobleman, suggests post-1600 revision of the text. In folk plays, such as Peele's *Old Wives Tale*, both *has* and *does* had been in sparing use since 1590.

2. Third pers. sing. pres. indic. of *do: Does* outnumbers *doth*, of which only two examples were noticed (750 and 2380), in the first and last parts of the play, where the work of the author seems to have been best preserved. Subsequent revision affected mainly the middle of the play.

3. Third pers. sing. pres. indic. of *notional verbs*: -*s* endings are regular, even with *say* and *dare*; please*th* (108) is accounted for by the sibilant stem-final.

4. Solecisms of concord, so common in plays before 1600, in which plural subjects are in agreement with apparently singular verbs, were noted as follows, and are in the mouths of all social ranks:

557 be shrowe the churles that *makes* my queene so sadd

938 his cursses *frights* not mee

1097 the dukes of yorke and lancaster / who as I guess Intends to ryd with hime

1103 what revells *keepes* his flattering minions
1116 (400) Archers In a guard *attends* them
1324 at one feast *was servd* (10000) dishes
1623 our owne hands *undoes* us
1892 we (4) *comes* presently
2037 those about hir. *feares* hir sudden death (The intrusive full-stop is a feature of the punctuation)
2091 some sports *does well*
2134 so many wyld boores *rootes* & *spoyles* our lands
2706 the warrs *has* don
2746 those fflattering mynions that ore *turnes* the state

5. The conjunction *whilse* (1827), or a spelling variant of it, is regularly used instead of *while* or *whilst*.

Some *orthographical features* noted are:

1. The copyist puts numerals in brackets throughout.
2. He has a fondness for capital *I*, sometimes even in the middle of a word e.g. 890 *enIoy*. Generally he prefers the prefixes *im-*, *in-* to *em-*, *en-*.
3. In the preterites and past participles of weak verbs there is the same regularity of inflexions as is found in *Richard II* (Q₁): with one exception (1448 earn*t*), *-d(e)* is used after voiced stem-finals, and *-t(e)* after unvoiced, *-ed* being reserved for instances where the ending is required to be syllabic, e.g. 545 learn*ed*. As consistency is maintained throughout the play, the copyist seems to have been responsible. His system dispenses with the necessity for apostrophes, the rare instance 568 *disgrac't* possibly denoting omission of *s*, as *gracst* is the spelling in line 439.
4. Unlike Munday's, the copyist's marks of elision are confined almost entirely to the colloquial and poetical contractions, but their incidence is most irregular, and often misplaced. This may be attributed to his lack of experience of the forms, the author's being probably void of elisions and distinguishable in such orthographies as *ath*, *eth*, *en* (= even), *efaith*, *ats* (= at his), *tayne*, etc.
5. Author-spellings are a matter of conjecture, but the following are idiosyncratic: 113 *boeth* (both), 137 *byssye*, 199 *wardropp* (wardrobe), 228 *vissett*, 341 *surssarays* (certiorari), 454 *hosse* (hose), 475 *collomes*, 497 *otians* (ocean's), 539 *swome* (past participle of swim), 652 *teranaye* (tyranny), 692 *higth* (height), 845 *descifard* (deciphered), 991 *dyneing Rome* (dining-room), 1038 *Royatous* (riotous), 1108 *pickes* (peaks), 1128 *sigth* (sigh), 1149 *grasher* or

1558 *Graysher* or 1575 *gratier* (grazier), 1245 *varlott*, 1322 *Rueind*, 1372 *cronicld*, 1409 *strocke* (struck), 1460 *scilence*, 1604 *benydissete* (benedicite), 1615 *puuding*, 1658 *nosses*, (noses, cf. 454), 1708 *casses* (cases), 1710 *whissells*, 1733 *caves* (calves), 1764 *gitt*, 1843 *dromes* (drums), 1922 *subsites* (subsidies), 2104 *a massed* (amazed), 2163 *vinards* (vineyards), 2265 *Aretchmaticke*, 2298 *dossen* (cf. 454, 1658).

The irregularity of the spelling and orthography of contraction compels the conclusion that the extant manuscript of *Woodstock* is a good example of stratification, the final version being prepared not earlier than about 1607. The naive and idiosyncratic elements appear to be the author's. As there is in dramatic works a progressive increase of contractions and elisions, as well as modernization of spelling, with each decade of the period 1590–1620, it is logical to infer that the simpler use of apostrophe antedates the more sophisticated, and that archaic spellings precede those which are more up-to-date. Most professional scribes about this time used Italian script and revised glaring irregularities. The copyist of *Woodstock*, however, was a literary man, with a good English hand, but no pretensions to skilled editing. He made as faithful a copy as he could of his material, which was in the hand sometimes of the author, sometimes of the playhouse editors, who had prepared and perhaps altered the play for performance. This, in itself, appears to have been a composite business on the lines of Dover Wilson's 'continuous copy', and dictated by the needs of presentation over a period of years. The original author was given to colloquial contractions, and the improvers continued in that spirit with more up-to-date forms. The dramatic stock-in-trade of cant phrases, oaths, clichés and contractions was gradually built up, and individual authors and producers followed the current fashions. Even such improvements as a copyist might have made would have been the result of improving notions of orthography, under the influence of practising literary men, such as Jonson, and reputable printers, such as Field, rather than of grammarians.

A verse characteristic of *Woodstock* is the frequency of lines with light, weak and feminine endings, a somewhat nerveless verse that anticipates the manner of Fletcher e.g.

1124 ere many dayes agen Ile vissett *ye* (light ending)
1497 Ile duble his reward thers (12)pence for *ye* (weak ending)
1135 our guard of Archers, keepe the doores I charge *ye* (feminine ending)

Lines with weakened *you* have been selected, because it is note-worthy that, in the same circumstances (there is one within-the-line exception (1786)), the full form *them* is retained, as one believes it to have been in Shakespeare's drafts, e.g.

523 we lett ye know those guifts are given to *them* (weak)
1988 we shall with greater ease arrest and take *them* (feminine)

Had *Woodstock* been re-written in the second decade of the seventeenth century, when Fletcher had succeeded Shakespeare as principal play-wright of the King's Men, the new contraction *em* of *Demetrius and Enanthe*, or its variation *um* found in *Bonduca*, would almost certainly have appeared in the falling rhythm of line-endings such as those cited.

The so-called Fletcherian line was, in fact, no innovation. It occurred in plays of the fifteen-nineties, such as *Woodstock*, which aimed at securing a type of verse approximating closely to the natural rhythms of speech. Wilson Knight in his essay 'Henry VIII and the Poetry of Conversion' (*The Crown of Life*, pp. 267-9) rightly points to the inci-dence of such lines in Shakespearian plays from *King Lear* to the end of the dramatist's career. What is characteristic of Fletcher, however, is the higher percentage of such lines, and the combinations of the final falling rhythm with colloquial contractions, especially *em* and *ye*.

Comparing the chronicle-tragedy *Woodstock* with the comedy *John a Kent*, it becomes apparent that the use of colloquial contractions depends not simply on the material handled, or the characters and setting of the play, but on the peculiar style and taste in language of the author. Additions and alterations, *ex hypothesi*, preserve the spirit of the original; but if they are as much as twelve years later, as is suggested in the case of *Woodstock*, the earlier contraction types would be overlaid by later ones, and especially by a different orthography and more pre-cise use of the apostrophe. Thus, in *Woodstock*, *shalls*, *th'are*, *hang um* and *I'me* are probably later than the other contractions, and so are the forms *has* and *does* for the author's *hath* and *doth*. These additions and revisions affected mainly the Nimble and Tresilian scenes, which pro-vide the comic relief.

When alterations to a play become extensive and complicated, or the theatre copy worn through much handling, a fresh draft becomes an important desideratum. What degree of regularization in the ortho-graphy then takes place depends on the experience and professional competence of the copyist. But a copyist, even of Ralph Crane's stand-ing, would not venture to modify much more than spelling, marks of

D

elision and punctuation. The copyist of *Woodstock* was not nearly so enterprising, and indeed must have been rather slavish. The frequent use of full-stops, where a modern editor would use a comma or no stop at all, seems to have been a theatre practice, sometimes varied with colons, intended to mark the rhythmical units for the actor's delivery. The alternative is to suppose that what are now periods were in the original draft imperfectly tailed commas, which the maker of the fair copy misinterpreted.

If *Woodstock* had gone to the printer, the latter would have removed the brackets from the numerals, reduced the unnecessary full-stops, modernized the more inconvenient of the author's archaic spellings, increased the apostrophes, regularized the capital letters at the beginning of verse lines, and confined them in the body of the sentence to certain classes of nouns (see Chapter 8). But, here again, the extent of improvement would depend upon the professional competence of the printer's staff. The setting up of *Hamlet* (Q_2), as Dover Wilson has shown, was the work of an apprentice compositor; the printing of Field's quartos of *Venus and Adonis* and *Lucrece* was another matter. Field's printing of poems reached the educated classes; but unfortunately plays did not always fall into the hands of reputable printers.

Chapter 7

The Manuscript Play *Sir Thomas More*:
List of Contractions in dramatic
use by 1600

SINCE 1911, when W. W. Greg prepared his valuable reprint of *Sir Thomas More* for the Malone Society, many able minds have been at work on the text. The most important results of the preliminary findings were contained in the symposium *Shakespeare's Hand in Sir Thomas More*, which was followed for several years by supporting articles and rejoinders, summarized by R. C. Bald in 1949.[1] Most scholars now appear to accept the conclusions that there were five dramatists and a playhouse scrivener involved in the preparation of the extant manuscript. A necessary preface to any further contribution is, therefore, a statement of what is already known, accepted or conjectured with most probability about the composition of this interesting play.

Sir Thomas More was probably written between 1593 and 1598, though some critics have argued for a date as late as 1600. The manuscript consists of twenty-two folio leaves, of which one and two are the wrappers. The original text is now only thirteen leaves, the missing folios 6–9, 12, 13 and 16 having been supplied by later insertions. The play was the property of the Chamberlain's Men, Shakespeare's Company, but was never performed; apparently it was abandoned in the process of revision, because it was found impracticable to meet the demands of the cautious censor, Edmund Tilney, who held the office of Master of the Revels from 1579 to 1610. The manuscript is a composite one and contains a few passages repeated in a different orthography. Six different handwritings have been identified, the original fair draft or nucleus of the play (placed first in the Malone Society reprint)

[1] *Shakespeare Survey* 2 'The Booke of Sir Thomas More and its Problems', pp. 44–65.

consisting of 1986 lines written by scribe S,[1] whom Greg identified as Anthony Munday. Munday was, however, only part-author of what he transcribed. There are also six additions in the hands of five other persons, called A, B, C, D, E. A and B, whose identity some still regard as uncertain, are confidently believed to be Chettle and Heywood respectively.[2] C was a theatrical scribe, D is presumed to have been Shakespeare, and E was Dekker.

E. H. C. Oliphant maintained that the original text transcribed by Munday contained, besides his own work, contributions by A (Chettle) and B (Heywood), and that when the play was revised, each was invited to make replacements in or additions to his part, his argument being 'that there was no difference in style between most of the added passages and the scenes in which they were to be imbedded'.[3] Shakespeare's contribution to the play was purely *ad hoc*; he was called upon to augment a crowd-scene, in the writing of which he was esteemed pre-eminent. Dekker's work was a rewriting of Scene VIII, for the original of which he may or may not have been responsible; his work was, however, transcribed by scrivener C, and then resubmitted to him, and augmented in his own hand, which accounts for the paucity of the lines definitely identifiable as Dekker's.

	Original Play	Addition I	Addition II	Addition III	Addition IV	Addition V	Addition VI
i. Munday	1–734*		66–122		1–26		
ii. Heywood	876–1156		1–64*				2–73*
	1603–1986						
iii. Chettle	1156–1602	1–71*					
iv. Shakespeare			123–270*				
v. Dekker					1–242†		
? Munday or Dekker	735–876						
? Dekker or Shakespeare				1–22			

* Autograph.   † Lines 212–242 autograph.

All the remaining lines are alleged to be transcription, in the first column Munday's, in the Additions Scribe C's.

[1] I have preserved the designations of the handwritings in Greg's Malone Society reprint, 1911.

[2] See S. A. Tannenbaum 'More about *The Booke of Sir Thomas More*', *P.M.L.A.* XLIII (1928).

[3] See E. H. C. Oliphant, 'Sir Thomas More' *J.E.G.P.* XVIII (1919), p. 228.

This is a reasonable explanation of the play's composition; but the intervention of amanuenses to make fresh drafts complicates the problem of authorship. In Appendix IV is given the most plausible analysis of the work of the five authors, according to Greg, Oliphant, Tannenbaum, Bald and others, of which the above is a summary:

It is outside my purpose to discover, in Munday's original transcription of *Sir Thomas More*, the work of Heywood and Chettle, as this to be convincing would involve detailed investigation of the known plays of each author. It will be sufficient to note the characteristics of the independent contributors, and to study passages re-written in a different orthography, one aim· being to illustrate the possibilities of mutation when a scene passes through different hands.

(i) *Munday*

As Munday transcribed the first version of the play, the evidence of his orthography should be plentiful; and it is. Especially noticeable are the regularity of the preterite and past participle inflexions of weak verbs, and the *u* spelling for *o* after initial *w*. His comparatively modern spelling and punctuation are everywhere. His use of apostrophe is extended to the combined contractions, for the reason that the use of these is more frequent in this play than in *John a Kent*. The first 734 lines of the original text are indisputably his own composition, since they contain *all* the idiosyncrasies of grammar and contraction in *John a Kent* (see Chapter V), and no novelties except the following:

Grammar
1. 3rd pers. sing. pres. indic. of *have* and *do*: 251, 293 *has* (used by Suresby and More, the gentry class); 651 *does* (used by Doll Williamson); elsewhere *hath* and *dooth*.

Contractions
2. *Pronouns: Thou:* 225 *Th'*art
          He: 357 (twice) *a*
          It: 128, 294 too'*t*, 463, 466 on'*t*, 376 for '*t*; 641 deny'*t*; 650 had'*t* (cf. ift in *John a Kent*)
          They: 448 *th'*are
3. *Auxiliary verbs: Would:* 294 I*de*, 540 they'*d*
4. *Verb 'to be': Are:* 214 you'*r* (cf. they'*r* in *John a Kent*)

The extension of the use of *has*, and of the contractions, which are practically all in the combined class, is undoubtedly due to the raciness of the dialogue, but also to the fact that Munday's contribution to *Sir Thomas More* was probably written seven years later than his *John a Kent*.

Hence also the conventional *th'are* in the latter for *they'r* in the former.

Under (iv) I have attempted to show that Munday's own composition extends beyond line 734 of the original version of the play, as far as line 876, i.e. he was actually the author of scenes I–VIII.

(ii) *Heywood*

In Scene IV (lines 412–52) Heywood gives evidence of his literary supervision. He takes Munday's scene and rewrites it with the sole purpose of replacing the outbursts of the mob by some witty remarks of a Clown (see Addition II, lines 1–64, in Heywood's own hand). Not only is the Clown's part more racy, but the language is charged with adages and proverbial phrases, the use of capitals is capricious, and the spelling oddly individual compared with Munday's. It is instructive to compare his transcription of some of Mundays' lines in the Heywood orthography:

Munday
> Doll. Peace there I say, heare Captaine Lincolne speake
> Keepe silence, till we know his minde at large.
>
> (Orig. 412–13)

Heywood
> Doll. pease theare I saye heare captaine lincolne speake.
> kepe silens till we know his minde at large.
>
> (Addition II, 9–10)

In the next speech of Lincoln, Heywood corrects the verse lineation of Munday, but does little else, allowing only one stop in seven lines:

Munday
> Lin. Come gallant bloods, you, whose free soules doo scorne
> to beare th'enforced wrongs of Aliens.
> Add rage to resolution, fire the houses
> of these audacious stangers. This is St. Martins
> And yonder dwelles Mewtas a wealthie Piccarde, at the greene gate,
> De Barde, Peter van Hollock, Adrian Martine,
> with many more outlandish fugitives.
>
> (Orig. 415–21)

Heywood
> lincol. then gallant bloods you whoes fre sowles doo skorne
> to beare the inforsed wrongs of alians
> ad rage to Ressolutione fier the howses
> of these audatious strangers: This is St martins
> and yonder dwells mutas a welthy piccardye

at the greene gate
de barde peter van hollocke adrian Martine
wth many more outlandishe fugitives

(Addition II, 13–20)

It is clear from the spelling, punctuation and capitals of the above why Munday was given the task of copying out the play. Not only was his hand more legible, but despite the limitations of his original talent, he was a scholar and student of grammatical conventions, excellent qualifications for a scrivener. The lack of apostrophe in Heywood's second line leaves doubt as to the delivery of the line, whereas Munday's elision makes it clear that the poetic past-participle inflexion has to be sounded. Examples, such as this, are of value in construing some of the lines of the Shakespearian good quartos. It is interesting to observe that Munday's *th'are* (448) is transcribed by Heywood *theyre* (58).

In lines 2–73, Addition VI, Heywood's own work is autograph, and the following characteristics appear:

Contractions

Pronouns:	He:	7, 16, 58 *a*
	It:	19 *tis*; 45, 56 *t*was (cf. Addition II, 64 *tis*)
	Us:	17 *gives*, 65 *lets*
Auxiliary verbs:	Will:	32 *ile* (cf. Addition II, 2 *wele*)
	Have:	56 god *a* mersye; 62 *ha* (cf. Addition II, 53 *ha*)
Verb 'to be':	Been:	13 *bin*
	Is:	28 that*s*, 36 what*s* (cf. Addition II, 35 that*s*); 71 sargin*s* (= sergeant is)
	Are:	18 *ther* 20s wantinge (presumably assimilated contraction = there are)

Grammar

The only 3rd pers. sing. pres. indic. of *have* is *hathe* (22); for notional verbs the ending is always -(e)s, e.g. 16 *sayes*.

In line 2 the common provincialism *be* for *are* after *Where, Here, There* etc. occurs.

Orthography

1. The favourite letter for capitalization is *R*, which occurs ten times; there are also seven instances in Addition II, lines 1–64, in which Heywood transcribed Munday.

2. The only punctuation marks are commas, colons, and full-stops. The last is several times employed where a lesser stop, such as a comma or semicolon, would suffice. There are no apostrophes. The same pointing, but more economical, appears in Addition II, 1–64.

3. Preterite and past-participle endings of weak verbs are regular: -*d(e)* after voiced stem-finals; -*t(e)* after unvoiced stem-finals; -*ed* or -*id* for syllabic inflexions. The ending -*id* occurs three times: 9 entreat*id*, 46 disseau*id*, 59 larn*id*. This -*id* orthography is not found in Heywood's revision of Munday.

4. Idiosyncrasies of spelling are: 2 *theis*; 7 *angills* (which varies with *angells*); 11 *neclegens*; 13 *other wies* (cf. 45 *wieslye*); 14 *curius*; 18 *suer* (= sure); 25 *rishes* (= rushes); 26 *hoo* and 42 *ho* (= who); 28 *hard* (= heard); 33, 53, 70 (twice) *ar* (72 are); 33 *fuer* (= fewer); 36 *haist*; 44 *Risseaue* (cf. Addition II, 44 *Risseude*); 45 *plaist*; 54 *dunn*; 59 *larnid*; 63 *sarvd*, 71 *sargins* (= sergeant is).

Heywood's independent contribution, although too scant for generalization, shows that he does not employ combined contractions, except of the conventional forms found in the poetry of the time, such as *tis, ile, whats* etc. There are no double contractions, such as *ith*, and no elisional apostrophes. If he wrote any part of the original play transcribed by Munday, his fondness for capital *R* and his peculiarities of punctuation and spelling were lost in the process of transcription. On the other hand, when he transcribes Munday, he is to some extent influenced by his copy; he writes *whoes* (Addition II, line 13), where his own spelling is *hoo*; and his old-fashioned use of the -*id* inflexion for weak verbs gives way to -*ed* (e.g. 14 *inforsed*). He does, however, let slip an occasional *ar* or *theis*, spellings for the commoner words. These last spellings were cited as abnormal in Dover Wilson's treatment of the supposed Shakespearian contribution to the play (see below), as were *straing* and *Iarman*. But similar spellings are characteristic of Heywood; for the holograph passage yields the orthographies *haist, plaist* and *hard* (heard), *sargin* (sergeant), in which the radical vowels are comparable. In fact, when the latter pair are placed beside *larnid* and *sarvd*, it becomes apparent that this *a* spelling, probably influenced by regional dialect, is an idiosyncrasy of Heywood's.

Coming to the portions of the original version of the play which are claimed for Heywood by Oliphant, viz. Scene IX (lines 878–1157) and Scenes XIV–XVII (lines 1603–1986), it is not possible to do more than note those features which are not characteristic of Munday. Scene IX is largely devoted to the play within the play, called *The Marriage of Wit and Wisdom*, which begins at line 1030. This is not the play now so entitled, but consists of a prologue of eight lines from *The Disobedient Child*, followed by Heywood's own version of an episode from *Lusty Juventus*. As the language and versification of this interlude are deliberately archaic, they should not be used as evidence of what Heywood usually wrote. The play itself, with some interruption from More towards the end, runs to line 1134, and the scene concludes twenty-three lines later, but was augmented by Addition VI (considered above) in Heywood's own hand, in order to depict in a colourful episode More's bounty, and his servant's niggardliness, to the players. Scenes XIV–XVII add to the conviction that the author's function in the play, whether he was Heywood or not, was mainly to characterize the central figure in all his domestic charm and diversity, to show More as the humane, humorous and generous person that compelled popular admiration. Munday's creative talent was too pedestrian for this purpose.

The following are the characteristic features that emerge from the scenes just mentioned:

Contractions
   Combined forms: preposition and def. article: 920 *o'th.* (This occurs in the title of a play.)
   Prepositions: Of: 1863 *a*
   Pronouns: It: 1019 in'*t*, 1819 And'*t*, 1863 is*t*
      You: (pl.) 1710 *y'*are
      They: 946, 947 *th'*are
      Them: 1630 *am*
   Auxiliary verbs: Would: 1026 I*de*, 1929 you'*ld*. (The -*ld* spelling of the contraction is found in Shakespeare only in the F$_1$ plays, the earliest citation in any work in O.E.D., she'*ld*, being from *Two Gentlemen of Verona*.)
The weakened pronoun *ye*, and the form *bin*, occur very frequently. I have not included the conventional verse contractions, such as *Ile, ther's, twas, ore, twixt, gainst, bove*, which are common to almost every dramatist and poet, and therefore seldom shown with marks of elision.

Oaths: 895 *Gods me*; 937 *bir Lady*; 1125 *In troth*; 1149 *by my troth*; 1013 *Gramercies*; 1673, 1731, 1915 *a Gods name*, 1698 *Before God*

Grammar:
(1) 3rd pers. sing. pres. indic. of *have:* 1144 (and 9 other uses) *hath;*
         1023 (and 4 other uses) *has;*
      ,,   ,,   ,,   ,,   ,,   ,,   *do:*   1018, 1122 (More) *does;* 1854,
         1897 *dooth*
(2) Preterites: 891 *bad*, 968 *drove*, 1149 *sweat*, 1152 *spake*
      Past participles: 937 *loden*, 1137 *holpe*, 1644 *tane*, 1717 *bestowne*
Spelling
Unusual forms: 1152 *extemprically*, 1913 *arrand*, 1986 *prograce*

Punctuation

Marks of syncope and elision in past participles and contractions are comparatively regular, except in the conventional verse forms of the latter, e.g. *Ile*. In the last four scenes there are 9 uses of brackets for parenthetical phrases and sentences; but these, like the elisions, were undoubtedly supplied by Munday, since they appear in his own and Chettle's portion of the play, in his transcription. The work of the original author is much overlaid by Munday's orthography.

There is nothing conclusive about the above evidence, and Heywood's independent work elsewhere needs careful investigation. The contractions *am* for *them*, and *-ld* for *would*, are not found in Munday's own work; neither are the oaths *Gods me* and *Gramercies*.

(iii) *Chettle*

Oliphant assigns to Chettle scenes X–XIII of the original version transcribed by Munday (lines 1158–1602), and if this can be maintained, it is obvious that Chettle's function was the clear-cut one of providing the portion of the play concerned with More's indictment, fall and consignment to the Tower. A conspicuous feature of these scenes is the very high percentage of speeches that are rhymed, either as a whole or in part, such speeches being easily distinguished from the occasional ones in Munday's and Dekker's parts that merely end in a rhymed couplet.

In the last of these scenes Chettle, whether he was the author of the original four scenes or not, saw fit to add a domestic episode between More and his lady, immediately prior to the Chancellor's disgrace. This Addition I (of 71 lines) was wrongly inserted in the manuscript as folio 6a, but there is no doubt that it was intended to replace lines 1471–1516, deleted, on folio 19a; it has the same partiality for rhyme as the original scene, of which it is a revision. As the Addition is in Chettle's own hand, I have noted its characteristics first:

Contractions

   Prepositions: *To:* 63 *t'*inrich
   Pronouns: *It:* 21 wer*t* (= were it), 33 *t*is
   Verb '*to be*': *Is:* 3 here*s*, 44 there'*s*, that*s*

Grammar:

(1) 3rd pers. sing. pres. indic. of *have:* 28 *has,* 52 *hath*
     ,, ,, ,, ,, ,, ,, *do* 15 *doth*
    2nd ,, ,, past ,, ,, *be:* 5 thou that *wert*

Spelling

Chettle's spelling is even more modern than Munday's, and is remarkable at this time for the comparative absence of the long spellings, especially in monosyllabic words, characteristic of Shakespeare, e.g. *sunne* for *sun*. The endings of preterites and past participles of weak verbs are regular, in the manner of Munday.

Punctuation

Though the pointing is economical, it is modern, the chief absence being that of commas. There are five semicolons in the 71 lines, and they are intelligently used. There are only two colons, not dramatic or rhetorical, but used as a temporal semicolon, a stop half-way between a comma and full-stop. The use of the apostrophe in the possessive genitive *Stuart's* in line 59 is the first I have found in drama, though it occurs occasionally in the Prayer Book of 1549.

Vocabulary

Though the spelling *dreep* for drip (see *overdreep* in line 11) is common enough in the Standard English of literary authors until the late seventeenth century, it is of dialectal origin, and does not appear in Shakespeare.

Returning to the original scenes X–XIII, one finds that such features as survive Munday's transcription, are wholly consonant with Chettle's authorship.

Contractions
Articles: The: 1542 *th'*other
Prepositions: To: 1247 *t'*appeare
            On: 1263 *a* fishing
                 1187 *gainst*: 1197, 1480, 1512, *twixt*, 1590 *twixte*
Adverbs: 1224 *oft*, 1291 *ere*, 1592 *nere*
Pronouns: It: 1165, 1560 *ist*, 1405 labour'*t*, 1188 *tis*, 1292 *twas*, 1566 *twill*
            Us: 1176, 1376 let'*s*
Auxiliary verbs: Will: 1264 etc., *weele*, 1575 *Ile*
Verb 'to be':   Is: 1168 ther'*s*, 1211 *hees*, 1274 who'*s*, 1328, 1596 what'*s*,
               1348 that'*s*, 1357 *thats*, 1360 title'*s*, 1424 honor'*s*

Grammar
(1) 3rd pers. sing. pres. indic. of *have*: 1191 etc. *hath*
   „   „   „   „   „   „ *do*:   1168 etc. *dooth;* 1332 *does*
   „   „   „   „   „   „ *notional verbs*: 1251 (stage direction) *riseth*,
                           1394 *pleaseth*
   „   „   „ past   „   „ *be*:   1339 *wast*
(2) Verb preterites and past participles: 1193 *sluic'de*, 1322 *defac'de*
                              1565 *spic'de*, 1590 *commenc'de*
                              1297 *bare*, 1308 *sunck*

(3) The usual spelling for the past participle of *be* is *bin*

(4) The conjunctional adverb *whilste* (1243, 1323) is preferred to *while* or *whiles.*

(5) *Yond* is used twice adverbially (1163, 1173) and once as a demonstrative (1563); *yonder* (1478) is used once adverbially. Munday's form in *John a Kent* is *yon.*

(6) *An* is used before words beginning with *h*; 1244 *an* hipocrite, 1474 *an* hundred. *A* is used before *one*: 1226 Such *a* one.

(7) The compound prepositional prefix to the infinitive (*for to*) is three times used for the sake of metre, and adds to the general impression of metrical nervelessness in Chettle's verse:

1283 Madame, what ayles yee *for to* looke so sad

1548 But if you now refuse *for to* subscribe

1557 readie *for to* arrest you of high treason

cf. the use of the compound conjunction in the following:

1387 we shall meete one day, *though that* now we part

(8) Possibly the very frequent use of weakened *ye* for *you* (not found in the 71 lines in Chettle's own hand) is Munday's.

(9) The use of the periphrastic auxiliary verb *do* is slight.

Spelling

The spelling is usually Munday's, but the following may be Chettle's: 1195 *Germanie*, 1232 *Germaine*, 1202 *discide*, 1307 *circkled*, 1434 *skrewe*, 1449 *laborinth*

Punctuation

This is again Munday's, the chief evidence being the numerical frequency of all the stops, with the exception of the semicolon, which was noticed only twice (lines 1389 and 1399), the first being unnecessary and the second calling for the shorter comma. Munday's rhetorical colons are everywhere, and many are inexplicable (e.g. in lines 1299–1308). Most interesting is the resumptive use of the colon after similes (e.g. lines 1218 and 1337), as this is a frequent occurrence in the quartos of Shakespeare's narrative poems *Venus and Adonis* and *Lucrece.*

Oaths

1284 *Troth*, 1368 *Tush*, 1408 *a Gods name*, 1588 *Gramercies.*

There can be little doubt that Scenes X–XIII are Chettle's. The characteristics of Chettle's work in *Sir Thomas More* are (a) the frequency of rhymed speeches; (b) the slight and conventional use of colloquial contractions, *t* for *it* and *s* for *is* being the principal; (c) the infrequency of the periphrastic auxiliary *do* in metrical emergencies, and preference for compound conjunctions and prepositions; (d) a considerable partiality for the spelling *bin*; (e) correct use of the semicolon, which he prefers to the colon; (f) meagre employment of oaths. Even a play such as Chettle's *Tragedy of Hoffman*, though probably written half-a-dozen years later, and not published until 1631, does not refute the above evidence.

(iv) *Scribe* C (copyist of work of Munday, Dekker and Shakespeare)

Lines 66–122, Addition II, are unaccountable, since they bear no apparent relation to the received text. They are written out by C, but are almost certainly the work of Munday, as is C's other transcription, the twenty-six lines of Addition V. The style and grammatical features of both passages are Munday's (e.g. the use of self-reflexives, *toward* without final -*s*, and a liking for syllabic past-participle endings); but the orthography is not. There are no punctuation-marks other than full-stops, no apostrophes, and a most irregular use of capitals, with a distinct preference for *I*, even in such unimportant words as *Into* (80) and *If* (102). Munday's spelling has been somewhat edited, e.g. 77 *tane*, for the author's usual *tayne*. The second personal pronoun is unfortunately not used in the first passage, and only once in a stressed position (*you*, line 5) in the second; there are no colloquial contractions. It is hard to believe that C, whose hand first appears in Addition II, was a professional scrivener of any standing, or even the Company's prompter, since his punctuation could have been of little theatrical value. It is more probable that he was a minor actor with a good hand and some experience in the preparation of 'plots' (see Appendix IV, 4).

C also transcribed the major portion of Addition IV, and most illuminating are lines 6–20 and 93–112, where he repeats passages in Munday's hand in the original version (lines 741–56 and 767–86). The first is reproduced for purposes of comparison:

Munday

                       ... or else thou'lt nere
be neere allyed to greatnesse: obserue me Sir.
The learned Clarke Erasmus is arriu'de
within our Englishe Courte, this day I heare,
he feasteth with an Englishe honourd Poett
the Earle of Surrey, and I knowe this night
the famous Clarke of Roterdame will visite
Sir Thomas Moore, therefore Sir, act my parte,
there, take my place furnishte with pursse and Mace.
Ile see if great Erasmus can distinguishe
merit and outward ceremonie: obserue me Sirra,
Ile be thy glasse, dresse thy behauiour

according to my cariage, but beware
thou talke not ouermuch, for twill betray thee.
who prates not oft, seemes wise, his witt fewe scan,
whilste the tounge blabs tales of th'imperfect man.

(Orig. 741-56)

. . . or ells thoult nere

be neere allied to greatnes. observe me Sirra
the Learned Clarke Erasmus is arived
wthin o^r english court. Last night I heere
he feasted wth o^r honord English poet
the Earle of Surrey. and I learnd to day
the famous clarke of Rotherdam will visett
Sr Thomas moore, therefore sir take my seate
yo^u are Lord Chauncelor. dress yor behaviour
according to my carriage but beware
yo^u talke not over much for twill betray thee
who prates not much seemes wise his witt few scan
while the (tog) tongue Blabs tales of the Imperfitt man.
Ile see If greate Erasmus can distinguishe
meritt and outward Cerimony

(Addition IV, 6-20)

Of the superiority of Munday's orthography there can be little dispute; but C is obviously transcribing a revision. The reviser had rearranged lines, inserted a few words such as 'you are Lord Chauncelor', substituted *you* for *thou* in More's instructions to his servant, changed the time of the verb *feast* in line 745 and transposed the epithets in the same line, so that 'an Englishe honourd Poett' becomes 'our honord English poet.' A similar transposition occurs in line 768 of the original, where 'learned woorthie' becomes 'worthy learned'. It is hard to believe that these transpositions are such as an author would later make in his own work, and I hold on more substantial grounds that the original Scene VIII (lines 735-876) was written by Munday, and revised in Addition IV by Dekker, the first 211 lines appearing in the transcription of C. Unfortunately, both Munday and Dekker cultivate a habit, found elsewhere in their independent plays, of ending a verse speech, the last line of which is unbroken, with a rhyming couplet. But the evidence that a different author was called in for revision rests upon style, supported by contractions and grammatical forms.

Lines 735-876 (Munday's original, though incomplete, version) contain *thou'lt* (741), *Ile* (750), *twill* (754), *twere* (792), *oft* (755), *th'imperfect* (756), *th'offenders* (834), *Hees* (772), *ist* (802), *er't* (817), *wilt* (860), *bear't* (865), *t'abuse* (853). These, with the exception of the last, are precisely the contractions found in *John a Kent* and the first seven scenes of *Sir Thomas More*. Of the other forms, there occur frequently *ye* for *you* (singular), and predominantly *hath* and *dooth* (there is a single use of *doo's*), which are characteristic of Munday also.

If, now, one turns to Addition IV, the greater vigour of the style is at once apparent. Dekker's purpose in adding thirty-one lines to C's transcription of his revision was to alter Faulkner's attitude from contrite submission to immediate defiance, until the cranky servant realized that perversity was to cost him his position. Incidentally, Dekker's punctuation is superior to C's. But wherever, as in the Faulkner episodes, Dekker is completely re-writing his predecessor's work, and not merely touching it up, as in the interlude with Erasmus and Surrey, new linguistic features catch the eye. In the thirty-one lines written in Dekker's own hand, are to be found:

> *Contractions:* 215 *a* (twice) and 234 *ha* (twice) for *have*, 229 *Ime*
> *Oaths:*   213 *nayles* and 227 *Sbloud*

In the Morris and Faulkner Scenes of Addition IV there are the following:

> *Contractions:* 26 *Ime*, 27 *Ide*, 27 *em*, 181 *thar* (= they are), 191 *this* (= this is),
>   the last two being used by More
> *Oaths:*   26, 42, 50 *sbloud*, 207 *shart*, 74 *troth*, 210 *hange me*
> *Adverbs and Prepositions:* 83 *besids*; 134, 205 *allwaies*, 166 *tweene*

Of the contractions only *Ide* and *th'are* are found in Munday's part of the play (lines 1–876) and, the latter's oaths are *bir Lady, marie, i(n) faith, (be)fore God, A gods name, A murren on't*, used sparingly and mainly in the insurrection scenes. Munday, as has already been pointed out, never uses oaths with initial *s* (= Gods). Nor does he favour the *-s* endings in such words as *besides*.

It is apparent, then, on stylistic and linguistic grounds, that the whole of Addition IV is Dekker's, and that he was enlisted, when Munday's name disappeared in Henslowe's books, to revise scene VIII. His instructions must have been to give life to the colourful Erasmus and Faulkner episodes, which illustrate More's love of jest, and which the scholarly Munday had treated too unimaginatively and sedately. Dekker's handling of the Erasmus scene is perfunctory, but he found Faulkner a man more to his taste.

Similarly, but probably later, Shakespeare was given the insurrection scene to refurbish, the play having then passed from the Admiral's to the Lord Chamberlain's Men.

The remaining transcription of C, Addition III, consists of only twenty-two lines, and they seem to me to be in the style and spirit of Shakespeare. Dyce and Tucker Brooke insert the passage before Addition IV of Dekker just considered, which opens with More jestingly coaching Randall in the deception of Erasmus, and this agrees with the apparent intention of the Company; with the result that this passage is generally also given to Dekker. But this is a soliloquy of quite another temper, More reflecting on the cares of office, the dangers of high place, and the mutability of all things; the object of the insertion seems to me to emphasize More's dignity and responsibility when called to the Chancellorship, that he should not appear merely as 'a fellow of infinite jest'. In fact, the lines are a natural continuation of the spirit in which More made his insurrection speech (see V), the suppression of the May Day Riots leading directly to his promotion in the king's counsels.

Though the passage is too short for any final judgment, it is worth remarking that its twenty-two lines contain practically nothing to identify them, in orthography or grammar, with Addition IV of Dekker. But there are verbal clues that link the passage with Shakespeare, the words *dexter* (12), *accite* for 'excite' (17), and *maxime* (20). Schmidt's *Shakespeare Lexicon* gives only one citation of *dexter* and *maxim*, and both are from *Troilus and Cressida*, written about 1601, which is roughly the date I believe should be assigned to Shakespeare's accepted Addition to *Sir Thomas More* (see V). The earliest occurrence of *dexter* in *O.E.D.* is dated 1562, and the citations are all in technical language until Sir Thomas Browne's use in *Pseudodoxia Epedemica* in 1641. The word is thus rare enough to be a nonce use in Shakespeare's acknowledged works, and may be considered unlikely from the pen of Dekker, until someone has located it. *Maxim* came into English about the second quarter of the fifteenth century, as a technical term of logic and rhetoric, being extended to legal use in the late sixteenth and early seventeenth centuries. Gabriel Harvey and Drayton used it in a literary sense, but the word must have been rare with dramatists who had not Shakespeare's range of vocabulary. The spelling *accite* is not given at all in the *O.E.D.*, and I have been able to find only one other instance of it, in Shakespeare's 2 *Henry IV* (Q), II.2.65:

. . . and what *accites* your most worshipfull thought to thinke so?

Three such unique Shakespearian phenomena in twenty-two lines seem at least presumptive evidence that the passage was another Addition by Shakespeare, transcribed by C in order to get it onto the lower part of folio 11b. The scribe did not, however, indicate precisely how and where the insertion was to be made, because he could find no logical or dramatic transition from the passage to the Erasmus scene; consequently he made no alteration of the stage direction at the beginning of Addition IV. This is probably one of the unfinished seams of the Shakespearian revision.

(v) *Shakespeare*

Addition II, lines 123–270, is the passage most frequently regarded as Shakespeare's, and a full account of its linguistic and other features is therefore appended. Citations are from Greg's Malone Society reprint pp. 73–78.

(a) *Contractions*

Articles: *The* (proclitic): 140 *thipp* (= the hip), 217 *th*apposlte, 246 *th*offender

The (enclitic): 180 by*th*, 199 too*th*

Prepositions: 218, 228, 229 *gainst*, 162 *ore*

Adverbs: 143 *ev'* (= ever. This is probably a graphic abbreviation; it is not recorded in O.E.D.); 217 *oft*

Pronouns: *Thou:* 181 *th*art

He: 165 *a* (twice; but the first is Dyce's reading, the character being no longer decipherable); so 264

It (proclitic only): 132, 216 *t*is, 218 *t*were

Us: 152, 165 *letts*, 211 *lets*

You (plural): 139 *ye* (Dyce's reading)

Auxiliary verbs: Will: 203 I'le; 153, 155, 160, 264 weele; 242, 264 *youle*

Verb 'to be': Is: 131 what*s*, 211 that*s*, 270 ther*s*, 212 *this* (= this is)

Been: 189 *bin*

Notional verbs: 189 *tane*

Nouns: 196, 244 *matie* (= majesty), 224 *matie.* (The full-stop to denote abbreviation.)

(b) *Grammatical forms*

(1) 3rd pers. sing. pres. indic. of *have:* 134 *has*; 196, 221, 223, 225 *hath*

3rd pers. sing. pres. indic. of *notional verbs:* 264 *saies;* the inflexion is -(*e*)*s* throughout.

3rd pers. sing. pres. indic. of *do* does not occur.

(2) Periphrastic auxiliary verb *do* in affirmative statements: used in lines 184 and 217 only, an infrequent incidence for Shakespeare.

(3) Orthographically consistent is the notation of preterite and past-participle endings of weak verbs, whether in verse or prose. After

E

voiced stem-finals -d is used, e.g. 202 *clothd*; after unvoiced stem-finals -t, e.g. 201 *sylenct*. The full orthography -ed is always syllabic, e.g. 134 *infected*. Precisely the same system obtains in Shakespeare's *Richard II* (Q_1), *Thomas of Woodstock* and in the manuscripts of Antony Munday.

(c) *Spelling*

(1) There is a distinct tendency to write initial C as a capital, which Dover Wilson remarks also in the good Shakespearian quartos.

(2) Though *i* and *y* were interchangeable in Elizabethan spelling, the *y*-spellings are abnormally high, unless compared with those of the earlier half of the sixteenth century, in such works as *The Prayer Book*. They would probably have exceeded the capacity of a printer's box at the end of the century. There are, for example, 13 *y*'s in lines 200–202, the spellings *sytt*, *desyres*, *aucthoryty*, *quyte*, *sylenct*, and *opynions* illustrating the idiosyncrasy.

(3) The spellings *shoold* and *woold* appear consistently.

(4) Dr. Johnson maintained in his *Dictionary* that no English word should be spelt with final *c*. I have counted six examples in the 148 lines, viz. 162 *obedyenc*, 217, 236, 237 *obedienc*, 204 *insolenc*, 250 *ffraunc* (= France). I cannot find the seventh such spelling which Dover Wilson claims.[1]

(5) The common words *ar* (8 times), *wer* (3 times) and *on* (twice) = one, are more frequently in the spelling without, than with, final -e. If the consonantal endings predominated in Shakespeare's manuscripts of the Good Quartos, spellings must have been normalized by the printers, though *on* is not uncommon. In most words, both monosyllabic and polysyllabic, the author's use of final -e in this Addition is very irregular.

(6) Notable spellings: 124 *a levenpence*; 129 *loff* (= loaf); 130 *straing* and 193, 197, 242 *straingers*; 134 *theise*; 176 *deule* (= devil); 208 (three times) and 269 *sealf*, 228 *himsealf*, 169 *sealves*; 173 *scilens*, 192 *geat* (= get), 244 *liom* (= lyam or leash), 251 *Iarman* (= German).

(d) *Punctuation*

(1) There is not a single colon, exclamation or interrogation mark, in spite of the numerous occasions for use, as illustrated in any edited text of the play, such as Tucker Brooke's in *The Shakespeare Apocrypha*.

(2) There are three semicolons, one in a deleted line (236), and the others (132, 245), by Jonson's or Crane's standards, inappropriate.

(3) There is an average of one comma to every five lines, a lower ratio than in any of the Good Quartos, and about one-sixth of the rate of use in a normally punctuated First Folio text.

---

[1] *Shakespeare's Hand in Sir Thomas More*, p. 124.

(4) Full-stops do not occur in lines 123–144, 147–172, and 174–229 (except for one abbreviation). Of the ten full-stops found, two are normal uses (173, 253), two mark abbreviations (146, 224), one is in a garbled and deleted line (236), three should be commas (230, 260, 270), one should be an exclamation mark (145), and one should be a mark of interrogation (248) [1].

(5) There are but two apostrophes, *ev'* (143) and *I'le* (203).

This analysis, while it does not disturb the massed evidence in favour of Shakespeare's authorship of lines 123–270 of Addition II, necessitates some modification of views often held in regard to Shakespeare's methods of composition in his acknowledged plays. On the ground of punctuation alone, either he did not write the Addition in the hand of D (which I have not the temerity to propose), OR he made his contribution to *Sir Thomas More* with more than ordinary haste and indifference, OR the claims of some editors in regard to the subtlety of Shakespeare's pointing should be revised. I prefer a compromise between the last two alternatives.

The pointing in the long, and therefore deliberately broken, oration of More on 'order and degree' (lines 169–270) hardly displays the sensitiveness that A. W. Pollard saw in the punctuation of the set-speeches of *Richard II*[2] and believed could only have been devised by an author skilled in the requirements of production. Even the light punctuation of *Hamlet* (Q₂), a play that Dover Wilson claimed to be nearer to Shakespeare's manuscript than any other printed text, surpasses in weight and in style the inadequate pointing of the three Shakespearian pages of *More*. Wilson's contention that the punctuation of these pages bears comparison with that of *Richard II* (Q₁) and *Hamlet* (Q₂)[3] can hardly be based on a detailed scrutiny. Without a preliminary survey of the diverse punctuation of both Good Quarto and First Folio texts, it seems audacious for individual editors to discover Shakespeare's hand in orthographically disparate works. By various critics his idiosyncrasies have been seen in the quartos of *Venus and Adonis*, *Richard II* (1597), *Hamlet* (1604) and the First Folio texts of *Antony and Cleopatra*, *Coriolanus*, and *The Tempest* (the copy for the last being almost certainly

---

[1] My criterion is the developed standard of punctuation already in use by the time of the printing of Jonson's and Shakespeare's first folios (1616–23). A history of the evolution and nomenclature of stops in English is contained in Appendix VI.

[2] See Introduction to *Richard II, a New Quarto* (Quaritch, 1916).

[3] *The Manuscript of Shakespeare's Hamlet* (Cambridge, 1934), Vol. II, pp. 196–7.

a transcript of Crane's). But the same hand could not have been responsible for the different practises there demonstrated, as comparison of the following passages will illustrate: *Richard II* (Q₁) III.3.142–58, *Hamlet* (Q₂) I.2.129–59, *Antony and Cleopatra* (F₁) III.4.1–9, *Coriolanus* (F₁) III.3.67–73, *The Tempest* (F₁) I.2.53–87. Most puzzling is the diversity in the use of colons, semicolons and parentheses, the first and the last being absent in the Shakespearian lines of *Sir Thomas More*; but even such commonplace stops as the comma and the period are capable in Shakespearian texts of considerable variation. Allowing for an author's progress and differences of pattern in the thought and style of his plays, one finds fundamental changes of method in Shakespeare that do not always coincide with the chronological development of his work. The punctuation of the set-speeches of *Richard II* (Q₁) is, for instance, more advanced than that which appears in similar passages of *Hamlet* (Q₂).

The conclusion seems inevitable that the last refinements of punctuation in published plays were, with some reservation for scholarly authors such as Munday and Jonson, added by playhouse editor, scribe, or printer. The possibilities of mutation are of Darwinian complexity, and the elements of chance too considerable for anything but conjecture on the part of the scientific student of textual history. In a published play the identification of a stratum as the author's can only be justified where there is bibliographical evidence that the printing was directly from his manuscript. The best that can be achieved through an examination of Shakespeare's punctuation, as is realized by that shrewd and cautious scholar Peter Alexander, is a comparison of Good Quarto and First Folio texts, with the ultimate object of discovering the process of editing the latter, and of grouping all the Folio plays according to the origin of the copy from which each play was printed.

The spelling of the pages attributed to Shakespeare has been so thoroughly examined by Dover Wilson in *Shakespeare's Hand in Sir Thomas More*, that comment alone is desirable. He defines 'abnormal spellings' in the Good Quartos as those 'that a reputable compositor of Shakespeare's day is not likely to have wittingly introduced into the text himself.'[1] Yet compositors, he rightly shows, were more up-to-date and consistent in spelling than the general run of authors whose work they had to print; and the chaos of forms presented in manuscripts compelled them to be economical and systematize. Abnormal spellings, Wilson argues, invariably came from the manuscript, because they are of words that caught the compositor's eye; and the less skil-

[1] Op. cit., p. 114.

ful the compositor, the more closely he would cling to his copy, and the greater would be the number of abnormal spellings he would incorporate. The value of the latter, he says, is that they reveal an author's orthographic habits; and examining Shakespeare's Good Quartos, Wilson finds that the same peculiar spellings occur as in *Sir Thomas More*.

Wilson's list of abnormal spellings contains two not in my list, viz. *infeccion* (136), *noyce* (195), both of which, on the authority of the *O.E.D.* are said to be rare after the fifteenth century. But undoubtedly considerations of space compelled the editors of the Dictionary to discard quantities of material that had been collected for the sixteenth century.[1] A fuller acquaintance with Elizabethan popular literature, and especially manuscript plays, would probably reveal that the majority of the ten notable spellings in my list were used by other authors, whose education, like Shakespeare's, had compelled daily readings of religious works such as *The First Prayer Book of Edward VI* (1549).

To take Wilson's list of abnormal spellings seriatim (*Shakespeare's Hand in Sir Thomas More* pp. 124–30). He himself has shown that Gabriel Harvey spelt words such as *temperance* without the final *-e*, and *eleven* with *a* for the weak initial vowel. There is no need to go to Harvey for *ar* and *theise*, since like forms occur in the Heywood contribution to the same play (see (ii) above, Additions II and VI). *Wer* is in the *Prayer Book*, and *on* for *one* occurs in the works of Ben Jonson and many contemporary writers. There is nothing unusual in the spelling *deule* for 'devil', since even in dissyllabic uses of words of this type the transposition *-le* for *-el*, on the analogy of French words such as *people* and *couple*, is frequent. The spelling *-cc-* for (ksh), e.g. in *infeccion*, is regular in *The First Prayer Book of Edward VI*; using a verbatim and literatim reprint, one can find *subieccion*, *affliccion*, *benediccion*, *unccion* and *affeccions*. The *Prayer Book* also has *mealte*, *shead*, *leat* and *read* (red), corresponding to Shakespearian *sealfe*, words that were normally spelt *e* by the printers. *Noyce* is no curiosity, *s* and *c* being common alternative spellings for the sibilant; for instance, *noice* is the spelling of scribe C in line 46 of Addition IV, and both *preased* and *preaced* (= pressed) are found in the *Prayer Book*. *Straing* and *Iarman* are pronunciation spellings, equally used by Heywood (see (ii) above), the diphthong of the first probably being identical to that in *main, complain* etc. In regard to the second, the word only came into English in the latter half of the sixteenth century, and both pronunciation and spelling continued to be

[1] I had this information from one of the late editors, Sir William Craigie.

uncertain until the seventeenth century, when *J* was introduced for consonantal *I*, which had existed alongside of vocalic *I* in both Latin and English.[1] The pronunciation of the first syllable in the sixteenth century was either (yer-)or (yar-), vowel confusion being further illustrated in such sixteenth-century forms as *sterre* (star), *sarvent, desart*, and modern *clerk* and *sergeant*.

Dover Wilson has rightly established that Shakespeare's spelling was old-fashioned. He does not, of course, maintain that his abnormal spellings are exceptional in manuscript, but only in print after 1590. By showing that the same spellings occasionally slipped into the Good Quartos, he seeks to identify the 148 lines with the hand of Shakespeare. But the evidence must be inconclusive, as long as the spelling-habits can also be found in other Elizabethan manuscripts; and several of them can. An instance that has been regarded as rare and spectacular is the spelling *scilens*, which is found in the speech prefixes of 2 *Henry IV* as well as in the *More* Addition, and is cited in the *O.E.D.* no later than 1513. Without any search for parallel spellings, I have come across *scylens* in Rastell's 1533 edition of Heywood's *The Pardoner and the Frere* (line 257), and *scilence* in line 1460 of *Thomas of Woodstock*, almost contemporary with *Sir Thomas More*. A rarer spelling is *liom* (244), not mentioned by Wilson, of which the *O.E.D.* gives no instance, the usual spelling between 1400 and 1600 being *lyam*. Shakespeare's spelling must later have been *lym*, but so unusual was the form when he, for the nonce, used it in *Lear* III.6.72, that the Pied Bull Quarto of 1608 has *him* and the First Folio *Hym*.

Another nonce-word in Shakespeare is *pumpion* in the F$_1$ version of *The Merry Wives of Windsor* (III.3.34). The earliest citation recorded in *O.E.D.* is dated 1545, and its use in the drama must be rare, though Fletcher has it in *Rule a Wife* (*c.* 1623). The word occurs in line 138 of Addition II to *Sir Thomas More*.

Coming to the grammatical forms and contractions, the single use of *has* to four instances of *hath* calls for the observation that *has* first appears in a Shakespearian Good Quarto, though rarely, in 2 *Henry IV*, probably written *c.* 1597. *Hamlet* (Q$_2$) is the first play in which Shakespeare relaxed his preference for *hath*, and it is too much to assume that the various printers of all the earlier Good Quartos regularized the hypothetical use of the *-s* inflexion. *Has* in such early plays as *Henry VI*

---

[1] Cf. the spellings *Iibbit* (= gibbet), *Iurney* and *Iayle* in Munday's part of *Sir Thomas More* (lines 573, 578, 639, 869). Scribe C's spelling *germaine* is found in line 145 of Addition IV, though *Iest* occurs in the next line.

and *Two Gentlemen of Verona* only exists because they are First Folio texts, probably re-edited after *c.* 1600.

The combined contraction *thart* (181), however, appears in no Good Quarto at all, only in First Folio texts. The following quotations from *Richard II* (Q_1), a precise play orthographically, show that Shakespeare probably wrote out these combinations in full, relying on the actors to slur or syncopate them:

II.1.7. Where words are scarce *they are* seldome spent in vaine

V.6.28. For though mine enemy *thou hast* ever beene (unless *enemy* is disyllabic)

Apparently Shakespeare continued thus until the turn of the century, when he began to abbreviate the pronoun. Quarto texts were often revised before the printing of the First Folio, as is illustrated by the following:

2 Henry IV, III.2.174. What, dost thou roare before *thou art* prickt? (prose; F_1 *th'art*)

The assimilated form *this* for *this is* occurs in the Pied Bull Quarto of *Lear* (1608), and again in the First Folio; the earliest F_1 text containing its use is apparently *Measure for Measure*. In *Hamlet* (Q_2), however, assimilation is only implied e.g. IV.5.76 O *this is* the poyson of deepe griefe, it springs.

To sum up, there is no reason to reject the thesis that Shakespeare wrote the three pages in the hand of D in the *More* manuscript; but it does not appear that he could have done so earlier than about 1597, the probable year of the writing of 2 *Henry IV*. A date soon after 1600 seems preferable for his Addition.

Conclusions

1. The above analyses, if they prove anything at all, serve to confirm the triple authorship of *Sir Thomas More* by Munday, Heywood (?) and Chettle, on the lines indicated by Oliphant, and largely accepted by Greg. Munday was concerned with the London revolt and the period of More's office as Sheriff of the City, which led to the latter's promotion to the Chancellorship. Heywood dealt with More in the contrasting periods of prosperity and disgrace, enlarging his character, domestic life, humour, steadfastness and magnanimity. Chettle had the task of depicting the steps that led to his downfall; but he is strangely silent, where he might be expected to provide a cause, on the nature of

the documents to which More refused to subscribe. When the whole of this play had been transcribed by Munday (some important parts of his version are now lost), it may have been offered to Henslowe and declined. As a work possible for production by the Admiral's Men, it was palpably deficient; the shortcomings were mainly in the central figure, who lacked vigour and geniality, and were due to the pedestrian handling of the theme by Munday. Munday, therefore, revised two episodes himself, and another was added by Heywood, who had been given the task of literary improver. Heywood augmented his own part, and so did Chettle; but still the play was unsatisfactory. Dekker then took a hand in Scene VIII and added greatly to the force of the Faulkner scenes. Finally, the rejected play seems to have been disposed of to the Lord Chamberlain's Men, added to by Shakespeare in two places, not so much with a view to touching up the crowd scenes, as to filling out the conception of More and his high sense of office, and actually cast for performance. Scrivener C took a hand in this preparation, and saw that certain additions were properly transcribed and inserted. When, however, the last blow fell in the demand for the removal of objectionable parts by the Censor, the task of completing what was already an awkward collaboration, was abandoned. In my view, the original play was probably written between 1593 and 1597, and the revisions, at any rate Dekker's and Shakespeare's, between 1598 and 1601. In either case the later dates are to be preferred.

2. The composite manuscript of *Sir Thomas More* is a valuable document, as illustrating that (a) dramatic authors differed considerably in their spelling, punctuation, oaths, and use of colloquial contractions; (b) when a play or parts of it were copied, spelling and punctuation were freely altered, not always for the better; (c) the persons entrusted with the copying were only occasionally professional scriveners of repute, with a learned knowledge of the nicer points of grammar, elision, and the conventional modes of spelling and punctuation acceptable to the printers; (d) both Munday and Chettle, the first because he was a scholar, and the second because he had been engaged in the printing-trade, were superior in their orthography to scribe C; (e) some devotion to scholarship seems to have been a pre-requisite to interest in orthography; except in the case of Jonson, authors of original talent, such as Shakespeare and Heywood, went their own way; (f) from a comparison of such a manuscript with the printed work of the known authors, it becomes apparent that the number of author-spellings that survived the process of copying or printing, or both, cannot

have been high; and this observation applies even more to an author's punctuation.

Pollard was, therefore, justified in claiming that the Good Quartos of Shakespeare's plays were largely printed from his manuscripts, or from faithful fair copies. When it was necessary for theatre-copies to be sent to the printers of the early Shakespearian quartos, e.g. the 1600 group, many, if not all, of the author's idiosyncrasies had conceivably been removed. Theatre-copy nearly always formed the basis of the material assembled and edited by Heminge and Condell. The First Folio printers, who had the reading public in mind, carried the process of obliteration a step further. Important orthographical changes can, in fact, be observed in many of the First Folio plays, as the next Chapter will demonstrate. On the other hand, Heminge and Condell helped to preserve the Company's and sometimes the author's authentic acting text.

List of contractions in dramatic use by 1600, including 'Woodstock' and 'Sir Thomas More', but excluding the plays of Shakespeare.

In the following table the bucolic forms have not been incorporated.

1. *Vowel-weakening: ye* for *you* (favoured by some writers, not used by others)
   me for *my*
   bin for *been* (used by most writers, but may be a spelling variant)
2. *Loss of aspirate:*   *a* for *he*; *em, am* or *um* for *hem* (= them); *a* for *have*
3 (a). *Aphesis* (nouns and verbs omitted): *bove, bout, gainst, mongst, las* (= alas)
   (b). *Aphæresis* (nouns and verbs omitted): *tween, twixt*
4. *End-curtailment* (loss of *-en* in strong p. participles omitted): *ha* for *have*, *ko* for *quoth, ma* for *make, ga* for *gave, oft* for *often, ev'* for *ever, ope* for *open, a* for *of, o* for *of, a* for *on*
5. *Medial-curtailment* (nouns omitted): *ere, nere, een* or *en, ore, tane*
6. *Combined contraction*
   (a) *Single: Proclitic: th* for *the* (before words with initial vowel)
           t for *the* (before *one* or *other*)
           t for *it* (before certain forms of verbs *be* and *will*)
           *pers. pron. + are: yare, thart, th'are
             „   „   + *has, had, shas, shad*
           a or *o* for *of* (before nouns or def. article)
           t for *to* (before prepositional forms of verbs)
           i, e or *y* for *in + faith; a* for *at + do; a* for *in + gods-name*

Enclitic: th for *the* (after prepositions): by*th*, to*th* (permissible before words with initial consonant)
t for *it* (after verbs, prepositions and conjunctions)
a for *he, she, thou, you:* quoth*a*
s for *his* (after prepositions and verbs)
s for *us* (usually after *let*, but occasionally after *shall* and notional verbs)
By*r* (Ladie)
s for *is* (after nouns, pronouns and adverbs)
*r(e) for *are* (after pronouns): you'*re*, ye'*re*, we*re*, they'*r*
st for *hast* (after *thou*): thou*st*
I*ll* or I*le*, thou*lt* (thou*t* once), hee*le*, shee*le*, wee*le*, thei*le*
I*me*
I*de*, you*d* (you'*ld* once), hee*d*, we*de*, they'*d*

(b) *Double: hate* (= have it); *shat* (= shall it); *t'as* (= it has)
eth or *ith* (= in the); *ath* or *oth* (= on the)
These *-th* contractions are permissible before words with initial consonant

7. *Initial assimilation: h'as* (= he has); *had* (= he had)
8. *End assimilation: ther* (= there are); *this* (= this is)

Only where the above forms appear solely with apostrophe, have I preserved that orthography; the majority of the forms occur both with and without elision. A rare combination is invariably apostrophized. The contractions marked with an asterisk are interesting alternatives; but the first or proclitic group was that preferred by the Elizabethan printers, whereas the enclitic group has been favoured since the seventeenth century.

Many of the recognizably poetic contractions, some still in use, were in the late sixteenth and early seventeenth centuries used also in prose. Types 7 and 8 are rare, and the combinations in 6, in which a preposition is coalesced with contracted *the* before consonants (e.g. by*th*, o*th*), are uncommon before 1600, though they do occur sporadically in such Good Quartos as *Love's Labour's Lost* and *Romeo and Juliet*. Shakespeare's use of contractions before the turn of the century is limited and conservative; none that he uses in the acknowledged Good Quartos up to and including *Hamlet* is wanting in the above list.

Chapter 8

Shakespeare's Apparent Orthography in
Venus and Adonis and some Early Quartos

THE printer of the 1593 Quarto of *Venus and Adonis* was Richard Field, a Stratford man and (it is thought) a friend of Shakespeare. In 1579 Field was apprenticed to Thomas Vautrollier, a Huguenot who had been admitted to the Stationers Company in the very year of Shakespeare's birth. During the next twenty years Vautrollier became a printer of considerable standing, printing, besides musical, grammatical and religious works, North's translation of *Plutarch's Lives*, Ovid's *Poems* and Bright's *Treatise of Melancholie*. On the master printer's death in 1588, Field married his widow and acquired his business. W. W. Greg in 'An Elizabethan Printer and his Copy'[1] shows that Field was a printer of authority and readily edited the copy of Harington's translation of *Orlando Furioso* (1591), as regards punctuation and spelling. Fripp in 'Shakespeare's Pronunciation'[2] points to at least one important reason why Field had to shorten Shakespeare's spellings: he printed the concluding couplet of each stanza of *Venus and Adonis* to the right of the quatrain, and had difficulty in avoiding 'tucked in' lines. He undoubtedly 'improved' Shakespeare's orthography, and took some care with the general set-up of the verse lines and the metrical elisions, probably because the poem was in honour of the Earl of Southampton. Field in the care of his printing had an eye to the patron and the degree of literacy of his public.

The dedication to the nobleman is brief, personal and in prose; the printer had probably little reason to depart from Shakespeare's manuscript, from which both this and the dedication of *Lucrece* seem to be set up. These dedications and the first quarto of *Richard II* may be the most accurate representations of Shakespearian orthography extant; they conform in the use of accidentals to the standards of carefully

[1] *The Library*, Vol. IV, No. 2, September 1923, pp. 102–118.
[2] *Shakespeare, Man and Artist*. Vol. I, pp. 379–85.

prepared texts. If one is to divide the manuscripts used for Shakespeare's quartos into primary categories, 'fair copies' such as *Richard II*, and 'foul papers' such as *Romeo and Juliet* (Q₂), is the natural method of doing so.

Venus and Adonis is, however, superior to the Good Quarto plays in the care of its printing, the attention paid to marks of elision, the use of poetical contractions, and sometimes in its spelling. It is possible, I think, to perceive what is Shakespeare's behind the editorial practices of Field or his compositors. The following orthographical features provide clues:

(a) *Spelling.*

1. Shakespeare's preference for full spellings, such as *sonne, proppe, woorde, heere, hee, cheekes, ecchoes, onelye, dooth, goe*, is witnessed in the Good Quartos, thought to have author-manuscript as their copy. The intermittent use of shortened forms in the Quarto of *Venus and Adonis* would, therefore, imply the modification of the printer. Fripp's reconstruction of passages from *Venus and Adonis* and *Lucrece* in Shakespearian spelling is conjectural (see last footnote); but he may be right in attributing such spellings as *wo* and *fy* to one of Field's compositors, though the former occurs twice in the first two Acts of *Richard II*. Fripp shows how space compels the compositor on occasion to introduce & for *and*, or to do away with final *-m* or *-n* by placing the nasal abbreviation sign above the preceding vowel.

2. Shakespeare, on the same evidence, favoured final *-ie* (occasionally *-ye*) to *-y*, e.g. in *Venus and Adonis, dutie, onelye, laie,* and *-ll* for *-l* at the end of a word, e.g. *hopefull, portall.* Also such spellings as *hie* for *high, noyse* for *noise, deaw* for *dew, shewes* for *shows, chaunt* for *chant, ougly* for *ugly*, to name only a few. Many of his spellings are pronunciation spellings; hence the forms *ake, servill, quiet, daine*, the intrusive *d* in *frendzies* (740), and the omission of silent *b* in such words as *nums* (892) and *lim* (1067); but in line 1146 *dūbe*, & for *dum, and* probably shows the hand of a compositor.

3. In words of French origin, sibilant *c* (e.g. *centinell* (650)) is a common feature of Shakespearian spelling.

4. Interesting spellings such as *sacietie* (19) = satiety, *ceaze* (25), *sullein* (75), *murmour* (706), *skorne* (1084), are found on every page. Such forms are unorthodox, but it would be presumptuous to describe them as individualisms. Spellings equally unusual occur in the *Authorized Version of the Bible*, and some of the most curious orthographies in

Shakespearian quartos are, as the last chapter showed, paralleled in *The Book of Common Prayer*.

5. Shakespeare may or may not have shared the taste of his printer's house for visual rhyme; e.g. the rhymes *nye/eye, thine/eine, despight/ night, donne/sonne*[1] (mod. *sun*, 749–50), *Nuns/suns* (mod. *sons*, 752–54), *togither/whither, confesse/decesse* (= decease), *feare/seveare, convaide/aide*.

(b) *Syncope and elision.*

A feature of the dedications of *Venus and Adonis* and *Lucrece* is the absence of syncope in the spelling of weak past participle inflexions, e.g. *pleased, praised, honoured, deformed* in the dedication to *Venus and Adonis* and *assured* and *lengthned* in that to *Lucrece*. The single exception is *untutord* in line 7 of the dedication to *Lucrece*, which was due to the compositor's justifying his line. In prose the full spelling does not imply pronunciation of inflexional *e*, as it does in Shakespearian verse; in poetry a more precise orthography is necessary for metrical reasons. The ending in *unpolisht* (*V.A.*, ded. line 2) illustrates the spelling practice of the time of converting *-d* to *-t* after unvoiced stem-finals. The printing of past participle endings in the dedications to *Venus and Adonis* and *Lucrece* is at one with the usage found later in the *Authorized Version of the Bible*.

By the early sixteenth century syncope of *-e* in preterite and participial endings of weak verbs was probably universal in colloquial speech, except in endings *-ded* and *-ted*. By the beginning of the seventeenth century the full orthography *-ed*, or the conventional verse elision *'d*, had become the vogue of the printers, after both voiced and unvoiced stem-finals. Transitional varieties of ending are, however, found in *Venus and Adonis*, e.g.

290 a well proportione*d* steed (*proportioned* trisyllabic)
451 rubi-colour*d* portall
469 And all amaz'd, brake off
773 this black-fac't night

On the evidence of Field's treatment of Harington's script and the dedications to the two early Shakespeare poems, the marks of verse elision in *Venus and Adonis* appear to be the work of Field's compositor(s); but the second quotation (line 451) is probably as Shakespeare wrote it. In line 2 of the dedication to *Venus and Adonis* Shakespeare

[1] The late M.E. scribal practice of substituting *o* for *u* in spellings before and after m, n, v, w, was continued optionally in the New English period, where the pronunciation is obviously *u*.

must be credited with the pronunciation spelling *unpolisht*, and in the poem itself with *laught* (4), *blusht* (33), *pusht* (41), *stuft* (58), *kist* (59), *Forst* (61), *unaskt* (102), *blest* (328), *ceast* (119) etc. The compositor, however, probably inserted the unnecessary apostrophe in such past participles as *wreak't* (1004).

Richard II (1597) confirms that, in verse, Shakespeare preferred to omit the *e* for the normal syncope of speech, and to insert it only when he wanted the extra metrical syllable; in the latter case assimilation to -*t* after unvoiced consonants was impossible. This simple orthography saved the author the necessity of dotting the manuscript with marks of elision. Apparently Field's compositor(s) replaced an elided *e* occasionally to justify the line; more often, however, this unsounded *e* would slip into printed verse through the habit of setting up prose, or inadvertently. Jonson's folio of 1616 contains similar lapses.

Stems of weak verbs ending in a vowel or vowel-sound, were followed by the full spelling -*ed*, pronounced -*d*, e.g. *wooed* (97), *swayed* (109), *borrowed* (488), *glewed* (546). A typical pentameter in Shakespearian orthography (save for *top*) is line 1143.

> The bottome poyson, and the top ore-*strawd*

where *strawd*, instead of *strawed*, appears as the best orthographical visual rhyme for *fraud*..

Where the stems of weak and strong verbs ended in unstressed -*en* or -*er*, syncope of *e* may have taken place before the *n* and *r* of the suffix, instead of in the inflexional ending itself, e.g. *fastned* (68), *battred* (104), *gathred* (131), *falne* (monosyllabic, 354). *Proportioned* in 290 may, indeed, imply a final syllable (*shned*) rather than modern (*shind*). Orthographically, syncope involved elision of *e* only; hence the retention of the French *io*, as well as the sounded *e* of the participial ending.

A further suggestion that marks of elision were a sophistication unpractised by Shakespeare so early is to be found in the forms *curt'sie* (= courtesy 888), *Ne're* (1107), the plural *mouth's* (695), and the third person singular present indicatives *tell's* (587), *fall's* (594), *esteem's* (631), *root's* (636), *crop's* (1175). The apostrophe in these verbs, and in *mouth's*, marking elision of the original inflexional *e*, is a nicety with which a busy dramatist like Shakespeare, a decade before 1600, can scarcely have troubled himself.

In 1593, if a manuscript poem had to be press-edited in an Elizabethan printing-house, consistency was hardly to be expected. By 1604, however, when Field came to print Sir William Alexander, Earl of Stirling's,

Paraenesis and *Aurora* (Bodleian Library, Malone 239) the niceties of elision were well established; they may even, by then, have been cultivated by Shakespeare himself. The second quarto of *Hamlet*, haltingly printed as it was by Roberts, shows that dramatic orthography, in punctuation and elision, had by then been tightened. The influence of Jonson's newly printed 'humour' plays, and the emulation by court poets of respectable printers like Field, had emphasized the need to give more assistance to the reader. The copy of the Earl of Stirling's poems presented to the printer would thus have been much more precisely pointed than the manuscript of Shakespeare's earlier *Venus and Adonis* and *Lucrece*. In *Paraenesis* elision is carefully marked, especially of *e* in past participal endings. In these endings *t* is not substituted for *'d* after unvoiced consonants. The poem was dedicated to the King, and it may be supposed that the draft was as near letter-perfection as possible. A laxer orthography is noticed in the same poet's *Aurora*, a collection of miscellaneous poems.

(c) *Possessive Genitive.*

The apostrophe before *s* was not employed by Shakespeare and most of his contemporaries. Where it occurs sporadically, as in Ben Jonson,[1] it plainly signifies elision of *-e* of the old masculine genitive singular inflexion *-es*, used in Received English for all genders and declensions by the end of the fourteenth century. This elision resembles that of the plural *mouth's* indicated above. In printed dialogue spelling sufficed to show that the *e* had been dropped in unstressed inflexions, exceptions naturally occurring after *-ch* and *-s*, or other sibilant or affricative stem-finals. The same syncope is found in the third person singular present indicative of notional verbs, where, in spoken English, the Northern inflexion *-es* had superseded the Southern *-eth* (cf. Field's orthography *tell's fall's* above). The necessity for employing these marks of elision was not appreciated by most printers, and Jonson drew attention to it in his definition of *Apostrophus* in Bk. II, Ch. I of his *Grammar* (the name *apostrophe* was first used by his friend Howell in 1642). In practice, however, Jonson insisted mainly on the mark of elision for the possessive genitive of proper names derived from Romance languages, where such names ended in a sounded vowel, e.g. *Every Man in his Humour* I.1.140 (Herford and Simpson, p. 201) *Prospero's* invention. In other nouns, whether in the genitive singular or nominative plural, he

[1] See my *Accidence of Ben Jonson's Plays, Masques and Entertainments* (Bowes and Bowes, 1951) Section 12.

was apparently indifferent to the use of the apostrophe. But Jonson's use of the possessive genitive, in all its possibilities of variation and substitution, is pedantically learned, whereas Shakespeare's is extremely simple, consisting of the uniform addition of *s* for singular and plural possessives, and the absence of any inflexion whatever if the nominative already ends in *s*, e.g. *Venus and Adonis* 261, *Adonis* trampling Courser. The latter was, of course, a metrical device. Field's compositor preserves Shakespeare's orthography for all possessive genitives.

(d) *Punctuation.*

There is no reason to suppose that Shakespeare's punctuation in *Venus and Adonis* was more elaborate or different in intention from that of his plays. The poem can certainly not have been pointed by Shakespeare, as it appears in Field's printed version; for there are practices that do not occur again, except in *Lucrece*. To what extent Shakespeare's printed stanza verse employs a different system of punctuation from that of the plays appears in the following analysis.

The stanza form of *Venus and Adonis* consists of a quatrain followed by a couplet. About half of the couplets are loosely attached to the quatrain, being marked off only by a comma. The other half are self-contained, and are then commonly separated by a colon; less commonly by a full-stop, semicolon or question-mark. Enjambement at the end of the quatrain occurs only five times, and in two of these, at lines 406 and 1006, the stop has apparently been omitted by the author or printer. This conclusion is based on the evidence of stops in the 199 stanzas of the poem. Wherever a colon is used at the end of the quatrain, modern editors are at a loss what to do, sometimes converting it, sometimes retaining it; the former when the stop coincides with some sense relation between the parts, the latter where the pause is clearly a metrical one. All but seventeen lines of the poem are end-stopped, but a metrical pause is often inserted in the form of a comma where logical syntax does not require it, e.g.

37 The studded bridle on a ragged bough,
   Nimbly she fastens

Probably the comma here conforms to Shakespeare's practice, and indicates inversion of the normal order to emphasize 'Nimbly'. But there is much comma-pedantry, mainly syntactical, which appears to be Field's.

It is clear from the poem as a whole that the comma, especially at the end of a line, is overworked, and that by modern standards a longer stop, such as a semicolon or colon, is often called for. But the use of the semicolon as an intermediate time-stop, with co-ordinating effect, was not understood until Jonson used it with logical precision; and the colon seems to have been largely reserved for metrical or rhetorical function, to mark off elocutionary units of a poetical passage or speech. Another function of the colon, apparently known to Field's compositor, is to mark off a simile, especially if it is followed in the next line by the word *So*, e.g.

> 87 Like a divedapper peering through the wave,
>   Who being lookt on, ducks as quickly in:
>   So offers he to give what she did crave

Both the colon and *So* are here resumptive. In lines 815 and 928 a semicolon is substituted in this function.

In the stanza 751-6, the resumptive semicolon at the end of line 754 was misinterpreted in the Boswell-Malone Variorum Edition of 1821 and by succeeding editions, such as the Cambridge, Globe and Oxford:

> Therefore despight of fruitlesse chastitie,
> Love-lacking vestals, and selfe-loving Nuns,
> That on the earth would breed a scarcitie,
> 754 And barraine dearth of daughters, and of suns;
> Be prodigall, the lampe that burnes by night,
> Dries up his oyle, to lend the world his light.

This is, on the whole, good Shakespearian orthography; but the editors have destroyed what I believe is the poet's intended sense by substituting a comma for the semicolon after *suns*, and a colon for the comma after *prodigall*. *Venus*'s exhortation to 'be prodigall' is addressed, not to the vestals and other religious orders, but to *Adonis*, whom she adjures not to follow their example. Possibly the editors see *Be* at the beginning of line 755 as an indicative plural, not as an imperative, which vitiates the sense further. To secure the true meaning, 'Therefore' must be taken with 'Be prodigall' four lines lower; 'despite . . . suns' provides a long interpolation, and the purpose of the semicolon is to mark its end and pick up the imperative. This is a kind of rhetorical pointing, just as the semicolon in line 516, and the comma in line 774, are gesture stops. Whether the semicolon after *suns* in 754 represents the precise quality of stop employed by Shakespeare, is doubtful. The mass of evidence in the quartos thought to be based on his manuscripts suggests that he used four stops mainly in his writing, the comma, colon, period and

F

question-mark; he may have had recourse to the semicolon here and there for special occasions, where none of his regular stops seemed suitable.

It is notable that exclamation marks are used only three times in *Venus and Adonis*, twice when the exclamation, indicative of emotion, is inserted between parentheses (lines 38 and 635), and one faultily in line 985:

> O hard beleeving love how strange it seemes!
> Not to beleeve, and yet too credulous:

where the mark should come either after *love* or *credulous*, and has probably been inserted after *seemes* by the printer. Both Shakespeare and Jonson in their early quartos,[1] resorted to a lesser time-stop, such as a comma, after a simple interjection, as at lines 95 and 505-6 of *Venus and Adonis*. Where an exclamatory sentence or phrase began with an interrogative word, it was common practice to end with a question-mark, e.g.

> 574 What though the rose have prickles, yet tis pluckt?

The use of parentheses in the poem also suggests the sophisticating touch of the printer. It occurs
  (i) When a sentence, usually to indicate the speaker, is inserted in the actual words of a speech. This obviates the modern use of inverted commas for the speech, a device not yet discovered by the printing trade; e.g.

> 7 Thrise fairer than my selfe, (thus she began)
> The fields chiefe flower, sweet above compare

The comma after *flower* is a metrical pause, probably Shakespeare's.
  (ii) When a casual reflection, sometimes in the form of an exclamation, is interposed in the narrative: e.g.

> 38 The studded bridle on a ragged bough,
> Nimbly she fastens, (ô how quicke is love!)

Brackets, circumflex accent and exclamation-mark are here probably

---

[1] I have counted less than a dozen exclamation marks in the whole of the 1601 Quarto of *Every Man in His Humour*, and less than three times that number in the earliest Quarto of *Every Man out of His Humour* (1600), published by the Malone Society in 1921. The latter play is much longer than the second Quarto of *Hamlet*, and has many exclamations; but the appropriate mark appears mainly after the interjection O, though inconsistently.

the work of Field's compositor, and might be that of a modern printer. Yet the Globe edition unnecessarily improves to

> fastens:— O, how quick is love!—

which has nothing to commend it.

(e) *Capitals.*

Simon Daines in his *Orthoepia Anglicana* (1640) has the following interesting statement on the use of capital letters:

> The pronoune, or word (I) must alwayes be written with a great letter; so must every proper name, or peculiar denomination of every individuall: as all the Attributes of God Almighty, the names of Angels, Saints, and evill spirits; the titles given by the Heathens to their faigned Gods and Goddesses; the names of men and women of all sorts whatsoever; the names of moneths, winds, rivers, Cities, townes, Islands and Kingdoms: the particular name of any peculiar dog, horse, or beast of any kind soever: The first word of every verse, at least Heroique: any letter set for a number, as you had in the beginning of our Orthoepie: Any letter standing for any such, or the abbreviation as we there mentioned.
>
> Lastly, all names or Titles of Magistrates, Arts, Offices, and Dignities, in what respect soever taken. In these, I say, altogether consists the use of Capitall Letters, in all other we use onely the smaller.[1]

It is probable that, in the employment of capital letters for nouns other than proper names, there was some sort of printers' convention. The loss of grammatical gender by the end of the fourteenth century may have aided the convention.[2] Natural gender was often relinquished or made more specific by authors who indulged in personification, and in such circumstances words such as Mercy and Justice would tend to be capitalized. Wyndham in 1898 gave a useful classification of substantives that were normally capitalized[3] by the printers of Shakespeare's poems, and with some modification the list will doe for the nine quartos of plays based on Shakespeare's manuscript, printed up to 1604. My own list, which is illustrated by some examples from the Good Quartos, has the following dozen categories:

1. Personifications and images, especially if based on classical statuary, mythology and emblems; e.g.

---

[1] Op. cit., 'Certaine peculiar Rules of Orthography', p. 76.

[2] See my *Accidence of Ben Jonson's Plays, Masques and Entertainments*, Section 13, pp. 66–7.

[3] See *The Poems of Shakespeare* (Methuen) pp. 223 and 262.

V.A. 291 His *Art* with *Natures* workmanship at strife,
    147 Or like a *Nimph*, with long disheveled heare,
    103 Over my *Altars* hath he hong his launce,

2. Names of animals, birds, fishes, insects, plants, trees and flowers, especially if used in fables, emblematically, proverbially or typically; e.g.

V.A. 1105 But this foule, grim, and urchin-snowted *Boare*,
    55 Even as an emptie *Eagle* sharpe by fast,
R. and J. (Q₂) II.4.39 like a dried *Hering*
V.A. 798 As *Caterpillers* do
R. and J. (Q₂) I.4.68 an emptie *Hasel* nut

3. Names of precious stones and substances; e.g.

R. and J. (Q₂) I.4.56 in shape no bigger thẽ an *Agot* stone.
V.A. Or *Ivorie* in an allablaster (sic) band,

4. Names of arts, sciences and public entertainments; e.g.

Richard II (Q₂) II.1.12 The setting Sunne, and *Musike* at the close,
R. and J. (Q₂) I.4.48 And we meane well in going to this *Mask*,

5. Names of religions and their institutions etc.; e.g.

Richard II (Q₁) I.1.139 ere I last receivde the *Sacrament*
R. and J. (Q₂) II.2.114 Which is the god of my *Idolatrie*

6. Names of diseases, ailments etc.; e.g.

R. and J. (Q₂) II.3.30 Full soone the *Canker* death eates up that Plant
    II.4.29 The *Pox* of such antique lisping affecting phantacies

7. Terms of cosmology, heavenly bodies, time, and geography of the earth; e.g.

V.A. 1020 blacke *Chaos* comes againe
    492 Shone like the *Moone* in water seene by night
R. and J. (Q₂) I.2.10 Let two more *Sommers* wither in their pride,
Richard II (Q₁) II. 1.278 A *Bay* in Brittaine

8. Terms relating to kingship, chivalry, statecraft and government; e.g.

Richard II (Q₁) I.1.24 Adde an immortall title to your *Crowne*
    I.1.75 By that, and all the rites of *Knighthoode* else
    I.3.93 Most mighty *Liege*, and my companion *Peeres*,
R. and J. (Q₂) I.4.56 the forefinger of an *Alderman*

9. Professions, trades, occupations; e.g.

V.A. 220 Being *Iudge* in love, she cannot right her cause
R. and J. (Q₂) Made by the *Ioyner* squirrel
V.A. 849 Like shrill-tongu'd *Tapsters* answering everie call,

10. Technical terms (e.g. (a) Heraldic, (b) Printing and publishing, including book, volume, reader, (c) Rhetoric, (d) Duelling etc.)

Hamlet (Q₂) II.2.479 Now is he totall *Gules* horridly trickt
Richard II (Q₁) I.3.67 Oh thou the earthly *Authour* of my bloud
R. and J (Q₂) II.4.26–7 ah the immortall *Passado*, the *Punto* reverso, the *Hay*

11. Personal appellations and family relationships; e.g.

R. and J. (Q₂) II.4.182 Nurse, commend me to thy *Lady* and *Mistresse,*
Richard II (Q₁) I.4.19 He is our *Coosens Coosin*

12. Foreign words not yet felt to be naturalized; e.g.

Richard II (Q₁) I.1.105 Even from the tounglesse *Cavernes* of the earth,
I.1.192 Before this out-darde *Dastard?*
I.1.205 we shall see/*Iustice* designe the *Victors* chivalrie

That this system is apparent in all the Good Quartos of Shakespeare, printed by different houses before 1604, is not evidence in itself that he conformed to the convention in his writing. Autograph manuscripts of plays of the preceding decade are rare, and point to negligent use of capitals by authors, both in these categories, and at the beginning of verse lines. There is no ground whatever, except accident, for supposing that the capitalization of substantives before 1600, and even as late as 1610, indicated dramatic or elocutionary emphasis. Percy Simpson's treatment of emphasis capitals in *Shakespearian Punctuation* (1911) is based upon the practice of the Folio of 1623, and by the latter date capitalization had so increased, that it is possible to allow the emphasis thesis, with the proviso that *all* capitals do *not* emphasize. The influence of scribes, such as Ralph Crane, who cultivated the upper case as an ornamental feature of his calligraphy, probably had much to do with the practice of capitalization. Crane (see Appendix V) and Jonson account for many editorial practices of the First Folio, and their influence probably began to be exerted in the second decade of the seventeenth century. About this time there was a considerable importation into literary works of foreign words and technical terms, also capitalized; and if one adds the influence of Continental, especially German printing, the stage would logically be reached when it became convenient and time-saving for the printers to capitalize practically all substantives, and to italicize those of foreign origin. This was, in fact, the situation at the end of the seventeenth century. Though printers varied, the peak period for the use of capitalized substantives is found to extend from the Restoration to the middle of the eighteenth century.

(f) *Contractions.*

There is not a clear division between forms found in literary productions, such as *Venus and Adonis*, and those employed in plays; though naturally exclusively poetical prepositions, adverbs and conjunctions such as *twixt, tween, ere, nere, oft* and *where* (=whether) predominate in the poems. Apart from these there are twenty-six contractions in *Venus and Adonis*, proclitic *t* for *it* (14), proclitic *th'* for *the* (2), *'s* for *is* (4), and *Ile* for *I shall* or *will* (6). These four kinds are again in use in *Richard II* and *Romeo and Juliet*. The most notable additions in the early plays are colloquial weakenings of pronouns and prepositions: *s* for *us*; *a* for *he*; *yee, ye* and *y'* for *you*; enclitic *'t* and *th* for *it* and *the*, *i* or *y* for *in* (in the expression *ifaith, yfaith*), and *a* for both the prepositions *of* and *on*.

In *Romeo and Juliet* (Q₂) *a* for *he* is used by Mercutio, Capulet and Romeo familiarly, but by the Nurse only when angered, and mainly in the disapproving *quotha*; in fact *a* in this expression may stand for any weakened personal pronoun (for instance *you* in II.4.124). *Ye* for unstressed *you* is used principally, but not always, by the racier speakers, such as Mercutio and the Nurse.

Two interesting weakenings are erroneously indicated by elision in *Richard II*, probably not by Shakespeare himself:

I.3.180 Sweare by the duty that *y'*owe to God

Metre here requires *you* or the full unstressed form *ye*. Elision is marked because of the juxtaposition of the two vowels.

I.3.239 Oh had'*t* beene a stranger, not my child,

The apostrophe indicates weakening of the pronoun to [ət], not actual elision.

Shakespeare observes the full form *them*, not only in the poems, but in the plays, as is clear from the manuscript-based quartos. He probably felt that the accusatives *'hem* and *'em* would obtrude by reason of their frequency, without providing the metrical advantage of a decreased syllable. Even in the weakened double ending of the rhyme *between them/seen them* (*Venus and Adonis*, 355–7) Shakespeare retains the dignity of the full form, where Fletcher in his plays would have reduced to *'em.*

Weele and *theile* in the plays of the nineties are analogous to *Ile* in *Venus and Adonis*, but the modern orthography *'ll* for *shall* and *will* does not occur. Nor does *'m* for *am* and *'ld* for *would*; but contraction was probably achieved by slurring or light pronunciation in the following verse lines, where the full orthography appears:

R. and J. II.5.13 She *would* be as swift in motion as a ball
R. and J. II.5.54 Ifaith I *am* sorrie that thou art not well.

The general features which emerge from the above, and can be checked by constant reference to the Quartos thought to be based on Shakespeare's manuscripts, are clear. Shakespeare's spelling was old-fashioned in its attachment to full-spellings and its curious blend of Tudor, individual and pseudo-phonetic representations. His mind must have been well stored with books written and printed in a previous generation; and when he became fully absorbed in the business of writing and producing plays, he apparently had little time to read and to keep abreast of the newer developments in printing and orthography, until his contact with Ben Jonson about the turn of the century.

When Field received his manuscripts of *Venus and Adonis* and *Lucrece* he had no scruple in editing what he found, because Shakespeare's orthography seemed to him arbitrary. In *Richard II* (Q_1) Shakespeare or a careful amanuensis appears to have made a fair copy of his play. It is one of his most carefully prepared dramatic texts, another being *Hamlet* (Q_2). I imagine that he used capital letters regularly after full-stops, for proper names and titles of dignity, and possibly for emblematic and classical images. In marginal insertions of verse written out as prose, he may have employed a capital letter sporadically to indicate where a new line was to begin; and omission to do this would frequently have caused mislineation in the printing.

Chapter 9

Shakespeare's Versification and the Editing of the First Folio

THE technical nomenclature of the various modes of elision and contraction (or 'metaplasms' as they were called in imitation of the terms of the classical grammarians Priscian and Donatus) has so far been avoided, for the reason that few English poets between 1400 and 1600 deliberately employed the classical devices. The earliest verse orthographer among practising poets seems to have been Ben Jonson; and his desire for classical formality arose partly from his interest in the grammars of European languages. His own *Grammar* contains a chapter on 'Apostrophus', and he told Drummond of Hawthornden that 'he had written a discourse of Poesie both against Campion and Daniel',[1] which is lost. Jonson's theories began to evolve after 1600, and were fairly fully developed by the time he wrote *Sejanus*. They were a modified application of the principles of Italian syllabic versification to English dramatic poetry, and are logically illustrated in the texts of the plays printed in the Jonson folio of 1616.

The history of English verse orthography is related to the history of versification, from Chaucer to the present day. There has, since the fourteenth century, been a fluctuating struggle between syllabists and accentualists, in which the latter, with a measure of compromise, have finally triumphed. The dust and acrimony of contention have not been about barren issues; important principles of poetic technique are involved, and significant contributions to theory have been made by poets themselves, such as Milton, Coleridge, Bridges, Hopkins and Eliot. When poets theorize, it is usually to justify and explain their own (at the time) revolutionary practice. But the attempts of others to rationalize the progress of Shakespeare's versification have produced conflicting views, the causes of which are largely textual. The transmogrification of Shakespeare's blank verse about the time he wrote

[1] Herford and Simpson, *Ben Jonson*, Vol. I, p. 132.

Hamlet suggests that Jonson, like Bridges at the turn of the nineteenth century, was a catalyser for important changes in the practice of other poets, and that Shakespeare may have been in frequent contact with him for a number of years after the sponsoring by the Chamberlain's Men of *Every Man in His Humour.*

Chaucer, the first considerable English poet, wrote verse modelled on the French and Italian, the pattern of which was syllabic in intention. In verse of this type the line is conceived as a measure of syllables, having, for variety, upper and lower limits. Though the cadence of the verse often overflows the line, the rhythm is tightened by this quasi-mathematical principle to which the metre of the line has to conform. To assist the orthodox syllabic poet to maintain strict form, certain licences of elision and contraction are worked out, and applied in theory, though in reading they admit of a considerable degree of latitude. An elementary principle of elision is the reduction of vowels in unstressed parts of polysyllabic words and in stock combinations. Chaucer employs such well-known classical devices as syncope, aphæresis, ecthlipsis, as in the line:

Thestaat, tharray, the nombre and eek the cause (C.T. Prologue 716).

The weakening of redundant unstressed vowels may be complete or partial, according to the taste of the theorist or speaker, and is a prolific source of rhythmical variety or modulation. Puttenham says in Ch. XVII, Book II, of his *Art of English Poesy*: 'our odde sillable . . . is in a maner drowned and supprest by the flat accent, and shrinks away as it were inaudible, and by that meane the odde verse comes almost to be an even in every mans hearing'.[1] How variable this 'almost' could be was soon to be demonstrated by Milton, modelling his freedom of modulation on the Italian poets. Writing of the 'purpose and effect of these colliding vowels', F. T. Prince in *The Italian Element in Milton's Verse* (p. 134), says: 'neither of the vowels is suppressed or lost, but rather they glide into one another, giving an effect of indescribable suspense and fullness to the verse'. But in the earliest English blank verse this method of modulation is sparing and exceptional. The verses of Shakespeare's poems and sonnets, and of such early plays as *Richard II*, *Romeo and Juliet*, *The Merchant of Venice*, and *A Midsummer Night's Dream*, are of this type.

Shakespeare, however, in the words of T. S. Eliot, did the work of two poets. During his first 'lifetime' 'he was slowly adapting his form

---

[1] *Elizabethan Critical Essays* (ed. Gregory Smith), Vol. II, p. 135.

to colloquial speech: so that by the time he wrote *Antony and Cleopatra* he had devised a medium in which everything . . . whether high or low, 'poetical' or 'prosaic', could be said with naturalness and beauty. . . . The later plays move from simplicity towards elaboration. He is occupied with the other task of the poet . . . that of experimenting to see how elaborate, how complicated, the music could be made without losing touch with colloquial speech altogether.'[1] In this phase Shakespeare, in effect, liberated his blank verse from its syllabic limitations. Poetry, which had relapsed into what was metrically doggerel for a hundred and fifty years after Chaucer, was rehabilitated by Wyatt, Surrey, Sackville and Spenser. They regained its prestige by the use of predominantly two-syllable-foot measures, which made for stabler accentuation. They knew Chaucer, and Italian and French poetry, and were reasonably strict syllabists. But the drama called for greater naturalism, and the obvious medium for it was blank verse, especially after Marlowe had shown its possibilities of power, dignity and flexibility.

The bulk of Italian verse from the thirteenth to the sixteenth century had been in rhyme, to which the nature of the language lends itself ideally; so that the development of the appropriate English measure for drama and epic was the experimental work of mainly English poets.

Marlowe's rhythmical modulations were achieved by the rediscovery of principles not unknown to Chaucer: varying the position of the medial pause, occasionally inverting the stress of the first or third foot, and admitting a redundant syllable, when desired, at the end of the line. The power of his verse, however, arose from its elocutionary instinct for stress manipulation, requiring a minimum of three primary stresses within the line, and those to fall on the most significant words for rhetorical delivery. This was the pattern on which Shakespeare wrote the noble numbers of his own early verse plays. Several factors in this formative period may have induced Shakespeare to experiment. Though *Antony and Cleopatra* marks the culmination of his evolution towards accentual verse, the shaping period was Shakespeare's progress from *Henry V* to *Hamlet*. The rise of his Company coincided with the decline of rhetorical acting in the last years of the sixteenth century. He had been developing his gifts of expression and his range of experience, and had begun to create the taste by which the new art of the theatre was to be judged. Actors of the calibre of Burbage helped him

---

[1] 'The Music of Poetry', *Selected Prose* (ed. John Hayward), pp. 63–4.

to the conviction that the drama could sustain a freer treatment of verse, through individual genius for interpretation and the infinite modulations of the human voice. The critical period for the emancipation of blank verse was the first ten years of the seventeenth century, and the innovators were Shakespeare, Jonson and Webster. To quote an article by Kellog, the old prosody 'was fixed and traditional; only within very well-defined limits could the poet take liberties with it. The pattern of speech-accents, on the other hand, was not a matter of prosody at all, but of rhythm.'[1] In the words of Bridges, 'the rhythm over-rides the prosody that creates it'.[2]

After 1600 Shakespeare, Jonson and Webster were as solicitous as T. S. Eliot at the present time about the suitability of syllabic poetry as a medium for dramatic expression. While they wished the unconscious effects of poetic rhythms to do their work upon the audience, they realized that a good deal of the business of the drama is necessarily prosaic; a return to common speech would obviate the awkward transitions which most verse dramatists are compelled to make, even when they eschew prose altogether. Of Shakespeare, Eliot writes: 'He first developed conversational, colloquial verse in the monologue of the character part—Faulconbridge in *King John*, and later in the Nurse in *Romeo and Juliet*. It was a much further step to carry it unobtrusively into the dialogue of brief replies.'[2] But what further technical advances were necessary in those parts of the play where the emotional intensity called for the highest insights of poetry? The answer of Webster and Shakespeare, as of Donne, was a more dextrous manipulation of the incidence of stress and pause, so that rhythmical flexibility could make the utmost demands on the syllabic base, e.g.

Duch. of Malfi IV.2.274 Cover her face; / mine eyes dazzle; / she died young

The double-stressed ending was cultivated by Shakespeare, after *Hamlet*, e.g.

T. and C. I.3.68 To his experienc't tongue, yet let it please both

Inversion of stress in the second, and even the last foot, was another daring innovation which Shakespeare began to practise, e.g.

---

[1] G. A. Kellog, 'Bridges' *Milton's Prosody* and Renaissance Metrical Theory', *P.M.L.A.*, LXVIII, 1, (1953), p. 269.

[2] *Milton's Prosody* (1921), p. 36.

[3] *Poetry and Drama* (Faber and Faber, 1951), p. 16.

          x /   x /   x   /   x   x   /   x

T. and C. I.2.5 To see / the bat / tel: Hec / tor whose / pacience,

Extra unstressed syllables before the medial pause and at the end of the line became common features of his verse, e.g.

     T. and C. I.3.335 If not / Achil / *les*; thought be / a sport / full com / *bat*
     Macbeth I.5.17 What thou / art pro / *mis'd:* / yet doe / I feare / thy Na / *ture*

Similarly with inverted stress after the medial pause, e.g.

                     /   x   x /   x /   /   x   x /

    T. and C. I.3.5 Failes in / the pro/ mist large / *nesse,* / checks and / disas / *ters.*

Whether or not a *syllabic* base for this kind of blank verse can any longer be deemed to exist, is a moot point. For this reason F. T. Prince, in *The Italian Element in Milton's Verse* (pp. 139 and 144, footnote) rightly objects to Bridges's interpretation of Milton's prosody in terms of Classical iambic 'feet'; 'Something is clearly wrong,' he writes, 'when Bridges has to declare . . . that "Milton came to scan his verses in one way, and to read them in another". . . . The value of Milton's adaptation of Italian verse is that it enables us to dispense with all these impositions of arbitrary rules, and to read the verse . . . with a basis of very few fixed principles. . . . The metrical unit is . . . in the deca-syllable, the line itself, with all its possible variations, not the five "dissyllabic feet" which are said to compose it.'

Blank verse, as the Jacobean dramatists conceived it, is a malleable medium to which the writer must give form without finality. The ulti-mate aesthetic satisfaction is derived partly from the actor's, and partly from the listener's, contribution to perception of the rhythm; and it follows that a pattern too ready-made, as syllabic verse tends to be, is not in the interests of sensory co-operation between interpreter and audience. 'Speak the speech, I pray you, trippingly on the tongue' is a plea for naturalness, for the most effective speed of attack, and for sympathetic interpretation of the emotion that underlies the rhythm of the words. Verse dialogue on the stage can only be natural if it culti-vates the rhythms of ordinary speech. It needs all the nuances of value-stressing, of slurring and clipping, that accompany intelligent conversa-tion. It is consequently in the drama, and especially the verse drama, that the speech habits of any period are best preserved. The prose of poetic dramatists, from Jonson to T. S. Eliot, is literary and mannered; it is the product of schools that suppress natural tendencies to collo-quialism. But dramatic dialogue aims to conceal the artifices both of education and of metre, and to secure its aesthetic appeal through the subconscious layers of perception. Thus, in the development of Shakespeare's style, colloquial retrenchment of syllables is commoner in the verse than the prose, and as effective in the mouths of the great characters as in those of a grave-digger, an illiterate constable, or a gentle young lady's vulgar nurse.

Two phenomena in the development of Shakespeare's dramatic language are of considerable interest: firstly, the variety and frequency of colloquial contractions are greater after 1600 than in the plays written before that date; and secondly, the First Folio plays of whatever date have the contractions more punctiliously, as well as conventionally. marked by apostrophe than have the Good Quartos up to and including *Hamlet* of 1604. These variations are capable of no simple explanation, and will not even be self-evident until a detailed orthographical analysis of the Folio texts has been made to confirm their origin. Some plays of early composition appear nowhere but in the First Folio, where spelling and punctuation have been so modernized as to obscure the Shakespearian peculiarities of their originals. In such plays, however, the date of composition is roughly validated by the nature of the contractions, which both in number and kind are limited, and resemble those of the early Good Quartos. Contraction-frequencies are, indeed, inseparable from verse-tests. Cutting across the types of contractions are the methods of elision used in marking them. There is some variety in the notation of verse-elision in the First Folio; but one general principle actuates it, and comes out clearly in the reading of the plays of the mature later period. Its purpose is to make the freer accentual measures more respectable in the eyes of Renaissance syllabic prosody; and behind this seems to loom the authority of Ben Jonson.

The opposed theories of Shakespearian versification are too well-known to require elucidation, and have been represented in more recent English criticism by M. A. Bayfield and Richard Flatter. Bayfield was so convinced of Shakespeare's devotion to trisyllabic feet (or resolutions), that he anathemized the editors of the First Folio for correcting them. The printers of the Good Quartos were, in his view, only a little less culpable than the publishers of the First Folio. Despite all the evidence of contemporary dramatic autograph manuscripts, Bayfield supposed that the dignity of blank verse is disfigured by clippings, slurrings and other syllabic retrenchments, and that Shakespeare himself abhorred them.[1]

Flatter, on the other hand, is a fundamentalist who attacks the

[1] See *Shakespeare's Versification*, p. 292.

authority of the Good Quartos, as generally confirmed by biblio-graphical investigation. The orthography of the Good Quartos must, on the evidence of the most recent analyses, be nearer to the author's draft than the First Folio's, since the spelling of the latter is too modern, and the punctuation too fussy and sophisticated. Flatter, in a skilful argument from the nature of copyright, and a reconstruction of the Company's practice in transcribing and disposing of plays, suggests, however, that it is the Folio texts that, in general, have Shakespeare's imprimatur. He argues for the superiority of the Folio texts, precisely because they present verse of a more uniform syllabic character, which he identifies with the taste of Shakespeare. 'As long as we regard Shake-speare principally as a man of the stage,' he writes, 'we have, in search of the "True Original Copies," to look not to the Quartos, but to the Folio.'[1]

Flatter believes his view to be confirmed by the claim of Heminge and Condell that they offer the plays, for the first time in print, 'abso-lute in their numbers (versification), as he (Shakespeare) conceived them'.[2] The word 'conceived' can, however, argue no more than the editors' view of Shakespeare's intentions. It cannot be made to support a theory that the dramatist wrote the great mature plays in the blank verse of the earlier ones, with no other modulation than an increased use of the redundant syllable before the medial pause, or at the end of the line. Malone maintained that the Address of Heminge and Condell to the Great Variety of Readers was touched up, if not actually com-posed, by Ben Jonson.[3] Jonson's was, in fact, the only folio volume of plays that had been collected and printed for the reading public; and but a few years later friends and colleagues were doing a similar service for Shakespeare. The Jonson Folio of 1616 set a high standard of correct-ness. The text was submitted to a disciplined self-criticism, the punctua-tion designed to point the rhetorical and syntactical significances, the verses edited with a care for elision that marks the classical prosodist. Would not such an authority be consulted by the harassed editors of Shakespeare's manuscripts and multiform texts? And it would be sur-prising if Jonson did not anticipate the celebrated dictum: 'This will never do!' Confronted with such a manuscript as the three supposed Shakespearian pages of *Sir Thomas More*, Jonson would have recom-

---

[1] '"The True Original Copies" of Shakespeare's Plays', *Proceedings of the Leeds Philosophical Society*, VII, p. 41.
[2] Address 'To the Great Variety of Readers', prefaced to First Folio.
[3] See Chapter XV.

mended radical revision from the orthographical point of view, and lent the editors a copy of his own folio.

What was suitable for Jonson's severely modelled plays, carefully calculated to exhibit the arts of composition, was not appropriate to the dramatic poems of Shakespeare. Shakespeare, not being a scholar in the classical sense, had balanced the genuine expression of the emotions with the arts of rhetoric in a unique way. His versification, especially in the great tragedies and the plays that followed, was not capable of containment in any classical mould. Bayfield was, therefore, right in objecting to the unwarranted interference of the editors of the First Folio; wrong in asserting that Shakespeare must have avoided colloquial contractions altogether. Shakespeare, in all things a man of his age, was not one to reject what all dramatists from the author of *Gammer Gurton's Needle* to Henry Porter had found useful. Colloquial contractions are present even in *Venus and Adonis*; collaborated manuscripts, such as *Sir Thomas More*, show that the most varied contributors favoured them. Before 1600, Shakespeare's contractions had been cautious and sparing, employed mainly in the dialogue of character-parts to secure an atmosphere of worldliness or informality. The later increase was part of Shakespeare's plan to liberate blank verse by the employment of natural speech. But the orthography of contraction of the late texts of the Folio is so elaborate, and yet so cramping in its effect, that this can hardly have been Shakespeare's intention also.

Though the editing of the First Folio was niggling in its attempt to fit Shakespeare's subtly modulated accentual rhythms to the old Marlovian pattern of iambic pentameter, it was conscientious in its desire to preserve an honest text; and this was perhaps a major virtue. By 1623 the energies of Elizabethan romantic adolescence were sobering towards a classical reaction. A generation of well-printed classical texts from Italy and France, and the scholarship they evoked, had had its influence. That 'Shakespeare wanted art' was a criticism of Jonson as easily swallowed as T. S. Eliot's censure of Milton in our own time. The improvement of the Shakespearian texts for the First Folio would be a *sine qua non* of judicious editorship; but haste and divided labour produced a miscellany. The editing had one serious consequence; it has complicated the problems of chronology and recension. The orthographical features of such plays as *Henry VI* and *The Two Gentlemen of Verona* must be treated with the greatest reserve; the difficulty of the timing of their revision or modernization is as insoluble as that of Jonson's *Tale of a Tub*.

Chapter 10

Italian Prosodists and Types of Dramatic Elision in the English Drama of the Sixteenth and Seventeenth Centuries

It is only necessary to read the grammatical writings of Lily, Gill, Jonson, Daines and others to be convinced of the importance that was attached to orthography, and the extent to which their ideas were influenced by the classical grammarians. Italian syllabic prosodists, though not mentioned except for Scaliger by Sidney, were none the less the latest authorities on the application of Tuscan principles of metrical composition to vernacular poetry; they went beyond their French predecessors in making certain types of elision permissive; and this had a powerful influence on English rhetorical composition and poetic theory at the beginning of the seventeenth century.[1] The devices of elision and contraction were treated collectively in Renaissance Rhetoric under the heading of Figures of Grammar. All orthographical variations from the normal forms of words were explained and classified; and in verse every adaptation of a word or word-combination for metre or rhyme was considered a poetic ornament. 'Metaplasmus' was the name given to such adaptations by the Late Latin grammarians Donatus and Priscian, and since the fifteenth century the derived English technical term has been 'metaplasms'. Puttenham discusses them in Chapter XI, Book III, of his *Art of English Poesie*, and gives the devices English names, which have not survived. The Figures of Grammar are also glanced at in Alexander Gill's *Logonomia Anglica* (1621), Chapter XXVI, and more fully treated in Chapter II, Part II, and Chapter VI,

---

[1] The principal Italian prosodists were Minturno, Mazzoni, Scaliger and Trissino who produced their treatises between 1525 and 1590. The most comprehensive treatment of elision and metrical composition generally is to be found in the fourth book of Minturno's *L'Arte Poetica* (Venice, 1563), which I consulted in the Biblioteca Nazionale, Florence.

Part III, of Sister Miriam Joseph's *Shakespeare's Use of the Arts of Language* (1947). Those which concern elision and contraction are Aphæresis, Syncope, Apocope and Synaloepha.

Simon Daines in his *Orthoepia Anglicana* (1640) remarks of the first three of these figures: 'The Apostrophe or mark of contraction is variously subject (according to the place it possesses) to the three figures, Aphæresis, Syncope and Apocope: that is according as the contraction be in the beginning, middle, or end of a word.'[1] The examples supplied are respectively *'twill, strength'ning* and *th'intent*. But strictly the last is Synaloepha, or the obscuring (sometimes the elision) of the first of two coincident vowels at the juncture of words. Apocope is the curtailment of a single word by the loss of a syllable or letter(s) at the end. Campion, on the other hand, couples Synaloephas and Elisions together, and does not distinguish *ev'ry* and *admir'd* as Syncope.[2] It is clear, then, that the terms were of varied application.

Gill, who was Milton's schoolmaster, had written his *Logonomia Anglica* by 1619, and it appeared when the sponsors of the Shakespearian First Folio were busy with their task. The last section of his book (Chapters XXV to XXVIII) deals exclusively with prosody, and comments on the work of such scholarly poets as Spenser, Sidney, Jonson and Campion. Speaking of metaplasms, Gill anticipates Milton in his advocacy of the elision of naked vowels between words, and the reduction of weak vowels where unstressed syllables of single words end in the liquids *l*, *m*, *n*, or *r* (or what the Latin grammarians misleadingly called the semivowels).

The most consistent exemplar of the principles of Italian Renaissance prosody, as well as the most deliberate manipulator of stress and elision was Milton. The syllabic poet in blank verse, of which Milton in *Paradise Lost* is the model, permits trisyllabic feet only where elision is theoretically possible on phonetic principles, e.g. where open vowels are contiguous, whether within the word or between words; or where vowels are unstressed before the liquids *l*, *m*, *n* and *r*. Whether his practice is instinctive or deliberate is immaterial; but what certainly appears to be intentional is the fact that syllables supernumerary to the decasyllabic pattern always appear either at the end of the line, or after a medial pause. Most young poets serve a considerable apprenticeship to syllabic verse before experimenting with trisyllabic feet in normally

[1] Op. cit., ed. M. Rösler and R. Brotanek (1908), p. 72.
[2] 'Observations on the Art of English Poesy', *Elizabethan Critical Essays*, Vol. II, p. 355.

iambic measures. In strict syllabic verse such combined contractions as *i'th, o'th'*, especially before words beginning with consonants, are not permissible. Milton never uses them in *Paradise Lost*, though he does occasionally in *Comus*, because here is verse to be spoken by players, written under the influence of Shakespeare, Jonson and Fletcher. *Comus* is remarkable for two other characteristics justified in blank verse dialogue, the use by Milton of Jonsonian elision discussed under 4, at the end of this Chapter, and of considerably more feminine endings than he permits in the two great epics. In none of the Milton manuscripts is elision consistently marked by apostrophe; sometimes it is achieved through the spelling, as in Shakespeare's early Good Quartos, and sometimes it is not marked at all. Miss Darbishire in her Clarendon Press edition of *Paradise Lost* (Introd. p. xxviii) remarks: 'It is plain that Milton disliked the lavish contemporary use of the apostrophe and himself limited its employment to definite purposes.'

The differences between the First Edition of *Paradise Lost* and the First Folio of Shakespeare are sometimes obscured by the identities of their orthography. In *Paradise Lost* syllabic conformity was carried by the author himself to its logical limits; in the Shakespeare Folio syllabism was merely tentative, because the author's intentions were but partially understood, or misunderstood, by his editors. Milton's designs were interpreted by Bridges in the explanations (1) that he scanned his verse one way, and read it another, and (2) that his elisions and contractions are, in practice, optional. In the case of Shakespeare it is more than probable that the more difficult elisions were never even contemplated. For instance, in the passage cited by Bridges[1] from *Antony and Cleopatra* to illustrate the loss of accent on prepositions before and after a weak syllabic line of three accents, the full forms intended by Shakespeare are correctly given:

> We must return *to the* court of guard: the night
> Is shiny; and, they say, we shall embattle
> *By the* second hour, *in the* morn. (IV.9.2–4—Bridges has modernized spelling
> and punctuation).

In the First Folio this reads

> We must returne *to'th'* Court of Guard: the night
> Is shiny, and they say, we shall embattaille
> *By'th'* second houre *i'th* Morne

[1] *Milton's Prosody* p. 79.

No reputable actor would dare to clip the prepositional phrases in this fashion, nor is the prompter likely to have ordained such a notation for any seasoned member of his Company. If this is one of the plays directly printed from Shakespeare's manuscript, there was editorial interference in the process.

What should emerge from a study of the First Edition of *Paradise Lost* and the Shakespeare First Folio, and even more from the opposed views of critics like Bayfield and Flatter, is that the word 'elision' is a term of comprehensive use and misleading connotation. It has been used for two distinct purposes, and hence follows the heat of controversy about trisyllables and resolutions. Originally 'elision' must have meant the cutting away of some part of a word in order to reduce the aggregate of syllables in the verse line. Later (and probably with the rise of vernacular literatures) the usage was extended to include partial suppression or slurring of a syllable. Phonetically, the nature of this glide is of various types; but it involves the accommodation of the speech-organs in such a way as to swallow some part of a sound's normal value, but not to sacrifice it altogether. In colloquial forms such as *Ile* or *y'are*, the first kind of elision (complete dropping out of a syllable) probably results from the intermediate or slurred pronunciation, which was the first stage.

Prosodic elision, like that of the Tuscan poets or Milton, is not necessarily true elision; it is a device to make metrical conformity theoretically possible to an inner ear, that refers the spoken line to the basic pattern. Sprott in *Milton's Art of Prosody* (p. 74) has correctly said that 'in Latin the elision determines the rhythm, in English the rhythm determines the elision'. The degree of audibility of a syllable, prosodically elided, may vary considerably, and it is the knowledge of this fact that the great writers of blank verse, such as Shakespeare and Milton, employ constantly. The supreme master of syllable variation in the intimate lyric was, however, Donne; the great flexibility of his command of colloquial idiom is the reason for his rediscovery by the moderns. Poetry like Donne's makes its play of modulation largely by what classical prosodists call inversion of the stresses, often in unusual places such as the second, fourth or fifth foot. His poetry calls for very little elision of the actual kind. In line nine of the sonnet 'Death be not proud'

Thou art sláve to Fáte, Chánce, kíngs, and désperate mén,

there are twelve syllables. Theoretically *Thou art* is *Th'art* and *desperate* is *desp'rate*; actually there are six stressed syllables, calculated to prolong the dignity of the line. But there is no intention on the part of the poet that any less than twelve syllables should be spoken in the reading; and the only use for marking the elision would be to point the rhythm of the line for an ear unfamiliar with Donne's technique.

Such rhythmical resourcefulness is unlikely to have been lost on an ear like Shakespeare's. Both he and Webster imported the Donne technique into the drama without loss of masculinity, such as began to appear with Fletcher. But the undetermined question when the line exceeded the normal limits of ten or eleven syllables is the notation which the playwright himself adopted. The apostrophe, as used by the Italian poets and Jonson, stands for both kinds of elision, the complete and the partial. But within these two broad categories there are a number of shades of use and significance, which I shall endeavour to illustrate:

1. The most elementary elision was achieved without the apostrophe at all, actual pronunciation being conveyed by suppression of letters in the spelling, e.g. *Ile*, *labord*. This must have been Shakespeare's early method, and is indeed attested by the orthography of the Good Quartos before 1600, especially *Richard II* (Q_1). In the syncope of preterite and past-participle endings of weak verbs, many writers took advantage of a practice encouraged by printers, viz. the assimilation of the inflexion to the stem-final, allowing *d* if the latter was voiced, and *t* if unvoiced, e.g. *banisht*. Shakespeare may not have been consistent in the use of this; it is a supererogation.

2. Next comes the pointed elision of modern times, beginning to appear in the last quarter of the sixteenth century, and almost fully developed by the end of the seventeenth century. Here the suppression of a letter or letters is indicated by an apostrophe, borrowed originally from Italian printing of classical texts and grammars. Printers of standing, such as Richard Field, who printed Shakespeare's *Venus and Adonis* and *Lucrece*, were using the apostrophe fairly regularly in the 1590's, whether the elided letter(s) affected pronunciation or not, e.g. *perfum'd*, *parachito's* (plural), *Prospero's* (possessive), *'gainst* (aphesis), *wee'll* (colloquial contraction). The use of *'s* for the possessive genitive was extremely rare before 1600, and even after that date it was only employed by some sticklers, like Jonson, after proper names of Romance-language origin, ending in a sounded vowel. The possessive singular and plural were of identical form.

3. Grammarians probably influenced a kind of morphological

elision, in which the apostrophe purported to point the loss of a hypothetical stem-final or historical inflexion, e.g. *wil't*, (second sing.),
was't, *ha's*. This usage, which is pedantic, occurs sometimes in Jonson
and frequently in the transcripts of Ralph Crane.

4. It is impossible to discover the originator of Jonsonian elision,
referred to on page 35. Here the apostrophe is interposed between
the full forms of a colloquial combination, but its function is equivocal,
e.g. *ye'have*, *art'not*. I think this elision is a metrical fiction, designed to
indicate the desirability of retaining the full forms in reading. The
manuscripts of Donne's Holy Sonnets contain many examples, some
incapable of true elision, e.g. line nine of 'This is my playes last scene':

> Then, as my soule, *to 'heaven her* first seate, takes flight,

where the four syllables in italics require metrically to be reduced
to two.

5. There is another form of elision, not peculiar to Crane, but possibly thought of by him, in which the apostrophe marks the supposed
omission of a familiar word, such as a pronoun, or a colloquial corruption or it, e.g. *'has* for 'he *has*'. This, like 3, is pedantic, and probably
has no metrical significance whatever. In his transcript of Fletcher's
Demetrius and Enanthe, Crane's use of this elision is a species of colloquial shorthand, e.g.

> noe' *beleeve*' Sir, (M.S.R. 471)
> *'pray'* a word with ye (M.S.R. 3300)
> *art' thou* (= artow M.S.R. 2041)

6. Occasionally an apostrophe is used simply to indicate weakened
quality of a vowel through lack of stress; there is no elision at all. Thus
in Shakespeare's *Richard II* (Q₁) the following lines appear:

> I.3.180 Sweare by the duty that *y'owe* to God (This is a
> Synaloepha to avoid the conjunction of naked vowels; but it is of the
> pseudo-variety; in speech the actor might reduce the pronoun to
> [yə.]

> I.3.239 Oh *had't* beene a stranger, not my child, (No true elision is possible;
> all that is intended is the weakening of *it* by the neutralization of the
> vowel. (See page 78.)

Chapter 11

Syllabic Variation in the Quarto and Folio Texts of Shakespeare: Its Effect upon Prosody in *Hamlet* and *Troilus and Cressida*

I

THE ambivalence of words was a property much prized by the poets of the late sixteenth and early seventeenth centuries; it extended to meaning, form and pronunciation. Among the Figures of Grammar were certain morphological devices for enlarging the form, and therefore the pronunciation, of a word, without appreciably altering its meaning. These metaplasms were called prothesis, epenthesis, paragoge and diaeresis. *Prothesis* was the introduction of an extra syllable at the beginning of a word, e.g. Shakespeare's *e*nsky, *a*-cold, *b*eweep, and Spenser's *y*blent. *Epenthesis* was the introduction of an extra medial syllable, e.g. Shakespeare's Emper*a*tor for Emperor (*L.L.L.* III.1.187), curso*r*ary for cursory (H5 V.2.77), how*s*oever for however, etc. *Paragoge* was the introduction of an extra final syllable, e.g. gold*en* for gold, hast*en* for haste, content*ed* for content. Despite the different orthography of the following Shakespearian examples, metre calls for an extra syllable in both the genitive singulars:

L.L.L. (Q₁) V.2.332 To shew his teeth as white as Whal*es* bone,
M.N.D. (Q₁) II.1.4. I do wander every where; swifter than the Moo*n*s sphere

Diaeresis was the splitting of a single syllable into two parts, usually by the analysis of a diphthong into vowels, e.g. Shakespeare:

R. and J. (Q₂) I.5.105 Saints do not move, thogh grant for pr*ai*ers sake
(Diaeresis converts the normally monosyllabic word *praiers* to a dissyllable.)

Diaeresis is not in question in the following, since the normal pronunciation of *violent* is trisyllabic.

R. and J. (Q₂) II.6.9 These *violent* delights have *violent* ends. (In the first use of *violent* there are three syllables, in the second only two.)

These four metaplasmic variations are seen to be the opposite process of Aphæresis, Syncope, Apocope, and Synaloepha.

These devices, coupled with Diastole and Systole, two Figures of Grammar that permitted deliberate shift of stress from the normally accentuated syllables of words, contributed to the free adaptation of words, making Elizabethan English a very flexible language for poetry. Yet the flux was not formless, as it had been before the advent of Wyatt and Surrey. By Spenser's time the vernacular had been stabilized in its essential features; only out of a reasonable measure of conformity can grow the cultivated relaxations of prosody and rhetoric.

What reasons are there to suppose that *violent* was normally a tri-syllable, and *prayers* a monosyllable? The answer is supplied in an illuminating study of the Lutenist song-writers of the early seventeenth century by Evelyn H. Scholl.[1] The writer examined the musical settings of the various Books of Airs of twenty-one song-writers from William Barley's *New Booke of Tabliture* in 1596 to Walter Porter's *Madrigales and Ayres* 1632. The movement is reported to have practically ended with the publication of Campion's *Third and Fourth Booke of Ayres* about 1618. The song accompaniments of the time took whatever rhythm they enjoyed from the wording of the poetry. To quote the author, 'The lutenist air . . . impresses the hearer as not so much song, in our usual acceptance of the term, as speech to which definite pitch has been given. In the second place, it is very simple, presenting with few exceptions one note for one syllable of music. In the third place, it was composed by contemporary musicians who were peculiarly fitted to understand the poetry and to give it adequate expression. At no time, until very recently, has the relation between composer and poet been so intimate. . . . Since all the composers were associated with the court or with the great cathedrals, their pronunciation represents educated English. . . . It is possible to show whether certain syllables were elided or merely slurred; under what circumstances vowels were apocopated or syncopated; what was the syllabic value of certain combinations of vowels; what the probable pronunciation of certain consonants; and upon what syllable a word was usually accented.'[2]

[1] 'New Light on Seventeenth Century Pronunciation from the English School of Lutenist Song Writers', *P.M.L.A.*, LIX, 2 (1944), pp. 398–445.

[2] Op. cit., pp. 399–402.

In Appendix VI is provided a summary of Miss Scholl's findings; and as the evidence is important and sometimes contradicts Jespersen, Wyld, Van Dam and Stoffel, it should be studied in conjunction with what follows in this Chapter. Miss Scholl maintains that, through the Lutenists, especially Ferrabosco and Cooper, Italian prosodic influence was strong in England after 1600; but it is clear from their work that an apostrophe did not usually indicate true elision. Bayfield was therefore right in believing that an apostrophe in general signifies two light syllables forming one upbeat. English being even more flexible at the beginning of the seventeenth century than it is today, neither spelling nor syllable-counting may be relied upon to provide the correct pronunciation of words in which slurring is possible. The English ideal was not metrical regularity; consequently a word was never contracted simply to avoid an extra-metrical syllable. The reading and speaking of verse encouraged the use of glide sounds, rather than perfect elision; and in those vowel-quality was not completely levelled. In unstressed syllables *e* was the only vowel generally syncopated, principally before *r* and *n*. Fluidity and naturalness were greatly esteemed in early seventeenth-century poetry; doublets were deliberately cultivated for resourcefulness; but it was never expected that the speaker should substitute one form for another.

Miss Scholl condemns Van Dam and Stoffel's proposed elisions in *Othello* (F₁) IV.2.51.[1]

Given to Captivitie, me, and my utmost hopes

Here are thirteen syllables, and the suggested elisions are *gi'n captiv'tie, m'utmost*, two syncopes and a synaloepha. The assumption of Van Dam and Stoffel is 'that Elizabethan poetry was constructed upon a strict count of alternately stressed and unstressed syllables'.[2] Not even the most ingenious devices of elision will, however, make certain lines of Shakespeare or Donne conform to the basic pattern.

The revisers of Shakespeare's texts for the First Folio endeavoured in varying degrees to make his lines conformable; but what can be said of their work depends on agreement about the probable orthography of his manuscripts. Bayfield maintains that 'by the habitual use of certain abbreviations, the substitution of different words and the misdivision of lines in a printed edition it is possible to make a poet's verse assume a character very different from that which it had when it

---

[1] B. Van Dam and C. Stoffel, *Chapters in English Printing*, p. 92.
[2] Evelyn H. Scholl, op. cit., p. 425.

left his hands'.[1] The policy of all editors from Rowe to the present day, he adds, has been to reduce the resolved (or trisyllabic) feet to the barest minimum; their practice, however, pales beside the theories of E. A. Abbott in his *Shakespearian Grammar* and G. Koenig in *Der Vers in Shakesperes Dramen*. Such curiosities of elision as Koenig's *curios'ty*, *mag'cal*, *Jess'ca*, *ignom'ny*, *do'ng*, Bayfield rightly asserts to be impossible.

Bayfield's evidence on the combined contractions in Shakespeare and Jonson, and on the various types of elision found in the first Folios of both dramatists, is important, though its value is vitiated by the special pleading necessary for his theory of Shakespeare's versification. The axe that he grinds unceasingly is the falsification of a metric of infinite rhythmical resource by the pedantries of editors; and true as this is as a general statement, the conclusions, through want of systematic investigation, are often invalid in detail. He will accept as authentic only the most conventional poetical contractions that have persisted down to the present day; for instance, such forms as *tis*, *Ile*, *gainst*, *twixt*, *ore* and *nere*, which he rightly regards as independent words. But why should he assume that a resourceful dramatist, especially in comedy, would want to stop at these? Bayfield's unacceptable answer is that the rest were vulgarisms comparable in taste to *'taint*, *gimme* and *good un* in the speech of modern gentlemen. It is unthinkable that the Court English Puttenham advised Elizabethan gentlemen to cultivate was so inflexible as to be unaffected by the colloquial expressions of young men of London, by the inevitable clippings of gossiping speakers, and by the dialect peculiarities to be heard within walking distance of the City. *A* for *he* and later *'em* for *them* may not have been vulgar, but streamlined, forms; and both seem in turn to have been affected by some actors. Though there is reason to doubt *em* as an autograph Shakespearian form, little doubt exists about the dramatist's judicious use of *a*, by Mercutio and Hamlet, for instance, to represent the slang of young city men of fashion. *O'*, *i'*, *th'* and *t'* (= to) were certainly not vulgarisms, but conventional clippings in regular employment. They appear in prose to season the speech of garrulous characters like Pandarus, and may represent the individual style adopted by the actor who played the parts. In verse the principal use was syllabic variation, conferring the same potential for shortening as weak syllables in polysyllabic words.

Among the corrupting agents of Shakespeare's texts Bayfield counts the actor-scribe, who made contractions to save time, and his boy assistant, whose task it was to read over the copy. The latter is blamed

[1] *Shakespeare's Versification*, p. 3.

for introducing the slang characteristic of his own daily speech, as well as being a source of verse mislineation. But Bayfield clearly saw that the apostrophe was a symbol of manifold purpose, employed by Jonson in all its diversity, adopted in varying degrees by the editors and printers of the Shakespeare First Folio, and often misinterpreted by modern editors, whose conception of elision has the restricted meaning current since the age of Pope. For instance, in *h'had, this's, but't, th'civill, int' themselves*, found in Jonson's *Sejanus* and later plays, the elision is purely orthographical; in *yo'are* there may be combined contraction with phonetic weakening of some kind;[1] *to'undoe* (with Jonsonian elision) may actually be intended to point a resolution. In *a'most* the apostrophe indicates phonetic spelling; in *Agrippina; 'and*, it merely separates two identical contiguous vowels—a pedantry few but Jonson would have considered necessary. Some of the elisions in the Folio version of *Sejanus* are obviously errors of the printer resulting from the revision of the quarto by Jonson himself, and escaping his eagle eye in the reading of the proof.

The plurality of apostrophe's meaning is confusing to us; but it conferred the utmost freedom on Jonson and the scholar poets of the early seventeenth century. I doubt, however, whether its refinements appeared in Shakespearian autograph manuscripts. Both the Good Quartos and the three pages of *Sir Thomas More* preclude a belief in it. Scribes and printers airily employed elision with little grasp of its complex significance. The subtlety of range of this simple symbol was amply demonstrated by Milton in *Paradise Lost*. Since Pope, elision has meant one thing only, a letter or syllable lost in pronunciation. Bayfield goes too far when he claims that apostrophe with elision in Shakespeare 'was a recognized signal drawing attention to the resolution which we thought it was meant to abolish'.[2] One use of apostrophe appears, however, to have been overlooked, its occurrence in combinations of words phonetically impracticable to contract. Here it points to nothing more than a modification in natural delivery of the normal quality of a vowel or consonant in the isolated word; the nice appreciation of such modulations may even be part of what Shakespeare

---

[1] It is instructive to compare such alternative representations of combined contractions as *th'art* and *thou'rt, y'are* and *you're th'are* and *they're*. The first is, in each pair, the commoner, but it may well be that no difference existed phonetically, and that the different orthographies were simply printers' or scribes' conventions.

[2] *Shakespeare's Versification*, p. 311.

had in mind in his advice to the players to speak the speech 'trippingly on the tongue'.

II

Flatter's '"True Originall Copies" of Shakespeare's Plays' (see foot-note, p. 86) argues for two manuscripts of each of the dramatist's works, an Author's Autograph and a Stage Book, and assumes without evidence that it was the Company's invariable practice to employ a scribe to prepare the latter before a play was used in the theatre. The printed play might, however, derive from either source of copy, depending on public demand for the play and the Company's consequent need for the Stage Book at the time the copy had to go to the printer. *The Merchant of Venice* (Q₁) and *Macbeth* (F₁) represent for Flatter accurate versions of the Stage Book, and *King Lear* (the Pied Bull Quarto) is the almost perfect counterpart of the three Shakespearian manuscript pages of *Sir Thomas More*. *Hamlet* (Q₂) offers a transcription of the Author's Autograph, made at the behest of the printer by a literary scribe unconnected with the theatre. This last is a crucial test of Flatter's theory, which differs wholly from the view held by Dover Wilson and the bibliographical critics. The printer's reason for a preliminary tran-scription for Q₂ is unexplained; but the aim of the scribe is alleged to have been 'readability'. The scribe had his own ideas of punctuation and versification, and removed the extra-metrical iterations of the Prince, which Flatter attributes to Shakespeare himself, and not, as Dover Wilson does, to Burbage. Flatter's Q₂ scribe is said in the versi-fication to have treated the words *our*, *fire* and *hour* as dissyllabic; Shakespeare, according to Flatter, regarded them as monosyllabic. The following are examples of syllabic variation in the use of these words, which Flatter thinks support his theory that the First Folio offers the truer Shakespearian text of *Hamlet*:

I.3.120 (Q₂) You must not take for *fire*, from this time (dissyllabic)
       (F₁) You must not take for *fire*. For this time Daughter (mono-syllabic)

II.2.57 (Q₂) His fathers death, and *our* hastie marriage (dissyllabic).
       (F₁) His Fathers death, and *our* o're-hasty Marriage (monosyllabic).

IV.7.172 (Q₂) But *our* cull-cold maydes doe dead mens fingers call them (dissyllabic, but the line becomes an Alexandrine)
       (F₁) But *our* cold Maids doe Dead Mens Fingers call them (mono-syllabic)

V.2.326 (Q₂) In thee there is not halfe an *houres* life (dissyllabic)
       (F₁) In thee there is not halfe an *houre* of life; (monosyllabic)

Dover Wilson in the New Cambridge edition of *Hamlet* has adopted the Folio reading in all but the first of these examples, though his text is based on the Q_2 version of the play. His choice in II.2.57 and IV.7.172 is not motivated, but lines I.3.120 and V.2.326 are explained in *The Manuscript of Shakespeare's Hamlet* Vol. I, pp. 62 and 139–40. What he does not indicate, however, is that the Quarto reading of V.2.326 is equally likely to be Shakespeare's. Indeed, the Quarto dissyllables *fire* and *houres* (first and last examples) prove nothing but the flexibility of Shakespeare's practice, especially in those types of words Miss Scholl recorded. An examination of the First Folio text of *Hamlet* illustrates the poet's undoubted taste for syllabic variation. The following is the parallel evidence deduced from Act I of the Second Quarto version of the same play:

(a) *Fire* is monosyllabic in I.1.117.
    Fire is dissyllabic in I.3.120.
(b) *Power* is monosyllabic in I.1.163.
    Hour is monosyllabic in I.5.52.
    Hour is dissyllabic in I.4.3 and is not altered by the scribe or editor of F_1.
(c) *Prayers* is dissyllabic in I.2.119.
(d) *Spirit* is monosyllabic in I.1.138 and 161, I.2.255 and I.4.40.
    Spirit is dissyllabic in I.1.154 and 171 and I.4.6.
(e) *Violet* is dissyllabic in I.3.7.
    Violence is trisyllabic in I.1.144 and I.2.171.
(f) *Seeing* is monosyllabic in I.5.173.
    Being is dissyllabic in I.4.67.
(g) *Memory* is dissyllabic in I.5.96.
    Memory is trisyllabic, in I.5.98.
(h) *Desperate* is dissyllabic in I.4.87.
    Ponderous is trisyllabic in I.4.50.
    Leaprous is dissyllabic in I.5.64, erroneously, as the metre requires three syllables, supplied by the spelling *leaperous* in F_1.
    Sulphrous is dissyllabic in I.5.3, but the *u* is supplied in F_1, thereby resolving the foot.
(i) *Radiant* has monosyllabic ending—*iant* in I.5.55.
    Convenient has dissyllabic ending—*ient* in I.1.175.
(j) *Probation* has dissyllabic ending—*ion* in I.1.159, though usually the ending is monosyllabic. Dissyllabic—*ion* is common in Shakespeare's early plays, especially at the end of a verse line, infrequent in the later ones.

This seems to refute Flatter's statement that, if we accept *Hamlet* Q₂ as Shakespeare's autograph, 'we should have to take it that Shakespeare himself . . . (contrary to his own usage, which we find everywhere) treated *our*, *fire*, *hour* as dissyllabics, but that the theatrical scribe corrected him by turning those words into monosyllables, in order probably to make those passages sound more generally Shakespearian'.[1]

Dover Wilson's immense labours on the transmission of the *Hamlet* texts cannot be lightly dismissed. A theatrical scribe, as he points out, must have been responsible for the copy presented to Jaggard for printing in the First Folio, and I believe that copy to have been prepared rather late. Frequently, but inconsistently, either the scribe or the compositor substitutes *ha's* for *hath* (as at I.1.18). At I.2.85 he gives the more up-to-date inflexion in *passes* for *passeth*. He occasionally abolishes resolutions by means of combined contractions, e.g.

I.5.126 (Q₁) Why right, you are *in the* right,
      (F₁) Why right, you are *i'th'* right;

He once in Act I substitutes *ye* for *you*.

I.2.251 (Q₂) I will requite your loves, so farre *you* well:
      (F₁) I will requite your loves; so fare *ye* well:

He substitutes *It's* for *Tis* at the beginning of line I.5.35, and occasionally *I'm* for *I am* (as at I.5.109 and 134).

There is no doubt that characteristic iterations in Hamlet's speech were provided by Shakespeare himself, and worked naturally into the metrical scheme of the verse. In the First Folio version the scribe has expanded these iterations so that they are often extra-metrical; it is difficult to imagine what his purpose could be, were it not to record the version of the part as acted by Burbage. This kind of scribal modification may, therefore, be expected in First Folio texts based on late prompt copy; it was even adumbrated by Pollard and Greg, who were more conservative in their textual theories than Dover Wilson. That the actor had an important influence on the text as preserved in theatre-copy should be obvious; and this would be even less remarkable if members of the Company helped in the transcription. Here, too, is a possible explanation of some modifications of the texts in colloquial contractions, for instance the intrusive *em*'s and *ye*'s that confront the reader of the First Folio, but are inconspicuous or wholly absent in the Good Quartos.

[1] Op. cit., p. 40.

III

What light can the foregoing, read with chapters VIII and IX, throw on the general problem of Shakespearian textual variation? Comparing the Good Quartos with the companion texts of the First Folio, one finds that even where passages are verbally identical, there is considerable difference in the orthography. On the latter basis Folio texts can therefore be grouped and classified. *Troilus and Cressida*, though textually unique, is typical of the kinds of variation that appear when Quarto and Folio versions are collated. This learned play was probably written for performance at one of the Inns of Court shortly after *Hamlet*, as early as 1601. A comparison of the two substantive texts indicates that the Folio version is from a theatre manuscript, which looks as though it has been read with the Quarto of 1609. The Quarto has many indications of being nearer to the author's autograph than the Folio text, for instance, its spelling, punctuation and typical paucity of stage-directions; but there are also a few significant Quarto variations corrected in F1, which are too crass to be laid at the door of Shakespeare himself.

The following is an analysis of some of the orthographical and metrical variations found in Act I of the two substantive versions of the play:

1. *Elision:* Apostrophe to mark a letter lost in pronunciation is the regular policy of the editor(s) and compositor(s)[1] of the First Folio text of *Troilus and Cressida*, as well as of other plays in that collected edition.

> (a) Deliberate improvement is apparent in the use of apostrophe in the preterite and past participle of weak verbs. Where Shakespeare in his manuscript seems to have indicated elision simply through the spelling, the Folio uses the seventeenth-century printers' convention, e.g.

I.2.107 Q *praisd*   F *prais'd*
I.3. 76 Q *lackt*   F *lack'd*

> There is in both texts some inconsistency in these matters, especially in the Quarto, where the ending after voiced stem-finals is often '*d* (apostrophe probably the printer's), but after unvoiced stem-finals usually simply *t*. The inconsistency is

---

[1] The different compositors engaged in the setting up of First Folio texts have been discussed, *inter alios*, by Alice Walker in *Textual Problems of the First Folio* (C.U.P. 1953).

explained by the probability of two compositors being set to work on the Quarto text.

(b) Similarly the First Folio points syncope of the inflexion of the second person singular present indicative of verbs, and the super-lative of adjectives, e.g.

I.1.	53	Q *Powrest*	F *Powr'st*
	59	Q *Telst*	F *tel'st*
	62	Q *layst*	F *lai'st*
I.3.338		Q *deerst*	F *deer'st*

(c) Elision is marked by the editor or compositor(s) of the Folio version in the following instances, where an intermediate weak vowel is omitted for metrical reasons:

I.3.	91	Q *medcinable*	F *med'cinable*
	205	Q *mappry*	F *Mapp'ry*
	352	Q *conquering*	F *conqu'ring*
	374	Q *lottry*	F *Lott'ry*

In I.2.150 and 207 *marvel's* (= marvellous) and *shrow'd* (= shrewd) appear with apostrophe in both texts.

(d) More interesting is the pseudo-grammatical apostrophe of the following changes:

| I.1. | 68 | Q *has* | F *ha's* |
| I.2. | 9 | Q *goes* | F *goe's* |

(e) In the prose speeches of Pandarus the full prepositional com-binations are sometimes contracted, e.g.

I.1.	66	Q *in it*	F *in't*
I.2.264		Q *in th.'*	F *i'th'*
I.2.304		Q *I will be*	F *Ile be*

2. *Syllable variation in verse:* Two interesting examples of change are to be noted:

I.3. 56 Q Heart of our numbers, soule and onely *spright* (F *spirit*).

I.3. 67 Q (on which *heaven* rides) knit all the Greekish eares (monosyllable).
 For the use of *Greekish*, cf. line 221.
 F In which the *Heavens* ride, knit all Greekes eares (dissyllable).

It is worth noting that *heaven* is predominantly monosyllabic in Shake-speare.

3. *Extra-metrical and short lines. Troilus and Cressida* is the first play after *Hamlet* to experiment freely with the newer versification, the

force of which begins to appear in the long speeches of the Council scene (Act I, Scene 3), which contains the difficult oration of Ulysses on 'Order'. In this speech there are both Alexandrines and short lines; and it is possible to explain the latter as breathing points, which divide the oration into rhythmical paragraphs. When a speech is of this length, as Milton saw, some device of paragraphing becomes necessary, unless the address is broken by the interruption of another speaker. An Alexandrine of thirteen syllables occurs at I.3.51:

> And Flies fled under shade, why then the thing of courage,

At I.3.387 is found:

> Now Ulísses I begín to relish thy advíse,

This is a duodecasyllabic line clearly in the rhythm of natural speech, prosaic, and yet capable of scansion. Alexandrines were a source of trouble to the editor of the First Folio text. For instance, the first line of Act I, Scene 3, has twelve syllables in the Quarto; but in the Folio, to accommodate the double-column page, it is printed as two lines:

> Princes:
> What greefe hath set the Iaundies on your cheekes?

At I.3.324 the twelve-syllabled line

> True the purpose is perspicuous as substance

is improved, because of its metrical difficulty, to

> The purpose is perspicuous even as substance

The grammatical and verbal differences of these companion substantive texts are even more impressive than the variations of elision, but these are not relevant to my immediate purpose.

Chapter 12

Readings in Plays of more than one Authority for an Original-Spelling Edition of Shakespeare: *Othello*. Compositor Analysis

(The line-numbering of quotations in this and the next chapter is from Dover Wilson's *New Cambridge Shakespeare*.)

WE are apt to think of the term 'definitive', applied to an edition, as meaning 'authoritative', and also as embodying most of the relevant results of scholarship. For earlier English literature, 'definitive' implies, in addition, a critical text that does not neglect the conventions of grammar, spelling and punctuation of the author's time. A 'critical' text, in turn, is one based on substantive authorities only, and which offers a reasonable account of the probable history of transmission, aiming at the same time at restoration of the text as nearly as possible to the originals of the author. The term 'definitive' is, on this last account, relative. An edition cannot be final as long as textual study and methods progress, though it may be valid for a generation or two.

About the need for an old-spelling edition of Shakespeare scholars disagree. The objections to such an edition of Shakespeare arise largely from the alleged inability of an editor to produce consistency in his original-spelling text.

Skeat in his 'Introduction to the Notes on the Canterbury Tales'[1] believes that the term 'modernization', as applied to the currently used editions of Shakespeare, is a misnomer. 'In all that is essential', he says, 'it is the spelling of Shakespeare's time that has been adopted in modern English.' Wright, in his Preface to *The Cambridge Shakespeare*,[2] puts the case for modernization quite reasonably. We have, he main-

[1] *The Works of Geoffrey Chaucer*, Vol. 5, Section 23, p. xxv.
[2] Vol. I, c. Orthography, p. xvi.

H

tains, too little evidence of Shakespeare's spelling to submit his language arbitrarily to the use of it. 'Moreover, in many of the Plays there is a competing claim to guide our spelling, put forward by an array of Quartos, of earlier date than the First Folio. To desert the First Folio for these, where they exist, would be but an occasional, and at best an uncertain means of attaining the lost spelling of Shakespeare, while the spelling of our volume would become even more inconsistent than that of the First Folio itself. Add to this; there are places, though . . . not many, where we have had to leave the reading of the First Folio altogether. How then shall we spell the correction which we substitute?'

The variations in orthography noted by Wright are not, however, peculiar to the text of Shakespeare; they are common to most dramatists of the time, including Ben Jonson. It would be impossible to edit any pre-eighteenth-century work in the original spelling, unless an editor were permitted to rationalize, especially where he has not had access to an author's manuscript. Jonson presented to his editors, Herford and Simpson, for all the plays and masques later than *Catiline*, similar problems to those met by Shakespeare's modern editor. The extent of Jonson's linguistic revisions in *Every Man in His Humour* compelled the editors to print both the folio (or English) and earlier quarto (or Italian) versions of the play; they are a valuable indication of Jonson's self-criticism and development.

The orthographical divergences found in the Quarto and First Folio texts of Shakespeare's plays bedevil the work of every editor of Elizabethan and Jacobean works. In vocabulary, accidence, syntax, colloquial usage, spelling, punctuation, and handwriting, the period from Spenser's *Shepherd's Calendar* to the closing of the theatres was one of great flexibility, fluidity and change. A writer who began his literary career in one writing style might end it in another markedly different in its details.

Thirty years separate the earliest of Shakespeare's substantive authorities (the 1593 Quarto of *Venus and Adonis*) from the latest, the First Folio (1623). The First Folio, as Appendix II shows, is the sole authority for eighteen of Shakespeare's plays, which may be called single-text plays. I include here *The Taming of the Shrew*, supposing that *A Shrew* and *The Shrew* should not be regarded as the same play. Of the remaining nineteen multiple-text plays, four will certainly have the First Folio as their major substantive authority, namely, *2 and 3 Henry VI*, *Henry V*, and *The Merry Wives of Windsor*. There are also five multiple-text plays of mixed authority, *Richard III*, *2 Henry IV*,

Troilus and Cressida, Othello, and *King Lear,* which present some difficulty; but an editor who has weighed the evidence will, I think, select
the First Folio as the basis of his text for two, namely, *Richard III* and
King Lear, though all five will call for the exercise of his skill as an
eclectic editor. And so, indeed, will many of the remaining plays for
which an early good quarto is the main authority, especially *Romeo and
Juliet* (1599), *2 Henry IV* (1600), *Hamlet* (1604), and *Troilus and Cressida*
(1609).

The textual authority of the sources is thus divided roughly into two
groups of two thirds and one third, twenty-four plays in the critical
edition being based mainly on the First Folio, and thirteen plays largely
on an early quarto (including *Pericles,* which Heminge and Condell
excluded from the First Folio). The corpus naturally displays differences,
not only between the two groups, but between different texts in the
same group; and this is because of the complications of recension.

In the case of plays like *Othello,* where the two substantive witnesses
are of nearly equal authority, it is necessary to say why the chosen text
is to be preferred as the basis of an eclectic text. The Folio text of *Othello*
may be the better only from certain points of view, being the result of
collation of texts, and consequently corrected; it has, for instance, the
merit of revealing more accurately Shakespeare's grammatical practice,
which can be derived from the Good Quartos that, on biliographical
evidence, lie close to his autograph.[1] For instance, at I.2.59 we find the
following difference:

(Q_1) Keepe up your bright swords, for the dew will rust *em,* (verse).
(F_1) Keepe up your bright Swords, for the dew will rust *them.* (prose).

As the Good Quartos reveal, Shakespeare preferred the full pronominal
form *them* to the contraction *'em.* Both versions of the *Othello* text are
probably several years later than the playwright's death; but the evidence in favour of Shakespeare's use of *them* rightly influenced its
adoption in both the Old and the New *Cambridge* editions. Nicholas
Okes, the printer of the Quarto of 1622, or the scribe who supplied his
copy, must have altered *them* to *em;* the printer is known to have taken
liberties with his text, when he printed the work even of such an

---

[1] The early quartos of two of Shakespeare's poems, and nine, at least, of his
plays are believed by competent bibliographical scholars to represent a printing
from his manuscript. These quartos are *Venus and Adonis* (1593), *Lucrece* (1594),
Richard II (Q_1, 1957), *Love's Labour's Lost* (1598), *1 Henry IV* (1598), *Romeo and
Juliet* (Q_2, 1599), four quartos in 1600, namely *2 Henry IV, A Midsummer Night's
Dream, The Merchant of Venice, Much Ado about Nothing* and *Hamlet* (Q_2) in 1604.

exacting orthographer as Ben Jonson. Percy Simpson has checked the changes he made in the punctuation of the *Masque of Queens*, by comparison with the British Museum manuscript,[1] and shows that he varies where he does not understand Jonson's subtleties and takes them for errors. By 1622, Fletcher and the newest dramatic orthographers had influenced the printing of *em* (the colloquial form) for *them*, especially when the pronoun appeared as an unstressed syllable at the end of a verse line. The Folio, however, wrongly prints Shakespeare's line I.2.59, and the next two lines, as prose, and has a full-stop after *them* instead of a comma.

Another proof of Okes' muddling can be illustrated in the opening lines of the Quarto version of *Othello* (I.1.1–7):

> *Rod.* Tush, never tell me, I take it much unkindly
>   That *you* Iago, who *has* had my purse
>   As if the strings were thine, should'st know of this.
> *Iago.* S'blood, but you will not heare me.
>   •   If ever I did dreame of such a matter, abhorre me.
> *Rod.* Thou toldst me, thou didst hold him in thy hate.

The context, and Roderigo's emotional impatience, clearly demand *thou* and *hast* in the second line. But the compositor probably mistook the abbreviation of *thou* for *you*, and then dropped the *-t* from *hast*, thinking it grammatical to have *who* in the third person, because its immediate antecedent was *Iago*.

Conjectural restorations of the text must be consonant with the history of recension and apparent stratifications in the production of copy. Occasional readings and the use of accidentals, including spelling and punctuation, may here provide important evidence, as in the well-known crux in *Othello* (V.2.349):

> (Q_1)   one whose hand,
>   Like the base *Indian*, threw a pearle away,
>   Richer than all his Tribe:
> (F_1)   one, whose hand
>   (Like the base *Iudean*) threw a Pearle away (etc)

The acceptance of the First Folio reading has difficulties, because the definite article before *Iudean* implies a biblical or historical reference; in which case the line should allude to Herod or Judas. The word *Iudean* does not, according to the *O.E.D.*, reappear until the nineteenth

---

[1] Jonson, *Works*, Vol. VIII, p. 272.

century, but this cannot disprove Shakespeare's possible employment of it. *Enurn'd* (F_1), to replace *interr'd* (Q_2), in *Hamlet* I.4.49 was, similarly, not revived until the early eighteenth century; and yet it was probably Shakespeare's own improvement of his line. But the difficulty in *Othello* must have been the handwriting; the scribe who drafted the Folio copy may have intended *Indian*; but the compositor read the word as *Iudean*, in the belief that it was a Shakespearian innovation, partly because he saw *Pearle* and *Tribe* in the words that followed. The Quarto, however, came from theatre copy, and therefore preserved the form *Indian*, which the actors were in the habit of speaking. This seems to be the correct reading.

Finally, there is an instance of variant punctuation in *Othello* II.1.215–6 which deserves attention. Both versions are in prose.

(Q_1) First I will tell thee, this Desdemona is directly in love with him.
(F_1) First, I must tell thee this: Desdemona, is directly in love with him.

On the basis of the illustrations of internal punctuation inserted, and external punctuation omitted, which Professor P. Alexander has adduced,[1] it could be argued that the comma before *this* in the Quarto is an emphasising comma (internal), and that both passages mean precisely the same thing. But I think it unlikely that this kind of emphatic punctuation should have been retained so late as 1622. Whatever stood in the transcription, the compositor of the Quarto took *this* to go with Desdemona (as Shakespeare appears to have intended); for, in the scene, she has just left the company with Othello. The Folio compositor, however, had no stop at all in his script before *this*, but one erroneously after *Desdemona*. The colon was probably the insertion of the Folio editor, who took *this* as the direct object of *tell*. The colon converts the following sentence into direct speech, and is characteristic of this editor's pointing.

In *Othello*, evidence of what we can trace of Shakespeare himself from the verbal quality of either text is inconclusive, and so the adoption of a substantive authority is largely a matter of editorial predilection— except in one important consideration. M. R. Ridley is surely right in seeing the sophistication of the text by the Folio editors as a process of change to which there need be no logical limits;[2] and this consideration

---

[1] See *British Academy Lecture*, 'Shakespeare Punctuation' (1945) and his review of Flatter's *Shakespeare's Producing Hand* in *R.E.S.* (New Series) Vol. I, No. 1 (1950), p. 69.

[2] *Othello*, New Arden edition, 1958, Introd. p. xxxi.

argues for reliance on a good Quarto, with independent authority, and a measure of linguistic similitude to author's copy. Ridley justifies his preference for the Quarto by asserting that, with the latter, we know we are as near to Shakespeare as we can reasonably expect to get; whereas with the Folio the degree of intervention leaves us in considerable doubt.

The Quarto's sporadic use of *has* and *does* in preference to the more Shakespearian *hath* and *doth* has no significance for discrediting the text, because it simply tells us what the date of publication (1622) reveals, that the current Jacobean forms supplanted Shakespeare's usage in the hand of the copyist. To any student of Quarto orthography it will be evident that the minor sophistications of the scribe are not to be compared with the large-scale improvements of those responsible for the Folio version.

Ridley's warning about the refuge 'memorial contamination' to which some editors are prone, is salutary. Some of the so-called 'common errors' of Quarto and Folio *Othello*, to which Alice Walker drew attention in her article on the 1622 Quarto in *Shakespeare Survey 5*, are sometimes not common, and sometimes not errors, at any rate in the Quarto version, e.g.

> I.iii.231 the flinty and steele *cooch* of warre (idiosyncratic spelling of *couch*).
> I.iii.235 *This* present warres against the *Ottamites* (*This* is not an error of concord, but a weakening of the late M.E. plural *thise*, commonly used by Elizabethan dramatists, e.g. Shakespeare *Romeo and Juliet* V.ii.25, *Henry VIII* III.ii.360, and Jonson *The Case is Altered* IV.v.16, 'this contemplations'. *Ottamites* is probably a peculiar spelling of the author.)
> II.i.233 Love *lines* in favour, sympathy in yeares (The Quarto compositor's error is the simple one of reading *n* for *v* in the MS. Folio's *Loveliness* for *Love lives*, which last Ridley suggests in his footnote yet rejects in his text, has had a curious attraction for most editors. Yet the Quarto reading (but for the turned letter) of this and the preceding sentence is unexceptionable.)
> III.iii.440 If it be that, or any, *it* was hers, (*that* is probably the correct reading; but the Quarto compositor seems to have misread the contraction y^t for *it* in the M.S.)

The mild enough oaths of the Quarto, as Ridley maintains, do not vulgarize the text, much less the character of Othello, who is after all a blunt soldier driven to the extremes of moral perplexity. Nor is there anything wrong, as Alice Walker suggests, in the Quarto reading at

V.ii.324, 'And he himselfe confest it even now,'. The Folio collator inserted *but* after *it*, because he took upon himself the task of metrical improver, and judged Shakespeare's use of *even* to be monosyllable *e'en* (as it nearly always is in this play), instead of leaving the choice of alternative pronunciations to the requirements of the verse or the rhythmic sensibility of the actor.

Under the stimulus of W. W. Greg, Alice Walker and Fredson Bowers, eclectic editing of Shakespeare's plays of dual source has experienced a minor renaissance. *Othello* shows clearly that this was inevitable. It is not, indeed, a disaster to be thrust back 'into the eighteenth century confusion from which R. B. McKerrow sought to extricate us',[1] but a challenge to the skill, textual education and reasoning power of the editor. *Othello* demands from him decisive action, backed by expert justification of the crucial readings. It is a worthwhile exercise, therefore, to examine the selections of C. J. Sisson in his *New Readings in Shakespeare* and to place beside them the decisions of Alice Walker and M. R. Ridley in their respective New Cambridge and New Arden editions. The results reveal in their most exasperating form the inconclusive nature of modern Shakespearian textual scholarship.

One of the reasons for the present dubiety may be the expanding, but slenderly substantiated theories, erected on the shifting sands of compositorial analysis. Not only have assertions been made without adequate linguistic evidence, but published results have been hailed, less as tentative hypotheses, than as demonstrations of the irrefutable value of this work for the editor of an Elizabethan play. The likelihood that any reputable printing house, Tudor or modern, would place editorial responsibility of the kind that this new school allows in the hands of its compositors is hardly to be conceived. Compositors' errors and normalization of spelling are one thing; tampering with grammatical forms, lineation and scansion are quite another. As Alice Walker has wisely pointed out, orthography is a matter 'about which we as yet know very little'; 'an historical approach to a writer's language is fundamental to both textual and literary criticism'. The interesting discovery of compositors' errors is, in the last resort, a matter of literary judgment; so is the choice of variant readings. It has to be admitted that Shakespeare's spelling and punctuation are only partly recoverable, and we should be grateful if the *ipsissima verba* of his text can be restored to the extent of about ninety percent.

The investigation of preferential spellings of compositors is unlikely

[1] Fredson Bowers, *On Editing Shakespeare* (1955), p. 82.

to gain more ground for an editor than knowledge of the habits of quarto and folio transcribers, whose share in the copy of some folio plays may be more significant than that of the hypothetical compositors. Alice Walker's groupings of typical spellings of compositors A and B of the First Folio may be taken as an illustration:

A	B
doe	do
goe	go
yeere	yeare
deare	deere

If A is consistent in his spellings *goe* and *doe*, why should he be inconsistent in spelling *yeere* as B does *deere*, but *deare* as B does *yeare*. Alice Walker's reply would no doubt be: 'A pair of compositors might draw together over some spellings but apart over others, and how often their spelling changed in one particular or another is of as much importance as their fixed habits.'[1] But as the criteria of compositors' spellings are invariably their 'fixed habits', such an escape merely adds a further element of conjecture to the already hazardous task of clarifying the transmission of texts. I am not arguing against the existence of two or more compositors, but against the facile and inadequately supported way in which their stints are determined, while ignoring mere whim (e.g. the spellings *lite* and *light* in consecutive lines of C_3^v of the Quarto) or the possible hand of the transcriber in the characteristic spellings. Compositor analysis has, indeed, been used in fragmentary form to bolster the bibliographical machinery an editor has devised by instinct, taste or prejudice. The time that is expended upon it is time that could more profitably be applied to an investigation of Shakespeare's language, and its structural effects on 'style'.

Fredson Bowers in 'Shakespeare's Text and the Bibliographical Method' (*Studies in Bibliography*, University of Virginia, 1954) has made a necessary plea for the usefulness of compositor determination, but has not convinced the sceptic of the *scientific* value of the present method, which he claims to be comparable to the law of evidence. Some of the crucial evidence from 'mixed' spellings is derived by fallible inference; it is not empirical enough to serve as a groundwork for the hypotheses about transmission and printer's copy that have been erected upon it. It may be that Dover Wilson's theory of the single

---

[1] 'Compositor Determination and other Problems in Shakespearian Texts', *Studies in Bibliography* (University of Virginia), VII, 1955.

prentice compositor of the second Quarto of *Hamlet* will have to be revised, but not for the reason Fredson Bowers offers—that the novice is the figment of bibliographical fancy, impossible because no printer would have risked employing such a bungler. Charlton Hinman has recently drawn inferences about the same kind of novice (compositor E) at work in the First Folio.

Hinman in *The Printing and Proof-Reading of the First Folio of Shakespeare* (1963), Vol. I, pp. 180–226, shows that the evidence so far obtained from the collected edition is still inconclusive, even for some of the Folio plays that Alice Walker thinks were set up from corrected quartos. Two things only are certain, that the Folio spellings are mainly printing-house spellings, and that roughly half the plays were set up from printed copy, rather than manuscript. Dramatic manuscripts, whether scribe's or author's, must have contained many inconsistent spellings; yet Hinman holds firmly to the faith that the spelling of individual compositors would normally be uniform, apparently because consistency saves time. Many bibliographers are also prepared to rely on the limited evidence of the spellings of the three words *do*, *go* and *here* for the determination of the Folio's compositors A and B. 'Not that either man *invariably* spelt all of these words—or, indeed, any one of them—in one way only,' writes Hinman. 'It is demonstrable that both A and B now and again used non-characteristic spellings, and sometimes without ascertainable reason' (p. 185). The reasons usually assigned are (1) justifying the line, and (2) influence of the copy, such as a quarto, where it still exists for comparison. But in an interesting passage from 3 *Henry VI* (p. 187), Hinman shows that compositor A had neither of these reasons for using the spellings normally preferred by compositor B; 'men are men, and no two of them are alike' suffices to dismiss this anomaly.

The most revealing part of Hinman's account, however, is concerned with the explanation of numerous pages in the major tragedies, and in *The Taming of the Shrew*, *All's Well that Ends Well* and *King John*, in which mixed spellings prove an embarrassment to the classifier. To explain these the theorists have hypothecated further compositors C, D and E, whose general characteristic is that they follow the spellings of their copy almost slavishly, especially with *do* and *go*. Hinman says that in *Richard III*, *Richard II*, *Julius Caesar*, *Troilus and Cressida* and *Macbeth*, 'compositor B's spelling tends to be remarkably pure' (p. 191); but in what the 'purity' of an Elizabethan spelling consists, he does not explain. To what standard is fidelity supposed to conform?

About the spellings in the Folio texts of *Titus Andronicus, Romeo and Juliet*, the pre-cancellation pages of *Troilus and Cressida, Hamlet, Lear* and *Othello*, Hinman admits the following:

> .... it can scarcely be denied that spelling tests alone have so far proved unsatisfactory in this: that they have not enabled us to determine with any real confidence just who set the many pages in the Folio that contain decidedly mixed spellings. In fact spelling evidence has not even permitted us to say how many compositors worked on the Folio, and different investigators have reached different conclusions from the same data. . . . (footnote). A more comprehensive study of C, D, and E would be desirable, and above all a qualitative evaluation of their work. (pp. 192–3.)

Hinman has also been unable to explain at all why prose passages and long lines of verse 'affect the spellings of different compositors differently' (footnote, p. 197). The characteristic difference is, in these circumstances again, that the spellings are less 'pure'. In ten verse lines of the Folio text of *A Midsummer Night's Dream* (III.1.138–147) set up from the Quarto (1600), compositor D is *characteristically* exemplified, in that with all three words *do, go* and *here*, he inconsistently follows his copy in some cases, and his own bent in others (p. 199).

Compositor E, who was B's amanuensis, is the most contentious of the quintette, not only by his absence from the Comedies and Histories, but because his spellings are so 'mixed' that he is assumed to have been inexpert, even an apprentice (footnote 2, p. 213). His characteristic is that he follows his copy with slavish fidelity. But after a luckless eighty-five lines in Act III, Scene 2 of *Titus Andronicus*, set up from manuscript, the enterprise dared not employ him further, except on printed copy; Jaggard, in fact, never gave him a case of his own to work from; and his work always called for careful proofreading. He is supposed by Hinman to have set up four pages of the *Hamlet* Folio text, more than half of *King Lear* and most of the first Act of *Othello*.

Hinman's admirable caution and tentative conclusions on the relation of spelling to compositor-stints in the First Folio gives the analysts little cause for confident pronouncements. What is needed is a check on compositor analysis by different criteria; the limited spelling range leads to over-simplification, and determination from such slender evidence can hardly be classed as scientific. What has become clear from Alice Walker's admirable accounts of the usefulness of compositor analysis is, first, that an old-spelling edition of Shakespeare, based of necessity on substantive printed texts, cannot guarantee author-spelling or author-punctuation; second, that the most valuable habit of a compositor is fidelity to copy, the most difficult of all the inferences to substantiate; third, that the most slavish compositor's spellings of unusual words and proper names cannot tell us of an earlier stage of transmission, in which a scribe or prompter stands between compositor and author.

A sense of proportion in evaluating the significance of textual theories is sometimes forgotten. The integrity of Shakespeare's text had been established in the bulk of what matters to literature by the Old Cambridge edition of Aldis Wright and by Kittredge. The clearing up of obscurities that remain is unlikely seriously to affect the artistic value of what the world already possesses.

Chapter 13

Editorial Revision and Corruption
of Shakespeare's First Folio Texts: *Coriolanus*
and *Antony and Cleopatra*

THE reinstatement of the First Folio by most Shakespearian scholars has been a matter of necessity, rather than of choice. Considered in its orthography, line after line bears the stamp of post-Shakespearian modernization. The First Folio, is in fact, the first edited collection of Shakespeare's plays.

A disadvantage of First Folio texts is that they contain, *inter alia*, much edited punctuation and some modification of spelling; but as the volume was composite, there are degrees of variation. This means that the extent to which Shakespeare's orthography is obscured varies. In some texts we can see very little of it at all; other texts are of the translucent order, such as *Coriolanus* and *Antony and Cleopatra*. But I can think of no Folio text that, in its orthography, is as transparent as the first Quarto of *Richard II*.

Coriolanus and *Antony and Cleopatra*, as they are printed in the First Folio, are thought by good authorities to be from Shakespeare's manu-script. However this may be, Shakespeare's punctuation shines through but fitfully; and these plays are no exception to the rule that the point-ing of the First Folio was heavily revised, the work being mainly that of a logical punctuator, trained in the school of Jonson or Crane.

In the Folio texts of *Coriolanus* and *Antony and Cleopatra* there is observed a highly developed dramatic orthography, replete with con-tractions and elisions of all kinds, such as *a'th, and't, in't, to't, to'th' Capitoll, upon's, th' fire*, alongside of the more familiar *wee'l, they'l, y'are, hang 'em, ha's, ta'ne*. Three explanation are possible for this. The first is that Shakespeare had absorbed from others a new technique of colloquial clipping, and developed it independently. This should, I think, be accepted as probable; for he was always willing to learn from others, and had possibly discussed colloquial elisions with Ben Jonson, realizing the freedom and flexibility in dialogue that the extended system of contractions or slurrings conferred. Another possibility is that the foul papers Shakespeare had handed over were copied or edited by the Company's latest scribe, before Heminge and Condell handed the drafts to the publishers of the First Folio. The third possibility is that the copy for these plays was revised by the supervising editors of the publishers themselves.

Shakespeare's syntax in the tenser dramatic speeches, especially of the later plays, is sometimes difficult; and it certainly gave the Folio reviser much trouble, for example, in *Coriolanus* III.3.68–74:

> The fires i'th' lowest hell. Fould in the people:
> Call me their Traitor, thou iniurious Tribune.
> 70 Within thine eyes sate twenty thousand deaths
> In thy hands clutcht: as many Millions in
> 72 Thy lying tongue, both numbers. I would say
> Thou lyest unto thee, with a voice as free,
> As I do pray the Gods.

At this stage the punctuator had apparently tired of wrestling with his text; for the punctuation, even by his own earlier standards, is corrupt. He could not construe lines 70–72, as most editors have failed to do. When one cannot expound syntax, how is one to punctuate by the logical method? If the dramatic significance of the stops, especially the full-stop after *hell* in line 68, is to be argued, should not the experience of actors be invoked to elucidate the theory?

A similar difficulty occurs in *Antony and Cleopatra* III.4.1–10, as it stands in the First Folio:

> *Ant.* Nay, nay Octavia, not only that,
> That were excusable, that and thousands more
> Of sembable import, but he hath wag'd
> New Warres 'gainst Pompey. Made his will, an dread it,
> To publicke eare, spoke scantly of me,
> When perforce he could not
> But pay me tearmes of Honour; cold and sickly
> He vented then most narrow measure: lent me,
> When the best hint was given him: he not look't,
> Or did it from his teeth.

To maintain faith in Shakespeare's autograph, and in the dramatic significance of the full-stop after *Pompey*, or the colons after *Honour*, *measure*, and *him*, is tempting. But the passage is patently corrupt at three points, possibly four. A full-stop is by no means impossible after *Pompey*; but the next two words are curious, since Plutarch avers that Octavius took Antony's will (not his own) and read it publicly, to which the latter naturally objected. The emendation *ta'en* has been suggested. The line-arrangement has gone awry from *eare* in the next line, apparently implying a marginal insertion difficult for the compositor to read. *Them* should be read for *then* at line 8, and *took't* for *look't* in the next line.

When corruption of this kind has taken place, it is unwise to look for significance in the punctuation. Unaccountable periods in the middle of a sentence should not be taken at face value in First Folio plays, since by 1623 scribal practice was given to capitalization. Anyone who examines Ralph Crane's transcriptions will find that in mid-sentence he may capitalize any part of speech at random, for no other reason than that his calligraphy is prone to ornamental features. An imperfectly tailed comma, just before such a needless capital-letter, would naturally be taken by the compositor for a full-stop. I do not yet suggest that a scribe supplied the Folio copy of *Antony and Cleopatra*; but one seems to have made insertions from theatre-copy. Nor do I suggest it useless to look for author-punctuation in Shakespeare's early editions; but the place to seek it is undoubtedly in the Good dramatic Quartos, not the First Folio.

In grammar, particularly accidence, the interference of scribes and printers was not of real significance. Their principal liberty was to insert marks of elision and contraction where Shakespeare, as was his general practice, had omitted them; and sometimes his judgment is better than theirs. An interesting grammatical feature, in both Quarto and Folio texts, is the retention by Shakespeare of the old *-s* for *-st* inflexion after *thou* in the second person singular present indicative of verbs, for example in *Antony and Cleopatra* I.3.71 and 103:

> I go from hence
> Thy Souldier, Servant, making Peace or Warre,
> as thou affects.

and

> That thou reciding heere, goes yet with mee;

Modern editors do not always follow Aldis Wright in the *Cambridge Shakespeare* in printing *affect'st* and *go'st*. Some have reflected on the impossibility, for the actor, of such a tongue-twister as the last four consonants in *affect'st*.

These *-s* endings are not printers' or scribes' tricks, but genuine grammatical forms, which go back to Old English. The inflexion *-s* was actually the original, though *-st* joined it in Old English. In Middle English *-es*, *-is*, *-ys* were the regular terminations in the Northern dialects, and *-est* in the Southern and East Midland dialects. The latter eventually prevailed in Received English; but in Elizabethan verse drama *-s* was a licenced survival of the Northern inflexion. The inflexion *-s* was, in fact, consciously employed in sixteenth- and seventeenth-century poetry for specific purposes, (a) euphony, and (b) metre (the adoption of the *-s* ending reducing the syllables by one). Mainly, though not always, *-s* was used where the stem of the verb ends in *-t*, and the practice survived as late as Congreve. Jonson resorted to it less frequently than Shakespeare, whose instances above are both explicable. For the sake of euphony *affects* is preferred to *affect'st*; the full form of the latter would indeed be unmetrical. *Goes yet* gives a smoother poetical delivery than *go'st yet*, especially as *go'st* is in an unstressed position. Shakespeare never shrank from the licence of using the alternative ending when the verb was separated from its pronominal subject, as here.

In the well-known speech of Octavius in the next scene (I.4.55–71) beginning 'Antony, / Leave thy lascivious Vassailes.', Shakespeare, in varying *-st* with occasional *-s* inflexions, reveals himself to be as thoughtful a technician as Pope was. One has only to count the phonetically awkward *-st* endings the actor had to deliver in those lines to realize how necessary it was to soften *Wast* to *Was* and *browsedst* to *brows'd*[1] in lines 57 and 66. The phonetic simplification of such a word as *browsedst* was common in the past tense, though the licence was economically used. It is almost certain that this and the *-s* endings derive from the author, and should be retained as legitimate phonetic or grammatical variants of the time, exhibiting the technical preoccupations of the poet.

That even a good modernized Shakespeare, such as Wright's *Cambridge* edition, obscures important morphological and syntactical features of Shakespeare's English can be shown by a comparison of his text with the original editions. A few instances should substantiate W. W. Greg's plea for 'an accurate record of the transmitted form of the words'.[2]

---

[1] Shakespeare probably wrote *browsed*, a disyllabic form being required by the metre; the mark of elision would then be the work of the Folio editor.

[2] *The Editorial Problem in Shakespeare*, Prolegomena, p. lii.

The first stage direction in Act IV, Scene 9 of the First Folio text of *Antony and Cleopatra* reads:

Enter a Centerie, and his Company, Enobarbus followes

This entry may not, of course, be Shakespeare's; but it is interesting to note what the editors make of *Centerie* (apparently the officer-in-charge) and *his Company*, who, in the dialogue that follows, consist of first watch and second watch. Had Shakespeare, or the person responsible for the stage-direction, here in mind (for the officer) *Century*, the reading of the Third and Fourth Folios, and transferred the name of the Company to the man in charge, the *Centurion?* I think it likely, on the analogy of such spellings as *venter* for *venture*. An editor of an old-spelling edition would retain the original spelling and add an explanatory note. A modernizing editor has to choose *sentry*, *century* or *centurion*, or compromise by using *soldiers* for all three men, as Aldis Wright did.[1]

Negatives often present difficulties in the interpretation of Shakespeare's text. The logician's view that two negatives make a positive is foreign to the earlier history of most Indo-European languages. In sixteenth-century English, a double negative was an intensifier or reminder of what had been negatived earlier in the sentence. There were also, and still are, words like *but* which, in certain uses, have a negative connotation; and the ear of the modern editor of Shakespeare, attuned to modern syntactical constructions, is apt to forget that such combinations as *but if* may be compound conjunctions with a different meaning from that given to them today. Thus in *Antony and Cleopatra* at V.2.96 is found:

> *But if* there be, *nor* ever were one such
> It's past the size of dreaming: Nature wants stuffe
> To vie strange formes with fancie, yet t'imagine
> An Antony were Natures peece, 'gainst Fancie,
> Condemning shadowes quite.

The editors of the Third and Fourth Folios altered *nor* to *or*, and the

---

[1] Shakespeare himself usually speaks of *Sentinels*, not *Sentries*, e.g. *Centinell* (*M.N.D.* II.2.26), the spelling with initial *c* being common with words of French origin. But as the first citation of *sentry* in the *O.E.D.* (1611) is only three years later than the probable date of use in *A and C*, the word may have been current when Shakespeare wrote. The *O.E.D.* itself suggests that *senterie* and *century* (in a military sense) are seventeenth-century variants of *sentry*. The intrusive *e* before *r* occurs as late as the eighteenth century, cf. Shakespeare's *enterance*, *Henery*, and Milton's *sentery* (*P.L.* II.412).

latter has been accepted by *all* subsequent English editors, despite the fact that these late Folios are not substantive authorities. Thistelton in *Some Textual Notes to Antony and Cleopatra* (1899) p. 27, justified *nor*; and this is certainly correct, though not perhaps because of ellipsis of *neither* in the preceding conditional clause. *But if* means 'unless', and the following *nor* is a double negative.

An instance of opposite character, where the editors generally insert *not*, against the metrical evidence, where Shakespeare has a positive statement, occurs in the same play, II.2.52–4. The context reads:

> If you'l patch a quarrell,
> 53 As matter whole you have to make it with,
> It must not be with this.

The conjecture *not* after *have* has the authority of Dr. Johnson and other commentators. But Ingleby in *Shakespeare the Man* (I, 145) objected, as did Ridley in the New Arden edition, and both are probably right. The substitution *take* for *make* in the Second, Third and Fourth Folios has no value, and does not help. The passage seems to be correctly worded in the First Folio and means: 'If you want to patch a quarrel, you will have to make your *patch* out of the *whole* (affair), not out of this isolated instance.' The contrast is almost certainly between the noun *patch* (or 'part'), assumed from the verb, and *whole*. The latter is an adjective in post-position, qualifying *matter*. The play on words is a kind of semantic pun, involving different parts of speech, and shows the degree to which language could be stretched in Shakespearian and Elizabethan wit.

The original word or words of the substantive witness do appear in the footnotes to emendations in reputable modern editions; but words appended, without the historical setting of the original context, are unlikely to influence, much less restore for the reader, the sense and beauty of Elizabethan English. The illogicality of modernization is shown most convincingly, perhaps, in visual rhyme. Take this stanza from *A Lover's Complaint* (appended to the 1609 Quarto of Shakespeare's *Sonnets*), lines 85–91:

> His browny locks did hang in crooked curles,
> And every light occasion of the wind
> Upon his lippes their silken parcels hurles,
> Whats sweet to do, to do will aptly find,
> Each eye that saw him did inchaunt the mind:
> For on his visage was in little drawne,
> What largenesse thinkes in parradise was *sawne*.

The nonce form *sawne*, presumably created by Shakespeare as a poetic licence, is retained by the modernizing editors (a) for rhyme, and (b) because they are not sure of what verb it is the past participle. This is shown by the erroneous conjectures. It is almost certainly the past participle of *see*, by analogy with the preterite.

Equally banal is the occasional emendation *bin* for *is* in the song 'Hark, hark! the lark' in *Cymbeline* II.3.25:

> And winking Mary-buds begin to ope their Golden eyes
> 25 With every thing that pretty *is*, my Lady sweet arise:

Bin (= are), for alternate rhyme, is an impossible reading, and a fault of which the original *Cambridge* editors were not guilty.

Greg's reasons for an old-spelling critical edition of Shakespeare on pp. li and lii of his *Editorial Problem in Shakespeare* are persuasive, and it is a pity, in view of their importance, that he appended them merely as a footnote to his 'Prolegomena'. The fact that, in editing classical texts, it has long been the practice to normalize orthography, and modernize to the extent of supplying word-separation, accents and breathings, has small bearing on the Shakespearian problem. Classical editors are concerned with traditions of scribal transmission and with manuscripts in dead languages separated not only by geographical origin, but in most cases by centuries of time, and often inaccessible to the editors. The number of such manuscripts is often very great, and recension difficult; the range of possible variants, in consequence, assumes astronomical proportions (vide the article on 'Textual Criticism' in the *Oxford Classical Dictionary*, 1949). But Shakespeare's originals are all printed texts, separated in time by only thirty years; and this period already had printing-house conventions—a fact that Skeat probably had in mind when he said we were inheritors of the illogical Elizabethan spelling tradition.

No Prolegomena can provide a complete system for a definitive edition. Each problem is unique, and must be dealt with as it arises. The result will depend on the detailed Shakespearian knowledge which the editor has been able to acquire, on his alertness, intelligence, impartiality and patience. McKerrow's plan for an edition which concentrates on a sound text, an account of recension, *apparatus criticus*, glossarial commentaries, and omits aesthetic criticism, meets with general approval. But since the publication of his *Prolegomena* there has been a movement away from a conservative text, such as he proposed, and a belief in the wisdom of a more eclectic one.

Greg's 'Prolegomena' in *The Editorial Problem in Shakespeare* has been criticised by P. Maas (*Review of English Studies*, October 1943, January 1944) on the grounds that it would produce a hybrid of critical edition and reprint, would give the text a fallacious appearance of authenticity, and unnecessarily enlarge the bulk and price of the book. But the fact that a critical old-spelling text may resemble a reprint must depend entirely on the accuracy of the transmitted authorities; in fact, the ideally perfect original authority would present no critical issues at all, except aesthetic ones.

When criticism has restored the text as nearly as possible to the lost originals, the last touch of authenticity can only be added by preserving the accidentals, the spelling and grammatical details. Certain types of enquiry demand orthographical fidelity; it helps to an understanding of the author's methods of composition. The philologist who rightly resorts to original texts or facsimiles, to be sure of the authenticity of his forms, must have full knowledge also of the different sources of the texts. A reliable critical edition in original spelling would help him to that knowledge and to the proper utilization of his evidence.

Chapter 14

Dramatic Punctuation in Elizabethan Drama

IN the period 1520–50, when the names of punctuation symbols began to appear in English (see Appendix VIII), considerable advances were made by the printers in the use of stops: the comma (instead of the virgule), round brackets, the mark of interrogation (printed first by Pynson in 1521) began to be generally employed, even in black-letter or Gothic printing. Printers would not have cut types for new punctuation symbols, unless there had been a demand, which probably came from scholars reading new classical texts, printed on the Continent. Eminent Englishmen and men of letters employed little punctuation in their cursive writing, as is proved by the manuscripts of Queen Elizabeth's translation of Boethius (1593), and Milton's Sonnet *On the Attainment of his twenty-third year* (1631).[1]

Until 1580, the comma (or virgule), the colon, the period, the mark of interrogation, and round brackets, had sufficed for the printers of England. The semicolon seems to have been introduced accidentally by the printer (Richard Grafton) of Myles Coverdale's translation of the Bible in 1538, and not to have reappeared until *The Scepter of Judah*, printed by John Wight in 1584.[2] Its function was not understood, and Shakespeare himself seems to have employed it little in the early quartos until *Richard II* (1598), printed by Valentine Simmes for the publisher Andrew Wise. Here is a passage from Act II, Scene 3 of the unique Quarto of W. A. White, edited by A. W. Pollard in 1916:

> *Yorke* My Lords of England, let me tell you this:
> I have had feeling of my Coosins wrong,
> And laboured all I could to doe him right;
> But in this kinde, to come in braving armes;

[1] See *Queen Elizabeth's Englishings* (E.E.T.S.), p. 33, and G. H. McKnight's *Modern English in the Making*, p. 244.
[2] See Ames, *Typographical Antiquities*, pp. 512, 782 and 858.

> Be his owne carver, and cutte out his way;
> To find out right with wrong; it may not be:
> And you that doe abette him in this kinde,
> Cherish rebellion, and are rebels all.
>
> *North* The noble Duke hath sworne, his comming is
> But for his owne, and for the right of that,
> We all have strongly sworne to give him ayde:
> And let him ne're see ioy that breakes that oath.

The semicolon at the end of line 3 is the only modern usage. The other semicolons are actors' pauses, to mark off the elocutionary units for delivery. For this purpose the normal stop in the prompter's copy appears to have been the colon. The use of the semicolons in this passage may have been fortuitous, determined by a shortage of much-used colons in the compositor's box. In the first Quarto (1597) the only semicolon in this passage occurs after 'owne' in the second line of Northumberland's speech.

It is instructive to place beside this the same passage from the First Folio, printed by Jaggard and Blount:

> *York* My Lords of England, let me tell you this,
> I have had feeling of my Cosens Wrongs,
> And labour'd all I could to doe him right:
> But in this kind, to come in braving Armes,
> Be his owne Carver, and cut out his way,
> To find out Right with Wrongs, it may not be;
> And you that doe abett him in this kind,
> Cherish Rebellion, and are Rebels all.
>
> *North* The Noble Duke hath sworne his comming is
> But for his owne; and for the right of that,
> Wee all have strongly sworne to give him ayd,
> And let him neu'r see Ioy, that breakes that Oath.

Except for the colon at the end of line 3, and the improving marks of elision, the punctuation of this passage is modern. From the acting point of view, the most interesting change is the syntactical stopping, the guide to the actors, if any, being in the form of emphasizing capitals.

The inverted semicolon used for the query in the Quarto of *King Lear* and other books may also have been caused by a shortage of type. Marks of interrogation from various founts were brought into service. The demand was heavy in plays, as the symbol was also used for exclamations beginning with an interrogative word. In other circumstances exclamation marks were in use by the fifteen-nineties, for example in the 1593 quarto of *Venus and Adonis* (lines 38 and 635) and the 1598 quarto of *Edward II* (lines 1511 and 2028 of the Malone Society reprint).

After Aldus Manutius (see Appendix VIII Section VIII) and before 1650, the most useful sources for the study of punctuation adapted to English printing are Pierre de la Ramée (Ramus) in his *Grammatica* (1572), R. Mulcaster's *Elementarie* (1582), G. Puttenham's *Arte of English Poesie* (1589), and Ben Jonson's *Grammar* (1637). Ramus, as a logician, made some important contributions to syntactical punctuation, cut short by his death in the Massacre of St. Bartholomew. Unfortunately, these works give insufficient attention to the theory of function. The most precise statement of function comes from Puttenham. For him punctuation serves three main objects: (1) to allow leisure for distinct and agreeable utterance, (2) to relieve and replenish the breath, and (3) to enable the ear to detect the subtleties of syntax, clauses being varied in both their construction and meaning.

All these objects are concerned with language as speech, the first two the speaker, and the last the listener. But Puttenham concludes by saying that the fullest application of punctuation, considered as time pauses of three different values (comma, colon and period), belongs more to the orator or writer in prose than the poet, because, as he puts it, prose has more use 'for a commodious and sensible distinction of clauses'; whereas poetry, measured by its line division and internal caesura, employs rests that may be independent of sense development.[1]

Despite the rationalization of theorists, however, and even the force of literary and theatrical example, printing-houses seem to have called the tune, and to have re-modelled, in varying degree, what came to their hands. Nowhere does this become clearer than in the quartos of plays printed in the decade 1594–1604. The chronology of actual writing and production is complicated by the state of the accidentals in the printed version, especially the punctuation. Thus Kyd's *The Spanish Tragedy*, written before 1592, but printed by W. White for Thomas Pavier as late as 1602, seems to me more sensitively punctuated than Marlowe's *Edward II*, written 1591–3, and printed in 1594, probably by R. Bradock, for William Jones. A speech by Gaveston (lines 53–76) is here set beside one of Hieronimo (lines 2423–37), both excerpts being from the Malone Society reprints.

---

[1] *Arte of English Poesie*, Bk. II, Ch. V.

Gavest. Do: these are not men for me,
I must have wanton Poets, pleasant wits,
Musitians, that with touching of a string
May draw the pliant king which way I please:
Musicke and poetrie is his delight,
Therefore ile have Italian maskes by night,
Sweete speeches, comedies, and pleasing showes,
And in the day when he shall walke abroad,
Like *Silvian* Nimphes, my pages shall be clad,
My men like Satyres grazing on the lawnes,
Shall with their Goate Feete daunce an antick hay,
Sometime a lovelie boye in *Dians* shape,
With haire that gilds the water as it glides,
Crownets of pearle about his naked armes,
And in his sportfull hands an Olive tree,
To hide those parts which men delight to see,
Shall bathe him in a spring, and there hard by,
One like *Actaeon* peeping through the grove,
Shall by the angrie goddesse be transformde,
And running in the likeness of an Hart,
By yelping hounds puld downe, and seeme to die,
Such things as these best please his maiestie.
My lord, heere comes the king and the nobles
From the parlament, ile stand aside.

By modern standards, the above passage is not only inadequately, but inconsistently, punctuated. The stop-of-all-work is the comma; but a much longer stop is needed at the end of the lines ending 'clad', 'hay' and 'die'; a colon, if one emulates the practice of Elizabethan producers, a full-stop in a modernized version. Possibly this was prompter's copy, little touched by the compositor; the aim being to give fluency and continuity to the speech—a cue to the actor to speak it 'trippingly on the tongue'.

But even from the actor's point of view, the punctuation of Hieronimo's speech has more subtlety and modulation:

Hie. I, now I know thee, now thou namest my sonne:
Thou art the lively image of my griefe,
Within thy face my sorowes I may see.
Thy eies are gum'd with teares, thy cheekes are wan,
Thy forehead troubled, and thy muttring lips
Murmure sad words, abruptly broken off.
By force of windie sighes thy spirit breathes,
And all this sorrow riseth for thy sonne:

> And selfe same sorrow feele I for my sonne.
> Come in old man, thou shalt to Isabell,
>
> 2433 Leane on my arme: I thee, thou me, shalt stay,
> And thou, and I, and she will sing a song:
> Three parts in one, but all of discords fram'd
>
> 2436 Talke not of cordes, but let us now be gone,
> for with a cord, *Horatio* was slaine.

I cannot believe that the pointing of this speech is as Kyd devised it; the marking of balanced adversative phrases in lines 2433–6 looks like post-1600 sophistication. The short pause after 'fram'd' seems deliberate, to point the antithesis of 'cords' and 'discords'; and the comma before 'Horatio' in line 2437 marks an actor's pause, to give emphasis to the final sentence.

Possibly, however, the responsibility of the printer for variations in punctuation will appear more forcibly if the Gaveston speech is compared with another set-speech of Marlowe, The Duke of Guise's in *The Massacre at Paris*, written 1590–2, and printed by E. Allde for Edward White (*c*. 1598). The passage is from the Malone Society reprint (lines 168–85):

> I but, *Navarre*, *Navarre*, tis but a nook of France,
> Sufficient yet for such a pettie King:
> That with a rablement of his hereticks,
> Blindes Europs eyes and troubleth our estate:
> Him will we   *Pointing to his Sworde.*
> But first lets follow those in France,
> That hinder our possession to the crowne:
> As *Caesar* to his souldiers, so say I:
> Those that hate me, will I learn to loath.
> Give me a look, that when I bend the browes,
> Pale death may walke in furrowes of my face:
> A hand, that with a graspe may gripe the world,
> An eare, to heare what my detractors say,
> A royall seate, a scepter and a crowne:
> That those which doe beholde, they may become
> As men that stand and gase against the Sunne.
> The plot is laide, and things shall come to passe:
> Where resolution strives for victory.

This speech is dramatic, not effeminately sensuous, like Gaveston's. But the pointing belongs to a more decisive and disciplined school of production. The colons are elocutionary divisions of the speech into manageable units for effective delivery. Punctuation designed for the modern reader would dispense with most of them. But the doubt I wish to press home is whether the punctuation in the two Marlowe speeches, Gaveston's and Guise's, can be derived from the same source, namely, the author. I suspect that author-punctuation is overlaid by that of scribe, prompter or compositor, in some cases possibly all three.

Chapter 15

The Punctuation of Shakespeare and Ben Jonson

BEN Jonson, like Aldus Manutius, favoured the logical theory of pointing; Richard Mulcaster and Shakespeare preferred a *partly* rhythmical system, or what Mulcaster in his *Elementarie* called 'right and tunable uttering'. These were not regarded as rival systems, for the reason that each permitted much latitude in individual practice. The difference, however, became evident in the last decade of the sixteenth century, and the first twenty years of the seventeenth century; and the antithesis is exemplified in the Good Quartos of Shakespeare, on the one hand, and the First Folio of Ben Jonson, on the other. The contrast between the work, character and ideas of these two men is proverbial; that they held different views on the practice of punctuation should, therefore, surprise no one. Shakespeare's approach to language was humanistic, the product of his uniquely figurative imagination; that of Jonson academic, critical and logical.

It can be claimed with reasonable certainty that Jonson himself punctuated his plays published before 1616; but the uncertainty about the transmission of Shakespeare's texts makes conjecture about his pointing more or less inevitable. Since the publication of Percy Simpson's *Shakespearian Punctuation* in 1911, conflicting views have been taken about the degree of Shakespeare's responsibility for what appears in his texts. Simpson's title and treatment show that he defended the punctuation of the Shakespeare First Folio (not necessarily the author's), and sought to explain it by comparison with the practice of other contemporary writers, mainly dramatists. A study of the punctuation of the Shakespearian Good Quartos was not attempted either by Simpson or his predecessor A. E. Thistelton except in the latter's examination of the Roberts Quarto of *A Midsummer Night's Dream* (1600), published in his *Textual Notes* of 1903.

Few of the rules in the compendia offered by Thistelton and Simpson are based on elocutionary principles, but rather on structural ones or printers' conventions. And this is a pity, because an analysis of the stops in the Good Shakespeare Quartos might have shown (a) what precise elocutionary principles were involved, and (b) that Shakespeare's elocutionary notions of stopping were not, and could not be, exclusive of other ideals. He was an individualist, and found in punctuation the possibility of a shorthand for the producer and actor. The Good Shakespearian Quartos, in fact, carry the elocutionary principle much further than other printed texts.

The principal value of Simpson's tentative study was the interest aroused by the compendious, yet useful, statement: 'We base our punctuation now on structure and grammatical form; the old system was largely guided by the meaning.'[1] This modest generalization was tested by A. W. Pollard in 1916, in an edition of a newly identified Quarto of *Richard II*, dated 1598. He concluded not only that some of the copy used for printing Shakespeare's quartos must have been in his autograph, but that the punctuation of the set speeches was so sensitive as to confirm that it could only have been devised by an author skilled in the requirements of production. This led to Pollard's much-quoted conviction in *Shakespeare's Fight with the Pirates* (1920):

.... in Shakespeare's day, at any rate in poetry and drama, all the four stops, comma, semicolon, colon, and full-stop, could be and (on occasion) were, used simply and solely to denote pauses of different length irrespective of grammar and syntax. . . . But two points seem to emerge from the study of almost any early Quarto we take up. In the first place it seems clear that the value of all stops was greater than at present. The comma is often used where we should put a semicolon; the semicolon for a colon, the colon for a full-stop; while a full-stop is a very emphatic stop indeed . . . there is good evidence that Shakespeare preferred a light to a heavy punctuation.[2]

Dover Wilson, apparently a believer in Pollard's conclusions, in his New Cambridge edition of *The Tempest* (1921), expressed confidence in the Shakespearian origin of the punctuation to be found in his First Folio authority. He writes that if the reader 'will turn to the second scene (of Act I) and follow . . . the pause effects in the exquisite dialogue between Miranda and her father, . . . [he] will not only master [the] principles . . . but become a complete convert to Shakespearian punctuation.'[3] When he later came to edit *Hamlet*, he made similar claims for the punctuation of the Second Quarto.

[1] Op. cit., p. 16.   [2] Op. cit., pp. 90–2.
[3] New Cambridge Shakespeare, *Tempest*, p. lix.

It can be argued that the First Quarto of *Richard II* (not the Pollard-edited Quarto of 1598) and the Second Quarto of *Hamlet* may contain much of Shakespeare's original pointing; but the further contentions of Pollard and Wilson seem now to be overstated. For instance, Pollard writes in the introduction of his edition of *Richard II* (1598) that the system of punctuation in the First Folio 'is found full blown in the Heyes Quarto of the *Merchant of Venice*' (1600).[1] R. M. Alden in 1924 showed this to be incorrect.[2] The Folio contains many more semicolons and parentheses per page than will be found in the Heyes, or any other, Quarto of the plays. For the semicolon and the exclamation mark occur only fitfully in the early Quartos from *Venus and Adonis* (1593) to *A Midsummer Night's Dream* (1600), and the sporadic appearance indicates the intervention of a printer, such as Field or Bradock.

Even the obviously light stopping in the Second Quarto of *Hamlet* is, however, liberal when compared with that of the sparsely punctuated 'Shakespearian' pages of *Sir Thomas More*, a manuscript play by collaborators, never published and apparently never performed. A feature of this manuscript is the meagre use of the full-stop, the absence of a question mark, for which a semicolon is once used, and the paucity of commas. There is but one use, in the three pages attributed to Shakespeare, of a colon (and that uncertainly after a comma), which is significant, because the colon is a stop much used in Shakespeare's Good Quartos by all the various printers of his time. This stopping cannot be of the same vintage as that contained in Good Quartos like *Richard II*. The Shakespearian additions to *Sir Thomas More* contain, moreover, a long set speech on the divine office of kingship, spoken by More himself. To accept these additions as in Shakespeare's autograph, one must assume that the stop the dramatist was most familiar with was the comma, but that he did not care about it overmuch. The punctuation of the supposed Shakespearian additions to *Sir Thomas More* is, therefore, inadequate, even by the light standards in *Hamlet* (Q_2); the First Folio punctuation is, on an average, at least six times as heavy.

There is no means, either, of supporting Pollard's statement that stops had longer value in Shakespeare's time than they have in our own. The assumption increases the difficulty of reconciling the action-time of Shakespeare's plays with the 'two hours traffic of the stage'; and this applies especially to the more heavily punctuated and longer of the plays whose authority is the First Folio. The punctuation here varies,

[1] Op. cit., p. 29.
[2] 'The Punctuation of Shakespeare's Printers', *P.M.L.A.* (1924), p. 579.

but is usually elaborate, being designed, as the volume itself was, for the study and the reader.

The Folio's printer, Jaggard, it should be remembered, did not, until 1619, print plays, but only serious works. As early as 1599 he had printed illicitly the Quarto of *The Passionate Pilgrim*, which contained a sonnet, 'Two loves I have of comfort and despair,' reproduced as sonnet 144 in Thomas Thorpe's Quarto of Shakespeare's complete *Sonnets*, printed by G. Eld in 1609. The punctuation of Thorpe's version, though ten years later, resembles the pointing of *Richard II* (Q_1) and *Hamlet* (Q_2), and is without capitals and parentheses; whereas Jaggard's has fourteen capitals in as many lines, three parentheses and many more commas. Jaggard's compositor was evidently a man for elaborate pointing, and in his version can be seen the germ, though not all the niceties, of the punctuation of the Shakespeare First Folio. The two versions of the Sonnet follow:

Jaggard's   Two Loves I have, of Comfort, and Despaire,
(1599)   That like two Spirits, do suggest me still:
            My better Angell is a Man (right faire)
            My worser spirite a Woman (colour'd ill.)
            To winne me soone to hell, my Female evill
            Tempteth my better Angell from my side,
            And would corrupt my Saint to be a Divell,
            Wooing his purity with her faire pride.
            And whether that my Angell be turnde feend,
            Suspect I may (yet not directly tell:
            For being both to me: both, to each friend,
            I ghesse one Angell in anothers hell:
                The truth I shall not know, but live in doubt,
                Till my bad Angell fire my good one out.

The theory of Simpson that the First Folio capitals are for emphasis I have already contested (see Chapter 8). In the first line, the second comma is to separate co-ordinates, a syntactical usage of the punctuation of the First Folio. So is the use of parenthesis in lines 3 and 4, the bracketed phrases being balanced and contrasted. In the tenth line the compositor omitted the second bracket, and he also misread the sense of the next line, because his punctuation fails to elucidate it.

Thorpe's version reverts to some manuscript or manuscripts of earlier date, and illustrates a rhythmical punctuation for smooth and fluent speaking:

Thorpe's   Two loves I have of comfort and dispaire,
(1609)   Which like two spirits do sugiest me still,
              The better angell is a man right faire:
              The worser spirit a woman collour'd il.
              To win me soone to hell my femall evill,
              Tempteth my better angel from my sight,
              And would corrupt my saint to be a divel:
              Wooing his purity with her fowle pride.
              And whether that my angel be turn'd finde,
              Suspect I may yet not directly tell,
              But being both from me both to each friend,
              I gesse one angel in an others hel.
                  Yet this shal I nere know but live in doubt,
                  Till my bad angel fire my good one out.

In modern English, a longer pause than the comma would be asked for
at the end of line 2; and the colons which act as the fulcrum for
balanced antithesis and parallelism in lines 3 and 7 respectively, would
not be used at all. Some necessary commas, for modern sense, are
wanting in the last five lines; but the pointing is in keeping with the
lighter stopping of the fifteen-nineties, to which most of Shakespeare's
Sonnets seem to belong.

In the printing of Shakespeare's First Folio, the compositors undoubtedly varied in the value they gave to stops. Satchell in 'The
Spelling of the First Folio' (*Times Literary Supplement*, 3rd June 1920),
and Willoughby in *The Printing of The First Folio* (1932) showed that
two presses and three compositors (possibly four) were engaged on the
printing of this work. Compositor A had to re-set the type of the first
page of *Troilus and Cressida*,[1] and when he did so, frequently altered the
punctuation by using a stop of longer value. The evidence, then, is that
the compositor had a free hand, and used his discretion in the value of
the stops he employed.

On the whole, it may be said that the Good Quartos illustrate play-
house punctuation, designed for dramatic effect in giving to the actor
some lead as to how he should attack the passage and find the most
fitting modulation, emphasis and speed. The style of this punctuation,
as Pollard pleads, suggests that prompt copy (sometimes autograph)
was handed to the printer. But the Folio punctuation goes beyond this;
the playhouse pointing is, for many plays, the basis, but much has been

[1] See op. cit., pp. 16 and 65. The original setting of the page is found in a few
extant copies of the Folio.

grafted on to it. There is suggestion now of compromise between the rhythmical and logical systems. Old punctuation marks were not always deleted, which produces over-stopping and sometimes confusion. Brackets, for example, are used in some Good Quartos to indicate a drop or change in the voice. These reappear in the Folio, alongside of the use of brackets for syntactical parentheses in the form of interpolated phrases and clauses. The notable features of the First Folio pointing are (a) the subtler appreciation of the semicolon (as compared with uses in the quartos), and (b) the excessive use of parentheses. The first shows the influence of Ben Jonson, the second the authority of Jonson and Ralph Crane, one of the Company's scriveners after 1610.

Ames in his *Typographical Antiquities* (p. 942) says that the printer Henry Denham, whose work appeared between 1559 and 1591, was 'the first who used the semicolon with propriety'. He did not, however, print plays. The first dramatist to employ the semicolon with knowledge was apparently Ben Jonson. In the following excerpts from the 1600 Quarto of *Every Man out of His Humour* (lines 41–9 and 68–71 of the Malone Society reprint) his use is demonstrated:

> *Mit.* Forbeare good *Asper*, be not like your name.
> *Asp.* O, but to such, whose faces are all zeale,
> And (with the words of *Hercules*) invade
> Such crimes as these; that will not smell of sinne,
> But seeme as they were made of Sanctitie;
> Religion in their garments, and their haire
> Cut shorter than their eie-browes; when the conscience
> Is vaster than the Ocean, and devours
> More wretches than the *Counters*.
>
>   .   .   .
>
> [*Asp.*] Let envious *Critickes* with their broadest eies
> Looke through and through me; I pursue no favour:
> Onely vouchsafe me your attentions,
> And I will give you musicke worth your eares.
> O how I hate the monstrousnesse of time.
> Where every servile imitating spirit,
> (Plagu'd with an itching leprosie of wit)
> In a meere halting furie, strives to fling
> His ulc'rous bodie in the Thespian spring,
> And streight leap's forth a Poet; but as lame
> As *Vulcane*, or the founder of Criplegate.

This play, written in 1598 and printed for William Holme two years later, uses the modern co-ordinating semicolon, with longer time pause than the comma. But in the folio version of 1616, printed by W. Stansby, all the semicolons, except one, are converted to marks of exclamation. Does this indicate a whim of Jonson, or a shortage of semicolons in Stansby's box?

Jonson's skill and conscientiousness as a punctuator, and his insistence on accurate printing, were not fully appreciated until Herford and Simpson edited the works for the Clarendon Press.[1] Jonson's chapter on Distinction in the *Grammar* is based on Ramus; but his practice is subtler than his theory. The Quartos of his plays, from 1600, are assumed to have been printed from acting versions; their punctuation is more resourceful than that of the Marlow and Shakespeare Quartos, and is nearer to modern practice. As Simpson has pointed out, 'the semicolon bringing in a finer grading of the stops, started the logical system in use at the present day. It is characteristic of Jonson that he used it freely.'[2]

If one compares Jonson's use of the semicolon in the passage above with that in *Richard II* (1598) in the previous Chapter, it will appear that the semicolons in the Shakespeare passage have no logical or syntactical significance whatever. Jonson, more than other Elizabethan writers and scholars, superseded the elocutionary practice of the actor-producer, Shakespeare, by giving a logical twist to dramatic punctuation.

Between 1600, when Jonson began to take punctuation seriously, and 1616, when he piloted his First Folio through the press, his ideas on pointing advanced to the 'elaborate and overloaded system' that Simpson describes as 'ultra-logical'. In every respect the Folio of 1616 was intended to be a monument to his fame, not the least in the scholarship of its editing. He plagued his printer, William Stansby, with strict insistence on his stops and marks of elision. If he used a quarto as basis of his text, he revised it; his improved system of punctuation, as Simpson says, was 'designed to mark clearly the structure of the sentence'.[3] This punctuation was intended, not for the actor, but the reader. Many exclamation marks were introduced where semicolons had previously served; commas were used, somewhat paradoxically, to separate co-ordinate substantives joined by 'and', but also to mark

---

[1] See introductions to the *Grammar* Vol. II, and to *Every Man out of His Humour*, Vol. III.

[2] Ben Jonson, *Works* Vol. II, p. 432.

[3] Ben Jonson, *Works* Vol. III, p. 414.

off qualifying phrases and to point antitheses. Many changes were of the fussy, pedantic order, not vital; for Jonson already knew how to punctuate when he published his first Quarto, *Every Man Out of His Humour*, in 1600.

That Jonson was an innovator is clear from other evidence of revisions. Shakespeare's tentative and limited contractions and colloquial forms, especially of common words such as pronouns, articles and prepositions, he elaborated into a metrically resourceful device for bringing his literary dialogue down to the level of everyday life. Only after Jonson had shown the way did Shakespeare extend the range of his colloquialisms, noticeable in the plays after *Hamlet*.

The genesis of the pointing of the Shakespeare First Folio is not easy to trace in printed books of the time, nor even in the compositions Shakespeare himself could have seen through the press, such as *Venus and Adonis* and *Lucrece*. The elements were born in Jaggard's house, as is seen from the evidence of his printing of the 1599 Quarto of *The Passionate Pilgrim*; but the final product, varying according to the nature of the copy supplied, cannot be attributed entirely to this printer or to his compositors.

Sidney Lee and A. W. Pollard conjectured that Edward Blount, the bookseller, was the chief editor of the first collected edition of Shakespeare's plays. He may have suggested the exhortation to buy the book in the first paragraph of the 'Address to the Great Variety of Readers'; but he entered late into the syndicate that eventually published the Folio, Willoughby says after one third had already been printed.[1] Willoughby disposes of the idea that Heminge and Condell could have been responsible for the general editing; but he does not consider the possibility that the shareholders would consult the only dramatist who had collected, in scholarly fashion, and published his work, namely Ben Jonson. It is not suggested that Jonson shared with Jaggard's compositors and with the scrivener, Ralph Crane, the responsibility of editing the punctuation of the Shakespeare First Folio; but there are reasons for believing that he not only gave them advice as to how it should be done, but actually wrote four items of the preliminary matter to the volume, the two poems already known to be his, the Dedication, and the Address to the Great Variety of Readers.

Three times in the Epistle Dedicatory and the Address to the Great Variety of Readers it is stated that Heminge and Condell only *collected* the plays, an office explained as calling for the exercise of great 'care,

[1] *The Printing of the First Folio of Shakespeare*, p. 60.

K

and paine'. The reason for this is obvious; for scholarship has established that Heminge and Condell assembled a miscellany of printed quartos (some of them late and corrupt), prompt copies, scriveners' transcriptions and possibly some autograph. Johnson probably helped with advice in tidying up this diverse material for the press; others may even have worked under his direction. The two actors, Heminge and Condell, who left no literary remains, could hardly have coped with the manifold editorial problems, much less been responsible for the Dedication. In the class of conventional appeals to patrons, this can hardly be bettered in the prose of the period. It combines the qualities of dignified formality, deference, tact and verbal polish that honour the art of epistolary writing, as Jonson assessed it in his *Discoveries*.

The evidence of Jonson's conception extends to the style and punctuation of the Address to the Readers; for a Dedicatory Letter, followed by such an Address, is a feature of both *The Alchemist* and *Catiline*. At the beginning of *The Alchemist's* Dedication there is a reference (taken from Pliny) to the offerings of sacrificers in the ancient temples; and this, with slight modification, is repeated at the end of the Dedication to the Shakespeare Folio. But more convincing is the appearance of typical Jonsonian orthography in both preliminary documents: the carefully marked elisions, the hyphenation of compound words,[1] the scholar's spellings (Ded. 11 and 13) *prosequuted* and *exequutor* (with *qu* instead of *c* to mark their Latinity), and the punctilious orthography *sixe-pen'orth* (Add. 10). The logico-syntactical punctuation resembles Jonson's, too, especially the use of capital letters after colons and semicolons (Add. 1, 20, 29, 35), the wealth of semicolons and the excessive use of commas, with all the niceties of Jonson's First Folio. The punctuation in all Jonson's dedications is precise and elaborate, and differs in no material respect from that of the Shakespeare Dedication. Occasional lapses merely indicate that Jonson was not called upon to read proof.

The punctuation of Shakespeare and Jonson deserves study, because their partly opposed aims account for some of the illogicalities of the alleged 'logical' system of modern times.

Conclusion

Author's manuscripts written before 1600 show that the writer's

---

[1] One of the hyphens (*some-thing*, Dedication, line 10) was actually accepted by the compositor, though unusual in the printing of the time. It probably marked, in the manuscript, syllabic division at the end of the line.

punctuation (Jonson's excepted) was the barest necessary to avoid mis-understanding, and confined usually to commas, colons, periods and marks of interrogation. In the case of plays, additional punctuation on elocutionary or rhetorical lines was added to guide the actor in the speaking of his lines; it may be assumed that this was the work of the prompter-producer. As Shakespeare was apparently a trainer of actors, it is right to suppose that playhouse punctuation of his manuscripts, at any rate in the set speeches, was his own. A transcription (or fair copy of the 'foul papers') made by a professional scribe or member of the Company, would naturally contain some modification of the point-ing; for scribes, by the nature of their trade, were skilled in punctua-tion.[1]

After the prompter and the scribe came the printer's compositors, who were governed by the punctuation-practices of their house, and by the possible shortage of some symbols. Only such an editor as Jonson would keep the vagaries of the printing-house in check. Even he sometimes found his symbols changed by the printer, as is shown by Simpson in his edition of the *Masque of Queens*,[2] based on Jonson's autograph manuscript in the British Museum. This Masque was printed by Nicholas Okes, who also printed the 1622 Quarto of *Othello* (see Chapter 12), and Octavo 4 of *Lucrece* (1607).

Another printer who produced works of both Shakespeare and Jonson was Valentine Simmes, whose Quarto of *Richard II* is one of the best specimens of playhouse punctuation. In Jonson's ceremonial piece, *The Kings Entertainment* (1604), and in the masque *Hymenaei* (1607), which Simmes also printed, the punctuation is poles apart from that of *Richard II*, and is clearly Jonson's.

In the Punctuation of Shakespeare's First Folio there is not one sys-tem, but a synthesis, which may represent several stratifications, those of author, producer, scribe, editor and compositor, though some copy did not pass through all these hands. How are we likely to discover what part of the punctuation was Shakespeare's? The only author-punctuation of the time that can be studied with any degree of cer-tainty is Jonson's. It is not merely in verse that Jonson is important;

---

[1] This is shown in the manuscript of *The Birth of Hercules* (written 1590) in which the copy is that of a professional scribe, with the addition of stage directions in the hand of the prompter, and corrections by the author. Here the punctuation, which is good, and includes the use of the semicolon, is that of the scribe (see Introduction to Malone Society Reprint, 1911).

[2] Jonson, *Works* Vol. VII, p. 272.

when he chose he could write prose that is practically modern. Before him prose was addicted either to slavish imitation of Latin, or to Euphuistic variations of the principle of formal balance. R. B. McKerrow in his edition of the *Works of Thomas Nashe* (Vol. I, p. xiii) says of prose of the latter type that it 'can hardly be punctuated at all according to modern rules, and even when this is possible, such treatment tends to obscure the antithesis of phrase, often unreal, which is one of its chief characteristics'.

Shakespeare owed little to Euphuism; but in his most passionate outbursts his style could be tortured, and neglect its syntax. His is, perhaps, the most difficult of Elizabethan styles for the grammarian to analyse into recognizable clauses. There are passages of the writing so characteristically his, that no one else could have been responsible for them. These passages called equally for his own individuality of punctuation. It is, therefore, regrettable that this pointing can never be certainly recovered, to throw further light on the processes of his thought.

Chapter 16

Henry VIII: Linguistic Criteria for the Two Styles Apparent in the Play

I

THE disintegration of Shakespeare, which the eighteenth century began, was advanced by scholars of the later nineteenth century, among them Spedding, Hickson, Fleay and Boyle. The climax of speculative dismemberment was reached in the works of J. M. Robertson on the Shakespeare Canon. But the methods of all, except the first two, have been discredited, and there has recently been a commendable reinstatement of Shakespeare, based upon authority of the First Folio. But modern textual science and bibliography, set on a firm foundation by A. W. Pollard, W. W. Greg and R. B. McKerrow, has not altogether confirmed this reinstatement; it is only by demolishing what is monstrous in the old theories that indirectly they have helped to reintegrate Shakespeare.

The new attitude of conservatism is praiseworthy, because it assumes that Heminge and Condell, fellow actors of Shakespeare, in drawing up their list of plays for the First Folio, must have known what they were about; that the collection they produced was not simply an opportunist publication; and that, while Shakespeare's friends could not be expected to be systematic and reliable editors of the text, there is no reason to impugn their honesty in the selection.

Much as bibliographical science has done to elucidate the parts played by the Company's book-keeper and the playwright's printer, it has only theorized about authors' collaboration. The determination of so-called spurious parts of the Shakespeare Canon is, therefore, still an open question. No approach to Shakespeare, short of bardolatry or Baconianism, can escape the accumulated force of the arguments (after discarding the fantastic) that some parts of the doubtful plays can hardly be by Shakespeare's hand. The most objective and plausible of the theses is that of Spedding and Hickson[1] with regard to *Henry VIII*. G. E. Bentley's paper 'Shakespeare and the Blackfriars Theatre',[2] especially the penultimate paragraph, puts the case of Shakespeare's association with Fletcher in the latter days of his service to the King's Players persuasively, and does much to explain, from the theatre angle, the genesis of the last plays.

No serious scholar of Shakespeare now accepts the implications of Fleay that, because Shakespeare was a great dramatic artist, he could not sometimes have written what is indifferent or mediocre. But the problem in *Henry VIII* differs from that, for instance, of *Pericles* and *Timon*, in that most of the great speeches are by the sceptics given to Shakespeare's supposed collaborator. This strengthens the contention of the traditionalists that Shakespeare may well have written the whole play. So does the absence of evidence (apart from the doubtful authority of his name on a title page) that Shakespeare was ever a collaborator with other dramatists. The evidence that he began as a mender of old plays, though circumstantial, is conclusive enough for us to visualize the effect of some of Shakespeare's improvements; and the marked individuality of all he touched and adorned may well argue against collaboration at a later period.

There is therefore a *prima facie* case against the collaboration theory, and Peter Alexander has made it. In 1930 he wrote a study 'Conjectural History or Shakespeare's Henry VIII',[3] in which he controverted the theory of Fletcher's hand in the play; he reiterated his views, with enlargements, in a paper read to the Shakespeare Conference at Stratford on 16th August, 1948 (not printed). He appeared in these papers to base his case on three main assumptions:

(1) That only Shakespeare himself would have ventured to introduce this play in terms of the Prologue. In his second paper Professor Alexander went further: he suggested that Shakespeare not only wrote, but spoke, the Prologue, having been brought back from retirement specially for the purpose.

(2) That Fletcher could not, in the reign of James I, have presented such a eulogy of Queen Elizabeth as we find in Cranmer's speech in

---

[1] Spedding's paper 'Who wrote Shakespeare's *Henry VIII*?' (*The Gentleman's Magazine*, August 1850) and Hickson's confirmatory letter (*Notes and Queries* No. 43, August 24, 1850) are reprinted in the appendix to *Transactions of the New Shakespeare Society*, 1874, Part I, pp. 1–22.

[2] *Shakespeare Survey* I, 1948.

[3] *Essays and Studies of the English Association*, Vol. XVI, p. 85.

Act V, Scene 5; but that Shakespeare, as the elder and more experienced dramatist, could have done so without offence to the reigning monarch.

(3) That the metrical tests used by Spedding and Hickson are unreliable criteria of poetic style, especially in view of Shakespeare's metrical development from *Antony and Cleopatra*, and that the results of the tests, upon which Fletcher's claims to part authorship are based, are insufficient evidence by themselves of his hand in *Henry VIII*.

These arguments call for consideration before fresh evidence is adduced. As Alexander has suggested, the lost prologues and epilogues to most of Shakespeare's plays must have been valuable dramatic documents, which Heminge and Condell might well have let us possess. But have we sufficient of them to draw safe conclusions about Shakespeare's practice in complying with the conventional formula of the time for introducing and winding up a play? A study of Prologue literature suggests that an apologia for the play was a conventional dramatic courtesy, in the hope of a fair hearing, so that an echo of the prologue of *Henry V* in *Henry VIII*, calling for tolerance, is not necessarily proof of Shakespeare's habitual modesty. On the internal evidence of style, the Prologue to *Henry VIII* is generally given to Fletcher. The suggestion that the play was not expected to please is surely more explicable if we assume that the rising dramatist of the King's Players had here completed, not very successfully, the unfinished work of the acknowledged master.

If the fatal production of *Henry VIII* at the Globe on 29th June, 1613, was a special Shakespeare premiere, after an absence of the dramatist from the stage of more than two years, it must indeed have been 'an important occasion'. But the accounts of the fire, which took place on the opening night, make it all the more unlikely that Shakespeare was either present or spoke the Prologue. Jonson in *An Execration upon Vulcan* says that he *saw* the fire, but does not mention that Shakespeare was at the performance. Nor is Shakespeare spoken of in the old ballad *Upon the pittiful burning of the Globe Playhouse in London*,[1] which does, in fact, mention the presence of Burbage and Henry Condell.

Fletcher was born in 1579 and the spacious and patriotic days of the last decade of the century would have come to him at a very impres-

---

[1] Described in its title as 'A Sonnett', this ballad was first printed in *The Gentleman's Magazine*, February 1816, from an old manuscript volume of poems. From the evidence of its incidents and language it bears all the marks of genuineness.

sionable age. He could thus reasonably be credited with the panegyric on Queen Elizabeth contained in the last speech of Cranmer. On this point, however, as the conclusion of my paper suggests, Alexander's intuition may be valuable. There is little in the linguistic evidence against Shakespeare's composition of the speech, and much in the substance to suggest that he conceived it. But the rest of the scene is undoubtedly in the style of the second dramatist.

On the validity of the evidence of metrical tests *alone*, the arguments of Alexander are weightier; he has rightly pointed out the possibility of their fallaciousness. But in this he was anticipated by one of the contributors to the metrical apparatus, F. J. Furnivall, who said that 'Counting can never be a better judge than real criticism'.[1] It is impossible to apply the tests to isolated individual lines, as Boyle would do. But the arguments of Spedding and Hickson are on broader and more tenable principles. It is not necessary, however, to re-traverse the ground of the metrical evidence, because comparable results can be obtained by a different method of scrutiny.

II

Where two authors are thought to have been at work on a play, it seems fair to assume that small mannerisms of grammatical usage, easily passed over in the weightier aesthetic considerations, are most likely to betray their several hands. The quest is the more interesting because a writer of lesser gifts, like Fletcher, even if willing to accommodate his literary personality to that of the master in the interests of unity (of which there is not much evidence in *Henry VIII*), would be quite unconscious of his ingrained grammatical habits. But the difficulties in the way of such a linguistic analysis are palpable, and one must anticipate possible objections in order to remove the impression that they may have been overlooked in advancing this kind of testimony.

The first is the dominance of the printer in determining the practices of spelling and punctuation in the Shakespeare First Folio, as well as in other printed books of the early seventeenth century. The compositors who set up *Henry VIII* had some share in the variations of spelling,[2] and probably also in punctuation and line arrangement. It is unsafe, therefore, to reason about an author's work solely, or even largely,

---

[1] Appendix, *Transactions of New Shakespeare Society*, 1874, Part I, p. 65.
[2] See R. A. Foakes 'On the First Folio Text of Henry VIII', *Studies in Bibliography* (University of Virginia) Vol. XI, 1958, p. 55.

upon the evidence of punctuation or spelling, and this I have not attempted to do here. There is less tampering by the printer in the matter of accidence. But it has to be borne in mind that a large number of alternative forms were in use, and that the general attitude of the writer employed in his trade was one of indifference to the inflexible grammarian; so that a certain amount of normalization, however rudimentary (and sometimes of unconscious falsification) is bound to have taken place in the printing-house.

The next objection, which ought to be mentioned here, though not applicable to *Henry VIII*, is the variation to be found in the forms of words represented in the quarto and folio versions of the same play. The classical example of morphological revision with a deliberate object is Ben Jonson's *Every Man in His Humour*. Here, seemingly in response to the accusation that his plays smelt too much of the lamp, Jonson substituted in his First Folio an English version for the Italian one of the quarto of 1598, toning down the literariness of the conversation and substituting wherever possible the clipped and colloquial forms of the newly evolved dialogue of the stage. In no period of the history of English has change been more rapid, particularly in the direction of accepting colloquial as literary forms of speech, than in the last decade of the sixteenth and the first ten years of the seventeenth century; and for this the large dramatic output was undoubtedly responsible. So that morphological variations in the different editions of a play, where they exist in any number, may be of some historical interest, as they prove to be in *Every Man in His Humour*.

The last objection applies especially to the use of language tests as criteria of authorship in the case of collaboration. Cannot divergencies in grammatical usage be explained by the fact that a first draft of a play is separated by a considerable lapse of time from the final product; that in reality a single author has been at work at different periods of his development, but carelessly left his seams exposed for critical scrutiny? This theory has been overworked, I think, even by the highest authorities; but there are plays in which it can be argued with considerable plausibility. Jonson's *Tale of a Tub* was probably an old discarded thing refurbished after a lapse of many years; but the linguistic revision was very conscientious, and in fact deluded the early chronologers of Jonson's plays into believing that the *Tale* was one of his dotages, instead of, in its main features, early prentice work.

In *Henry VIII* the stylistic strata are differentiated, not in time, but by personal idiosyncrasy. From the linguistic evidence no part of the play appears to be earlier than 1604. Spedding, anticipating the theory of a previous draft of *Henry VIII* subsequently revised by Shakespeare, rightly objected that 'if he had set about the revisal of it on so large a scale in the maturity of his genius, he would have addressed himself to remove its principal defect which is the incoherence of the general design'.[1] But he goes on to say that 'the style of those parts which upon this supposition would be referred to the *earlier* period does not at all resemble Shakespeare's style at any stage of its development'. (My italics.) He therefore appears to suppose that the scenes he assigns to Fletcher would be those suggested as the basis of an earlier draft, whereas priority for the scenes he assigns to Shakespeare must certainly be argued from both the linguistic evidence and the metrical tests.[2] To be drawn into a non-statistical generalization from the latter is not my purpose. But what do the metrical tests on Shakespeare's work prove, if they do not show him, at maturity, working out in his own way similar theories of dramatic speech to those engaging Jonson, Webster and the newer school. Jonson and Shakespeare, lovers of speech and style to whom Massinger put himself to school, were trying to make blank verse less 'poetic' and more adapted to the needs of their own theatre. They were, as Professor Bonamy Dobrée suggests in 'Shakespeare and the Drama of his Time',[3] aiming at a form of verse-speech more natural, less obvious in its transitions from verse to prose, and sufficiently pliable to get the emphasis on the dramatic word rather than on the metrical syllable. Fletcher, without the discipline of the earlier blank verse which Jonson and Shakespeare had practised, carried the new modulations of the line to the verge of licence, and his level flights (e.g. in *Henry VIII*, Act I Scene 3), while clear syntactically —a prose virtue—are nerveless as poetry and barely distinguishable from prose.

III

Re-reading *Henry VIII* for the purpose of this analysis, I was struck by the fairly sharp transitions from one grammatical idiom to another. These divisions seemed to correspond to differences in the method of developing the thought through the style; in the one case involved,

[1] *Transactions*, p. 11.

[2] I find this view supported on other grounds (the internal evidence of the structure of the play) by Miss M. H. Nicholson in *P.M.L.A.*, Vol. XXXVII, No. 3, 1922, 'The Authorship of *Henry VIII*'.

[3] *A Companion to Shakespeare Studies*, p. 252.

though poetically pregnant; in the other, fluent and lucid in syntactical pattern, almost anticipating Dryden. Emerson in *Representative Men* noted a cognate difference in the styles when he said that Shakespeare's 'secret is that the thought constructs the tune, so that reading for the sense will best bring out the rhythm'; whereas in the Wolsey soliloquy and the following scene with Cromwell (Act III, Scene 2) 'the lines are constructed on a given tune, and the verse has even a trace of pulpit eloquence'. If it is not heretical to say so, Fletcher and Massinger, from the modern prose point of view, are more competent stylists than Shakespeare. Their style is constructed upon 'given tunes'; it is *set*, as the coiffure of society ladies follows the dictates of the temporary fashion, and the style of the leaders in *The Times* conditions that of its most recalcitrant contributors. Shakespeare cannot serve as a stylistic model for anyone, because his rhythms are individual and accommodated to the needs of the moment; his ideas outstrip his syntax. On the track of the telling and indelible image, he may leave behind anacoluthons and hanging relative clauses in the most inconsequent fashion; he compresses his meaning and tortures his syntax, so that while the effect of the passage may be poetically grand, the meaning is wrung from it with extreme difficulty. To compare the difficult syntactical progression of Shakespeare with the clarity of Fletcher, one has only to look at Act I, Scene 2, lines 177–99[1] and Act II, Scene 1, lines 100–36, the famous last speech of Buckingham, which is almost certainly by Fletcher.

Differences of grammatical idiom are more noticeable in their assessable details than the broader effects of style, though the one must condition the other. At the beginning of the play grammatical idiosyncrasy shows variations between one scene and another; such variations are very noticeable, for instance, as the reader of the first Act proceeds from Scene 2 to Scene 3. Shakespeare could command many styles for different dramatic purposes, and the conclusion is natural that in Scene 3 he is affecting another method to deal with more frivolous and satirical matter. But, as the play develops, it becomes clear that this is not the case, that the different grammatical forms and constructions occur in the speeches of the same character under similar dramatic conditions in different parts of the play. In Act III, Scene 2, we seem to have the first division of labour in a single scene. The division takes

---

[1] The First Folio has been used for the examination of this play, but for the convenience of readers line reference and scene divisions are taken from the New Cambridge Shakespeare.

place at the middle of line 203, and Hickson accordingly assigned the first half of the scene to Shakespeare and the second to Fletcher. Spedding was not at first sure, and tentatively suggested that this was 'a scene by another hand which Shakespeare had only remodelled, or a scene by Shakespeare which another hand had worked upon to make it fit the place'.[1] The latter of Spedding's alternatives proves to be the more tenable theory.

If one marks the uses of the periphrastic auxiliary verb *do*,[2] as a mere expletive in affirmative statements—a use of which Shakespeare, as a writer of the old school, was comparatively fond—no less than twelve uses turn up in the first half of the scene, namely at lines 32, 34 (twice), 60, 79, 92, 130, 146, 155, 182, 190, and 194. It is possible that some of the uses carry a mild degree of emphasis, as the first in line 34 and the examples in lines 60, 146 and 190; but such uses are mainly metrical, and it is precisely the frequency of this licence that distinguishes, in one of its aspects, the poetic style of Shakespeare and Fletcher. From line 203 to the end, which Hickson suggested as Fletcher's share of the scene, one finds only a single use of expletive *do*, in the last couplet. This distinguishing grammatical feature is not peculiar to Act III, Scene 2, but to the whole play, whenever the hands of Shakespeare and Fletcher are in question. In the whole play I find fifty uses of expletive *do*, forty-five in the parts which Spedding and Hickson assign to Shakespeare, and five in the parts which they assign to Fletcher (see tables near the end of this section). This predominance is weighted by the fact that they give only a little more than one-third of the play to Shakespeare and nearly two-thirds to Fletcher. Of the five uses in scenes presumed to be by Fletcher, one is in the song (Act III, Scene 1) 'Orpheus with his Lute', which has every likelihood of being Shakespeare's, another in the final couplet I have just mentioned (III.2.459), two are mildly emphatic (though also metrical) in the phrase 'I *doe* beseech' (II.1.79 and V.3.45)[3], and one in prose (V.4.44), where it seems to be occasioned by the inversion of the sentence to give the object special emphasis. It need hardly be said that neither the printer

---

[1] Appendix, *Transactions of the New Shakespeare Society*, 1874, p. 9.

[2] See Willem Franz *Shakespeare Grammatik* (4th edition, 1939), ss. 594–601 and my paper on the use of this verb in Ben Jonson, *Modern Language Review*, January 1948.

[3] Users of the First Folio will note that Act V, Scene 2 is made into two scenes by modern editors, thus disturbing the Folio's scene-numbering at the end of the play (cf. the New Cambridge Edition, 1962).

nor his compositor could have been responsible for all these uses of expletive *do* in the Shakespeare part, and the comparative absence of them in the supposedly Fletcher part; because if he had removed them from, or inserted them in, the verse, he would have marred the metre. The use of expletive *do* in Shakespeare is well attested by Franz in his *Shakespeare Grammatik* (§ 597). On the other hand, an examination of plays independently written by Fletcher will show that the use of expletive *do* is uncommon with him, except in one play, *The Faithful Shepherdess*. This work he obviously treated as a pastoral poem of great dignity, honouring the old conventions, and the language, in keeping with the lyrical conception and the rhyme, is slightly archaic. The play is, in almost every respect, an exception from Fletcher's usual dramatic practice. But in *Bonduca* (dated by E. H. C. Oliphant 1610–12) there are in all eight uses of expletive *do*, of which four are in the phrase 'I do beseech' (which seems to be not only a Fletcherian, but a courtly, cliché), and two in conjunction with the familiar down-toner adverb *but* (e.g. V.2.1: I did *but* see her, / And see her die) which is common with all dramatists.

Another verbal peculiarity worth noting is the use of *-th* inflexional endings in the third person singular present indicative, both of notional and auxiliary verbs. The use of *-th* for *-s* was by 1613 (accepted date for *Henry VIII*) old-fashioned and literary. By 'literary' is meant that it would be found still in the dedications of works to patrons, in officialese, in the higher language of the *Authorized Version of the Bible* (1611) etc., but only sporadically in plays, with the exception of *hath* and *doth*. Even *doth* is extremely rare in plays after Shakespeare's retirement, though *hath* lingered on for a considerable time. Notional verbs with sibilant or affricative stem-finals continued, with the stricter grammarians like Jonson, to take the *-th* ending, though generally this phonetic habit was falling into disuse too. Another curious relict of 'literariness' was the occasional ending of notional verbs in *-th* in stage directions, quite common in both Jonson and Shakespeare. Generally speaking, the *-s* inflexion, which was originally a colloquial one, had come to stay, and its ousting of the *-th* ending must have been hastened by the large dramatic output of the preceding twenty years.

In Shakespeare's verse the *-th* ending is comparatively frequent, especially in the earlier plays, though it is by no means regular. It is resorted to mainly when the poet wishes to express himself with dignity or solemnity. *Hath* and *doth* are commoner in Shakespeare than notional verbs with -*th* endings. Franz records sixteen uses of *hath* and eight of *doth* in the first Act of *Hamlet*; twenty-eight uses of *hath* and three of *doth* in the first two Acts of *The Merry Wives of Windsor*. Chronology seems to bear some relation to his -*th* and -*s* inflexions; for as he developed he was clearly catching up with, as well as creating, the new linguistic fashions. But the frequency with which *hath* continues to turn up in the later plays is proof that he still slipped back into his old poetic habits. In the parts of *Henry VIII* which Spedding and Hickson assign to Shakespeare there are twenty-two uses of *hath* to fourteen of *has*; in the Fletcher parts there are two uses of *hath* and thirty-three of *has*. As *doth* went out of fashion long before *hath*, it is not surprising to find only two uses of it in the whole play, and both occur in the Shakespearian part. There are only four uses of notional verbs ending in -*th* in the play, three in Shakespeare's portion, one in Fletcher's, and all occur in stage directions. It is possible that neither dramatist was himself responsible for these. The figures for Fletcher's *Bonduca* are: *hath* 1, *has* 31, *does* 10; there is no use either of *doth* or of notional verbs ending in -*th*.

The last of the tell-tale grammatical evidence is concerned with colloquial clippings of personal pronouns, which, as has already been shown, had become increasingly popular after the turn of the century, in order to bring the language of plays nearer to that of everyday speech. One need only look at the Italian version of Jonson's *Every Man in His Humour* and compare it with the revised English version to appreciate the extent to which colloquial changes could be made. But whereas Jonson, being a strict grammarian, wrote 'hem (a form directly derived from Old English and not a contraction of *them* at all), Fletcher wrote 'em, and he used this weakened form abundantly at his medial pauses and for feminine verse-endings. The use of both 'em and *ye* (the weakened form of *you*)[1] at such places in the line is extremely characteristic of the Fletcherian rhythm and cadence. In the portion of *Henry VIII* which Spedding and Hickson assign to Shakespeare there are twenty-three uses of *them* to five of 'em; in the Fletcher portion seven uses of *them*[2] to fifty-nine of 'em (nearly twelve times as many as Shake-

[1] *Ye* can, of course, be the grammatically regular form of the Nom. Plur. as consistently used in the *Authorized Version*; but I doubt whether it was ever so intended by the dramatists after 1610.

[2] Three of these uses of *them* (Prol. 27, IV.1.29 and IV.2.53) occur after vowels where 'em would be avoided for reasons of euphony. The example in IV.2.53 also bears the metrical stress.

speare's).[1] Similarly with the unstressed form *ye* for *you*; if verse elision is required, *ye* is further weakened to *y'*. Shakespeare's part of the play has only one use of *ye* and four of *y'*, Fletcher's seventy-two of *ye* and nine of *y'*.[2] The use of *ye* (in Shakespeare's plays always restrained) occurs in the very first line of *Henry VIII*; but I share the view of several other critics that the opening lines (1 and 2)of this scene are very unlike Shakespeare and probably represent the revision of the second hand. It is interesting to revert once more to the shared scene (III.2) and to note the number of times *ye* occurs as soon as Fletcher takes over. Seeing that it is found here in a solemn speech of Wolsey (III.2.236–50), there can be no question of a single dramatist accommodating his forms to a new vein. This colloquial weakening of the personal pronoun may be called into use by Fletcher on *any* occasion, no matter how dignified. His partiality for *ye* has already been observed in the Variorum *Beaumont and Fletcher*, and I note no less than fifty-eight uses in the first Act of *Bonduca*.

As these details appear to be significant, they are tabulated in full for closer scrutiny:

[1] The use of *'em* and *them* as a test was originally proposed by A. H. Thorndike in *The Influence of Beaumont and Fletcher on Shakespeare*, pp. 24–8. He examined *Cymbeline*, *The Winter's Tale* and *The Tempest*, in addition to *Henry VIII*, and found the same preponderant use of *them* over *'em* by Shakespeare. He then investigated some of Fletcher's plays and found *them* to be rare and *'em* numerous. Unfortunately, in testing for Massinger, he relied on the edition of Gifford, who had systematically altered *'em* to *them* wherever he found it. Thorndike had, therefore, in an errata slip, to withdraw his evidence in regard to Massinger on an examination of the original quartos. But this in no way invalidates his test of the use of the forms by Shakespeare and Fletcher. His figures are:

	SHAKESPEARE		
	Cymbeline	Winter's Tale	Tempest
Them	64	37	38
'em	3	8	13

	FLETCHER		
	Woman's Prize	Bonduca	Four Plays in One (last two)
Them	4	6	1
'em	60	83	15

[2] *W'* for *we* and *th'* for *they* are also to be found occasionally as verse elision in Fletcher's part of *Henry VIII* (e.g. Epil. 4 and 8 and I.3.15, II.2.52, V.4.82). But a more characteristic weakening (or loss) of the personal pronoun in Fletcher is *'has*, *h'as* or *ha's* (= he has), which occur in *Henry VIII* I.3.59 and V.5.75. The contraction is found 9 times in *Bonduca*.

HENRY VIII

Shakespeare's Part

Act	Scene in F_1	Expletive 'do'	Hath	Has	Doth	Does	Them	'em	Ye	'y	Notional vb inflected -th
I	1	10	5	4	–	1	5	2	1	–	1 (S.D.)
	2	3	3	1	1	1	5	2	–	–	2 (S.D.)
II	3	3	1	–	–	1	–	–	–	1	–
	4	12	3	2	–	1	7*	–	–	2	–
III	2	12	7	6	1	4	2	1	–	–	–
	(lines 1–203)										
V	1	5	3	1	–	2	4	–	–	1	–
		45	22	14	2	10	23	5	1	4	3

Fletcher's Part

Act	Scene in F_1	Expletive 'do'	Hath	Has	Doth	Does	Them	'em	Ye	'y	Notional vb inflected -th
	Prologue	–	–	–	–	–	1	–	2	–	–
I	3	–	–	2	–	–	–	7	–	–	–
	4	–	–	–	–	–	1	12	4	4	–
II	1	1	–	4	–	1	–	4	4	–	–
	2	–	1	9	–	1	1	2	3	–	–
III	1	1	–	4	–	–	–	4	20	–	–
	2	1	1	7	–	1	1	2	6	–	–
	(lines 203–end)										
IV	1	–	–	2	–	–	1	3	3	1	–
	2	–	–	–	–	1	2**	3	5	–	1 (S.D.)
V	2	1	–	2	–	1	–	6	12	1	–
	3	1	–	–	–	–	–	13	7	2	–
	4	–	–	3	–	1	–	1	6	1	–
	Epilogue	–	–	–	–	–	–	2	–	–	–
		5	2	33	0	6	7	59	72	9	1

S.D.   In stage directions
*   Five in stage direction
**   One in stage direction

From the foregoing tables it is clear that no completely satisfying explanation can be given for exceptional uses in *Henry VIII*, for instance the occasional appearance of *'em* and *ye* in the parts assigned to Shakespeare, and *hath* and expletive *do* in those assigned to Fletcher. These peculiarities are not exclusive, but preponderant, indicating individual preference. Nor can it be supposed that the parts of the play assigned to the two hands by Spedding and Hickson are altogether watertight. There may be intrusive elements throughout; obviously the author who had the final oversight of the play, probably Fletcher, must to some extent have worked over his predecessor's draft. But the grammatical peculiarities above noted seem to establish the presence of two hands, and they substantiate broadly the divisions of the play, made upon other grounds, by Spedding and Hickson.

IV

The commonest forms of colloquial weakening and contraction in *Henry VIII* are those that affect the personal pronouns *you* and *them*; but there are many others. Everywhere in the drama of this time suppressions and elisions abound, which originate in colloquial vowel degradation and consequent slurring of the definite article and pronominal forms. It has been suggested earlier that Ben Jonson, in his realistic attempts to represent contemporary speech, and his meticulous care in marking verse elisions, was mainly responsible for the importation of the fashion into the drama. The use of such contractions as *'tis, in't, to't, on't, knew't, i'th, o'th, to th', by th', on's* (= on us or on his), *in's cram's, let's* forms the subject of a paper by W. E. Farnham in the *Publications of the Modern Language Association of America, 1916*.[1] This writer, upon investigation of many plays, came to the conclusion that the use of these contractions points to the author's own habit of writing and not to the practice of his printer. A. W. Pollard is his authority for maintaining that the Good Shakespeare Quartos and the First Folio of Beaumount and Fletcher were probably printed from the writer's autograph. After comparing quartos and folios Farnham found that variations in these contractions were very slight. Whatever their source (Farnham believes them to be the authors'), the printer honoured these contractions, because they were a necessary part of the metrical structure of the verse. Differences in the use of the contractions in the parts of a collaborated play, he concludes, are 'too orderly to be ascribed to the vagaries of a printer.'[2]

Examining *The Merchant of Venice, Romeo and Juliet, Othello* and *The Winter's Tale*, he found that colloquial contractions are few in Shakespeare before 1600, but that there is an enormous increase in their use in *Othello* and subsequent plays, which he explains by the theory that Shakespeare gradually 'mellows into a more free-and-easy style'.[3] The proportion of colloquial shortenings in the Shake-

---

[1] *P.M.L.A.*, XXXI, No. 2, 'Colloquial Contractions in Beaumont, Fletcher, Massinger and Shakespeare as a Test of Authorship', pp. 326–58.

[2] Ibid., p. 332.   [3] Ibid., p. 342.

spearian parts of *Henry VIII* closely resembles that of *Othello* and *The Winter's Tale*.

At no time has Massinger anything like the proportion of contractions found in Shakespeare after 1604, and the *s-* contractions are altogether absent from his plays, i.e. the use of preposition or verb + *'s* (= his or us), e.g. *upon's* or *let's*. Assuming that the parts of *Henry VIII* assigned to Shakespeare by Spedding and Hickson must have been written somewhere between 1608 and 1622, he concludes that Massinger could have had no hand in them, because these scenes show regular use of many more of the contractions (including the *s* ones) than are found between those dates in Massinger. Massinger appears upon examination to be 'a decidely un-colloquial writer'.[1]

But, what is more significant, the scenes in *Henry VIII* assigned to Shakespeare are three times as prolific in colloquial contractions as those assigned to Fletcher, while the nature of the contractions is different too. Numerical differences cannot be accounted for by the temper of the scenes; forty-three of the seventy-seven contractions in the whole play are in any case in the mouths of the noblest characters, the King, the Queen, Wolsey and Buckingham. Fletcher's writing, Farnham finds on examination of other plays, is less addicted to *t-*, *the-* and *s-* shortenings than Shakespeare's after 1604, and is further distinguished from it by the infrequency of *t-* contractions with verbs (i.e. verb + *'t* for *it*, e.g. *know't*).

Beaumont, in his distaste for colloquial contractions, nearly resembles Massinger. He has far fewer shortenings than Fletcher, and is especially distinguished from him by the comparative rarity of *the-* contractions (i.e. preposition + *'th* for the definite article, e.g. *i'th'*).

But a most useful part of Farnham's paper is that which shows that the preference for these contractions, whoever the author may be, has nothing to do with subject matter or with people who talk *in character*. They are found in scenes of high tragedy and poetry, and had become an accepted poetical convention. Shakespeare's use of them 'is as much a characteristic of his development toward freedom in versification as the increase of run-on lines'.[2]

Whatever Shakespeare's actual orthography in this respect may have been, Farnham demonstrates that what must have been colloquial shortenings (because used in the racy prose scenes also), had come to be accepted as dramatic conventions adaptable to purposes of verse

---

[1] Ibid., p. 351.   [2] Ibid., p. 357.

elision. Shakespeare apparently concurred with Jonson and other play-wrights, that this was a source of freedom, and not a degradation of the verse. But he apparently thought otherwise about the use of *'em* and *ye*. They were mere colloquialisms, of no service for metrical elision, were less dignified than *them* and *you*, and would obtrude too frequently in serious verse. Shakespeare thus maintained his conservatism in the face of the practice of Jonson and Fletcher, and used *'em* and *ye* sparingly, if at all.

There being no Quartos after *Hamlet* certainly based on Shakespeare's manuscript, it is difficult to determine whether Shakespeare continued to *write* unstressed *them* and *you*, especially in extra-syllabic positions, after 1600. Even if he did, the full forms, according to Kökeritz,[1] may conceal a pronunciation *'em* or *ye* in unstressed positions. In *Henry VIII*, Act I, Scenes 1 and 2 (both attributed to Shakespeare) he sees this possibility in I.1.8 (saw *them*), I.1.26 and I.2.32 (to *them*) and I.2.46 (know *them*). The first, Kökeritz says, 'is obviously monosyllabic' and should be read *saw 'm*; though why he should prefer this contraction to *to'm* and *know'm* (which he suggests were deliberately avoided by the printer to prevent misreading), he does not explain.

On the other hand, Kökeritz maintains that *'em* and *ye* (or *y'*) may be simply typographical devices, not indication of some author's preference;[2] and this may apply to First Folio texts, in particular, for reasons of line-space. What Kökeritz has not explained, however, is the morphological reduction in certain parts of *Henry VIII* only, and those not uniformly consistent with a single compositor's stint.

Disregarding the views of E. K. Chambers, A. W. Pollard and others, Kökeritz asserts on page twenty-eight that all syncopations and contractions, 'undoubtedly imply the complete suppression of the elided vowel or syllable'. An actor who pronounces the full forms represented by the contractions, he adds, defies scansion, and must not 'claim that his reading agrees with Shakespeare's practice'. This view indicates, for me, insensibility to Shakespeare's skill in modulating the later poetry for dramatic purposes—an aesthetic gift to which systems of typography could hardly do justice.

The significance of *'em* and *ye* in suggesting Fletcher's hand in *Henry VIII* has also been taken up by R. A. Foakes in his Arden edition of the

---

[1] *Shakespeare's Pronunciation*, p. 30.

[2] Joseph Moxon in *Mechanic Exercises* (1683), discussing abbreviations (Vol. II, p. 368) states that *y^e* and *y^t* 'have been much used by Printers in Old Times to *Shorten* or *Get in Matter*; but now are wholly left off as obsolete'.

play in 1957. Treating these clipped pronouns as though they were the major, and not merely ancillary evidence, he sees them as probable modifications of the Folio scribe or compositors,[1] and draws attention to a manuscript copy of *Bonduca* in which *you* is used 172 times, where *ye* appears in the Beaumont and Fletcher Folio of 1647. The manuscript referred was made for a private collector between 1625 and 1635 by a scribe of the King's Men, Edward Knight; it was edited for the Malone Society by W. W. Greg in 1951. The transcript seems to have been made, not from the temporarily unavailable prompt-copy, but Greg thinks from foul papers;[2] these could even have been contemporary with the fair copy of *Henry VIII* presented for the First Folio.

If scribal transcripts for patrons, like *Bonduca* and *Demetrius and Enanthe* (made by Ralph Crane in November, 1624),[3] are used as testimony, scriveners of the third decade of the seventeenth century were not apparently consistent in the use of *you* and *ye*, and in Knight's case, of *em* and *um*. *You* occurs most frequently in the subject position (whether the syllable is stressed or unstressed), and *ye* nearly always as an unstressed enclitic object to an accented verb, or in feminine endings at the end of a verse line. Clearly, Fletcher increases his use of *ye* in the racy speech of the lower orders, such as Roman soldiers (see Act I, Scene 2 of *Bonduca*).

V

A Shakespearian peculiarity already mentioned is the syntactical difficulty with which the dramatist develops his ideas in verse. Since Dryden proposed syntactical correctness as the classical basis of Augustan writing, the reader has learnt to subsist on precise formalities of arrangement that make intelligibility their first aim. But Shakespeare inhabited another world—what Hardin Craig has called a pre-Cartesian, baroque world—and the effect of that ideological environment upon his style is remarkable. In his great speeches the thought is developed through the poetry itself, in momentous imaginative flashes, and actors had to be trained to speak them. A repertoire of such plays as the great tragedies required a high standard of acting and intelligent speaking of the verse, or they could not have held such a heterogeneous audience.

But the difficulty of interpreting Shakespeare remains, and the causes are sometimes peculiar to the age, sometimes to the dramatist himself.

[1] Introduction, p. XXI.
[2] See Introduction, M.S. Reprint.
[3] See Malone Society Reprint (ed. F. P. Wilson), 1951.

If language was, as T. S. Eliot says, 'at the tips of the senses', logical development of ideas could not have been regarded as one of its highest functions. Verbal magic and power were fascinations not confined to Marlowe, and on the analytical side subtle distinctions of meaning were a by-product of both. Elizabethan English shows language in a highly fluid state, moving in the next reign to a more normative stage of its development. The absence of any definite system of teaching grammar was both a drawback and an advantage: an advantage in that speech had few fixed *parts*; a disadvantage in that syntax, as conventional speech pattern, save for a diluted application of Latin, was almost unknown outside of the ecclesiastics, the dons and a few poets like Spenser. Words themselves were plastic, unstable, chameleon-like in their adaptability to individual needs. Shakespeare, finding the language at a malleable stage, bent it to his will, and made it a personal, though not an eccentric, instrument. Thus in *Henry VIII* are found:

I.1.18–21   . . . To day the French,
                   All Clinquant all in Gold, like Heathen Gods
                   Shone downe the English; and to morrow, they
                   Made Britaine, India:

II.3.103–4   . . . it faints me,
                   To thinke what followes

II.4.199–200   . . . thus hulling in
                   The wild Sea of my Conscience

V.1.156   He ha's strangled his Language in his teares

Such things were possible to Shakespeare, but they were not possible to any poetic dramatist after Dryden.

The power of Shakespeare's imagination, especially where the emotional tension of a scene is heightened, called for rapid transitions of feeling, thought and figure, and for these the syntax of the time, of any time, was too halting:

III.2.190–9   I do professe,
                   That for your Highnesse good, I ever labour'd
                   More then mine owne: that am, have, and will be
                   (Though all the world should cracke their duty to you,
                   And throw it from their Soule, though perils did
                   Abound, as thicke as thought could make 'em, and
                   Appeare in formes more horrid) yet my Duty,
                   As doth a Rocke against the chiding Flood,
                   Should the approach of this wilde River breake,
                   And stand unshaken yours.

Narrative, which requires an orderly development of details and events, is naturally tortuous in Shakespeare, and serves to distinguish him from most of his contemporaries. In *Henry VIII* several examples come to mind:

I.1.16–38
                    Each following day
  Became the next dayes master, till the last
  Made former Wonders, it's. . . .
            . . . The two Kings
  Equall in lustre, were now best, now worst
  As presence did present them: Him in eye,
  Still him in praise, and being present both,
  'Twas said they saw but one, and no Discerner
  Durst wagge his Tongue in censure, when these Sunnes
  (For so they phrase 'em) by their Heralds challeng'd
  The Noble Spirits to Armes, they did performe
  Beyond thoughts Compasse, that former fabulous Storie
  Being now seene, possible enough, got credit
  That Bevis was beleev'd.

I.1.75–80
               He makes up the File
  Of all the Gentry; for the most part such
  To whom as great a Charge, as little Honor
  He meant to lay upon: and his owne Letter
  The Honorable Boord of Councell, out
  Must fetch him in, he Papers.

Passages equally involved in their syntactical building are Buckingham's description of Wolsey's drafting of the treaty with France (I.1.158–90), the Surveyor's evidence against Buckingham (I.2.151–199) and the King's explanation to Cranmer of the necessity for restraining him in the Tower (V.1.95–108). Few dramatists, except Shakespeare, could have drafted such structurally entangled accounts of events. He tends to lose track of his relative clauses, especially if used continuatively and in proximity to participial phrases (or adverbial clauses) of time:

I.1.132–4
                 . . . Anger is like
  A full hot Horse, *who being allow'd his way*
  Selfe-mettle tyres him

I.2.164–7
  Whom after under the Commissions Seale,
  He sollemnly had sworne, that which he spoke
  My Chaplaine to no Creature living, but
  To me, should utter

I.2.180–2   . . . untill
It forg'd him some designe, *which being beleev'd*
It was much like to doe. . . .

I.2.194–9   . . . I would have plaid
The Part my Father meant to act upon
Th' Usurper Richard, *who being* at Salsbury,
Made suit to come in's presence; *which if granted*,
(As he made semblance of his duty) would
Have put his knife into him

It is not suggested that these constructions are either confined to Shakespeare or representative of him at his best. They are found in most of the dramatists of the time, including Jonson, but are much rarer in Jonson, Fletcher and Massinger than in Shakespeare. Many of the apparently anacoluthic constructions are historically traceable, as I have shown in two studies of Ben Jonson's grammar,[1] to the old habit of employing periphrastic relatives and to prevailing uncertainty about the use of relative pronouns generally. Equally unstudied in Shakespeare's time was the habit of making participial phrases do duty for temporal and conditional clauses. They tend to clog the meaning, and modern syntax avoids them in complicated sentence structures.

VI

Vocabulary, unless judiciously handled, may be an untrustworthy guide to authorship. The fact that a word is nowhere else used by Shakespeare is no proof that he could not have used it. Nonce uses are scattered throughout his authentic plays; and no evidence is to be deduced from the fact that such words are more frequently used in the works of other writers. But vocabulary may serve as a pointer to Shakespeare's reading, and investigations already made show that many uses attributed first to Shakespeare by the *O.E.D.*, or other authorities, have been ante-dated.

A large number of verbal clues to a possible second hand have been cited by Aldis Wright and Knox Pooler in their introductions to the Clarendon and Arden editions of *Henry VIII*. Wright, while regarding the play as a joint work, tactfully describes his list as 'un-Shakespearian words and phrases'. But in what sense, except a semantic one, *Office*

[1] *The Accidence of Ben Jonson's Plays Masques and Entertainments* (1953) and *Studies in the Syntax of Ben Jonson's Plays* (1953), both published by Bowes and Bowes.

I.1.44), *Papers* (verb—I.1.80), *Out-worths* (I.1.123), spand (= spanned, I.1.223), *solicited* (I.2.18), *Revokement* (I.2.106), *ruminate on* (I.2.180). *mounting his eyes* (I.2.205). *spleeny* (III.2.99), *hard rul'd* (III.2.101), *filed* (III.2.171), *Allegiant* (III.2.176), *glad* (= gladden, V.1.71) can be regarded as 'un-Shakespearian' I am unable to understand. *Filed* is an editorial emendation, generally accepted, for *fill'd* of the First Folio; and *glad*, from Old English *gladian*, occurs in Ben Jonson and elsewhere, such derivative weak verbs, without the formative suffix *-en*, being extremely common in Elizabethan English.

Knox Pooler suggests as Fletcherisms *ha's no Fellow* (I.3.41), which I find in *A Midsummer Night's Dream* (IV.1.38); the use of *else* at the end of a clause (I.3.65), which occurs, as he points out, in *The Tempest* (I.2.350) and is a regular idiomatic usage with Jonson and others; and the use of *'em* for *them*, which he says, erroneously, is not found in the non-Fletcherian parts of the play.

These instances emphasize the unreliability of inferences drawn from word comparison and parallel expressions. Boyle and Dugdale Sykes[1] use the latter a great deal to substantiate the hand of Massinger in *Henry VIII*. But the difficulty is that Massinger, in his own plays, reveals himself constantly as an imitator of Shakespeare, whom he appears to have studied closely. It has been shown that, after the publication of the Shakespeare Folio in 1623, his plays contain many more parallelisms than previously, and they extend to the great tragedies, as well as to *Henry VIII*. The subject of verbal parallels is complicated by the fact that Jacobean drama had inherited from Shakespeare, Jonson, Chapman, and their predecessors, a large number of words and phrases that had passed into the general coinage of the stage. Colloquialisms, expletives, clichés, class formulae, tricks of stagecraft and rhetoric, words strongly suggestive of dramatic tension, amorousness and comic levity, formed a common stock for all the practising dramatists of the time. So that, while Sykes produces from *The Two Noble Kinsmen* a convincing list of parallel phrases in Massinger's work to prove his partnership with Fletcher, Litledale outdoes him with a much more imposing list from Shakespeare.

[1] Sykes in his essay on 'King Henry VIII', *Sidelights on Shakespeare*, p. 28, points to 'a corruption of the text' in I.2.86—'In feare our *notion* will be mock'd, or carp'd at.' But he could not have consulted the First or three subsequent Folios, all of which have *motion*, the sense obviously required. Strangely, *notion* is found without a note (even in the addenda) of the *Cambridge Shakespeare* and the *Arden* edition of the play. Aldis Wright, however, corrected to *motion* (again without note) in the Clarendon text of *Henry VIII*.

On the other hand the use in *Henry VIII* of *one* as a substantive, (Franz, § 363, notes twenty occurrences in the play) of *thousand* without the preceding article, and of *A long farewell* are idiosyncrasies,[1] and they occur so frequently in the plays of Fletcher that they seem to be illuminating evidence of his hand in this play.

VII

The evidence for Fletcher's share in *Henry VIII* is thus broader-based than Alexander supposed: it rests on the results not only of metrical tests used by Spedding, Hickson and others, but of language criteria adduced by Thorndike, Farnham and in this chapter, and is supported by the use of iterative imagery[2] and internal evidence concerning the structure and characterization of the play, ably argued by Marjorie Nicholson in the *Publications of the Modern Language Association*, 1922,[3] In the face of the accumulated results, though they do not wholly agree about the parts to be assigned to Shakespeare and Fletcher, it is hard to see how Shakespeare's sole authorship can be reasonably maintained.

Why, then, did Heminge and Condell include *Henry VIII* in the First Folio? They must have done so because Shakespeare originally conceived and wrote about half the play, and it may even have been claimed as his at the first performance. But if Alexander claims too much in maintaining that Shakespeare wrote the whole play, a case might be made for allowing Shakespeare more than Spedding and Hickson assigned to him in the nineteenth century, especially in Acts III to V. That Shakespeare had a hand in the conception of Cranmer seems most probable; but Cranmer's advancement in the royal favour falls into the latter half of the play which, on dramatic principles at least, Fletcher in piecing together mishandled. Possibly much of what Shakespeare blocked out was over-written by his successor; and if this is what happened, it is difficult either on linguistic or metrical grounds to say how much was Shakespeare's original share. It is arguable, for

---

[1] They were first pointed out by Hickson in *Notes and Queries*, Ser. I, Vol. 3, p. 33.

[2] See Caroline F. E. Spurgeon's British Academy Lecture 'Shakespeare's Iterative Imagery', May 6, 1931, pp. 166–7. Spurgeon, not unjustly, sees more of Shakespeare in *Henry VIII* than is usually allowed to him, for instance the latter half of Act III, Scene 2, and touches in 11.2 and V.3. If Shakespeare had a hand in these parts they have been heavily revised, from the linquistic point of view, by Fletcher.

[3] 'The Authorship of *Henry the Eighth*', *P.M.L.A.*, Vol. XXXVII, p. 500.

instance, that Shakespeare originally had some hand in IV.2.1–82 (until the appearance of the vision to Katharine) and V.5.17–62 (Cranmer's last speech, which, incidentally, contains a use of *thousand* preceded by the indefinite article at line 19). On this theory the inclusion of *Henry VIII* in the Folio by Heminge and Condell may have been based on real knowledge of how much Shakespeare did write, and the exclusion of *The Two Noble Kinsmen* on the fact that their colleague wrote little of it, if anything at all.[1]

Is it, in all the circumstances, unreasonable to conclude that *Henry VIII* was an unfinished play, left at Shakespeare's retirement in the hands of his Company, and completed, perhaps with his acquiescence, by Fletcher, his successor as principal dramatist of the King's Players? There would have been sound business justification for retaining Shakespeare's name in connection with the new historical play, while paying Fletcher to complete it and giving him *carte blanche* to alter it as his talents dictated. In the last three Acts he must have made considerable modifications of the original plan, which would not have been to Shakespeare's taste. He may even have worked hurriedly.

This theory seems more probable than the one of simultaneous collaboration, especially if one accepts, as I do, the quite feasible idea that Shakespeare's comparatively early retirement to Stratford was due to overwork or ill-health. Every author, however premeditated his retirement, is bound to have on hand some unfinished work; and *Timon of Athens* is the best proof in Shakespeare's case. Parts of it are in such a rudimentary state, that they must have been abandoned. But the text of *Henry VIII* is in a much better condition, because it had to be acted, and was somehow put in order. The fact that the shares fall largely into whole scenes supports the notion that Shakespeare concurred in the Company's plans for completion, and tidied up his portion of the play before handing it over. But it is useless speculating too far along these lines.

Wilson Knight in *The Crown of Life* (1947) admits that there are two styles in the play, but claims that both are Shakespeare's. He believes that, in and after *King Lear*, Shakespeare developed 'a certain detectable rhythm concerned variously with a poetic self-pity or self-accusation',[2] and that this rhythm is mainly resorted to in argumentary or expostulatory speech. Shakespeare, he says, was probably the originator of this dramatic verse rhythm, and not Fletcher. But this, in my

[1] See Appendix VII.
[2] *The Crown of Life,* 'Henry VIII and the Poetry of Conversion', p. 269.

view, is a matter for detailed investigation; it cannot be decided by individual impression. It is certainly strange that one speaker, Cardinal Wolsey, in a single scene (Act III, Scene 2—his downfall), utters moving poetry in two different styles.

It is unnecessary to comment on Foakes's belief in Shakespeare's sole authorship of *Henry VIII*,[1] since this has already been done by R. A. Law in 'The Double Authorship of *Henry VIII*', *Studies in Philology* LVI, 1959; by Cyrus Hoy in 'The Shares of Fletcher and his Collaborators in the Beaumont and Fletcher Canon' (VII), *Studies in Bibliography* (University of Virginia), 1962; and by J. C. Maxwell in his Introduction to the New Cambridge edition of the play (1962).

[1] See Introduction to Arden edition, 1957.

Appendix I
Chronology of Shakespeare's Plays and Poems
The Variations from E. K. Chambers's order are marked
with an asterisk.

PERIOD I: before joining Chamberlain's Men
(most plays probably re-written after 1594)

	Probably written	First printed
2 Henry VI	1590	1594
3 Henry VI	1590	1595
1 Henry VI	1591 (possibly re-vised 1594)	1623
*King John	1591 (possibly re-vised 1594–6)	1591
Richard III	1592	1597
Venus and Adonis	1592	1593
Comedy of Errors	1592	1623
Lucrece	1593	1594
Titus Andronicus	1593	1594
Taming of the Shrew	1593	1594
Love's Labour's Lost	1593	1598

PERIOD II: 8 Years (two plays a year)

Two Gentlemen of Verona	1594	1623
Romeo and Juliet	1595	1597
Richard II	1595	1597
Midsummer Night's Dream	1596	1600
Merchant of Venice	1596	1600
1 Henry IV	1597	1598
2 Henry IV	1597	1600
Much Ado about Nothing	1598	1600
Henry V	1598	1600
Julius Caesar	1599	1623
As You Like It	1599	1623

	Probably written	*First printed*
Merry Wives of Windsor	1600	1602
Additions to Sir T. More	1600	—
Hamlet	1600	1603
*Twelfth Night	1601	1623
Phoenix and Turtle	1601	1601
Troilus and Cressida	1601	1609

PERIOD III: 5 Years (one play a year)

All's Well that Ends Well	1602	1623
Measure for Measure	1603	1623
Othello	1604	1622
King Lear	1605	1608
Macbeth	1606	1623

PERIOD IV: 2 Years (Four Classical Plays, two written in each year

*Pericles	1607	1609
Antony and Cleopatra	1607	1623
Coriolanus	1608	1623
Timon of Athens	1608 (probably incomplete)	1623

PERIOD V: 4 Years (Plays of Resignation, one written each year)

Cymbeline	1609	1623
Winter's Tale	1610	1623
The Tempest	1611	1623
Henry VIII	1612 (probably incomplete)	1623
Two Noble Kinsmen	1612 (See Appendix VII)	1634

Occasional Works

Sonnets	1589–1600	1609

Appendix II

Substantive Texts of the Shakespeare Canon, in probable order of Composition

17 SINGLE TEXTS (Authority, First Folio)
- (3) 1 Henry VI
- (4) King John
- (6) Comedy of Errors
- (10) Two Gentlemen of Verona
- (19) Julius Caesar
- (20) As You Like It
- (23) Twelfth Night
- (25) All's Well that Ends Well
- (26) Measure for Measure
- (29) Macbeth
- (31) Antony and Cleopatra
- (32) Coriolanus
- (33) Timon of Athens
- (34) Cymbeline
- (35) Winter's Tale
- (36) The Tempest
- (37) Henry VIII

10 MULTIPLE TEXTS (Main authority a Quarto)
- (7) Titus Andronicus (Q 1594) one scene from F_1
- (9) Love's Labour's Lost (Q 1598)
- (11) Romeo and Juliet (Q 1599) with some reference to Q 1597
- (12) Richard II (Q 1597) Deposition from F_1
- (13) Midsummer Night's Dream (Q 1600)
- (14) Merchant of Venice (Q 1600)
- (15) 1 Henry IV (Q 1598)
- (17) Much Ado about Nothing (Q 1600)
- (22) Hamlet (Q 1604) with reference to F_1
- (30) Pericles (Q 1609)

5 MULTIPLE TEXTS (Main authority, First Folio)
- (1) 2 Henry VI
- (2) 3 Henry VI
- (8) Taming of the Shrew
- (18) Henry V
- (21) Merry Wives of Windsor

5 MULTIPLE TEXTS (Mixed authority)
- (5) Richard III (basis F_1)
- (16) 2 Henry IV (basis Q 1600)
- (24) Troilus and Cressida (basis Q 1609, but Stage directions F_1)
- (27) Othello (basis Q 1622, with constant reference to F_1)
- (28) King Lear (basis F_1, with some additions from Q 1608)

Appendix III

Classification of First Folio Texts, according to the probable nature of copy procured by Heminge and Condell

1. Manuscript   (a) Shakespeare's foul papers.
   - (b) Fair copies (mainly in play-house use).
   - (c) Transcripts subsequently made for the Company, including abridgements and possibly assembled texts (i) pre-1612, (ii) post-1612, which may be classified according to scribal practices.
2. Printed texts (a) Good quartos faithfully reprinted from one of the above (probably play-house copy).
   - (b) Quartos with contemporary manuscript corrections (play-house copy).
   - (c) Good quartos collated with bad.
   - (d) Quartos with possible post-1612 modifications (play-house copy).

NOTE: 1612 is the assumed date when Shakespeare severed his personal connection with the Company.

Appendix IV
The Hands in *Sir Thomas More*

The following is the accepted division of the *handwritings* in *Sir Thomas More*, with the conjectured authorship of the parts they embody, the citations being from Greg's Malone Society reprint:

1. S (Original text transcribed by Munday): lines 1–1986, folios 3–5, 10, 11, 14, 15, 17–22a. Munday, who took no part in the transcription of the *additions*, has a careful English hand, with the admixture of some Italian characters for proper names and other special purposes. The spelling has little variation and is fairly modern; the punctuation is unremarkable, except for rhetorical colons, which he favours at the end of the penultimate line of a speech, without syntactical significance (see Chapter 5, *John a Kent*). Nine lines near the end (1956–64) are deleted and replaced immediately by a revised version, without important changes of spelling. Oliphant suggests that Munday himself wrote the first eight scenes, comprising lines 1–876 (folios 3–14a);[1] and Greg in his reprint that Munday subsequently replaced lines 453–72 by lines 66–122 of Addition II (folio 7b), and lines 844–76 by the whole of Addition V (folio 13a). But these revisions are in the hand of scribe C (see 4 (a) and (d) below), who copied the revisions simultaneously. According to Oliphant Scenes IX to XVII of Munday's transcription, comprising lines 878–1986, are the composition of Heywood and Chettle.

2. A (Chettle): lines 1–71, Addition I, pp. 66–8. This is written in a legible English hand with sparse punctuation. The addition is on one side of a single leaf (folio 6), and apparently represents Chettle revising his own original work and correcting his revision in the process, since corrections are of the type made in the course of composition. The leaf is wrongly bound, as the passage is to replace a deletion on folio 19a, lines 1471–1516, pp. 49–50. Oliphant gives Scenes X–XIII, lines 1158–1602, of the original version to Chettle.

---

[1] See E. H. C. Oliphant, 'Sir Thomas More' *J.E.G.P.* XVIII (1919), p. 228. On p. 230, however, Oliphant expresses the belief that Dekker's may have been a fourth hand in the original play, since he would hardly have been invited to revise a part that he had not originally had a hand in. Unfortunately his work survives only in the revised version, which replaces original lines 735–876 (see 4 (c)).

3. B (Heywood): (a) lines 1–64, Addition II, pp. 69–71, and (b) lines 2–73, Addition VI, pp. 91–3. This is a poor and probably hasty English hand, with practically no punctuation. In the same hand appear several marginal additions in the original version transcribed by Munday, which indicate Heywood's general literary supervision.

(a) The 64 lines of Addition II replace Munday's original lines 412–52 on folio 5b, but are not a significant change, since they are merely Heywood's transcription and simultaneous revision of Munday's work.

(b) The 71 lines in Addition VI (line 1 is prefaced by C) are the only ones on folio 16, and were intended to be inserted after line 1157 on folio 17a, i.e. at the end of Scene IX, which was, according to Oliphant, Heywood's original work. Deleted lines 21–35 of the Addition are without speaker's names, and the last five lines are repeated by the scribe C at the beginning of Addition V.

In addition to Scene IX, lines 878–1157, of the original play (folios 14b, 15a, 15b, pp. 30–5), Oliphant gives Scenes XIV–XVII, lines 1603–1986 (folios 20a–22a, pp. 53–65), to Heywood also.

4. C (Professional Scribe): (a) lines 66–122, Addition II, pp. 71–3; (b) lines 1–22, Addition III, p. 79; (c) lines 1–211, Addition IV, pp. 80–8; (d) lines 1–26, Addition V, pp. 89–90. The work is that of a finely formed, calligraphic hand in Italian script, with little punctuation beyond an occasional point placed rather high. Greg identified the hand as that of the unnamed theatrical scrivener who wrote the plots of *The Seven Deadly Sins* and *Fortune's Tennis*. C revised the stage directions throughout the manuscript, ensured that the additions were properly inserted, and added the speaker's names in the Shakespearian contribution (Addition II, hand D, lines 123–270, see 5), indicating that he was the final theatrical, as Heywood was the literary, supervisor of the text.

The authorship of the passages transcribed by C is uncertain, but

(a) Addition II, lines 66–122, was an attempted revision, abandoned, of the incomplete and cancelled Scene V, lines 453–72, Folio 5b, p. 16. Oliphant believes the author was Munday.

(b) Addition III, lines 1–22, was an insertion on a piece of paper pasted on the lower half of folio 11b, covering the deleted lines 761–96 of the original, pp. 26–7, and intended to precede the opening of Addition IV, folio 12a, p. 80. This insertion Oliphant appears to ascribe to Dekker, and Bald to Shakespeare.[1]

(c) Addition IV, lines 1–211, was an insertion of three and a half pages

[1] Op. cit., p. 54.

(folios 12a, 12b, 13a, top half of 13b) intended to replace cancelled lines 735–876, folios 11b and 14a, pp. 25–30. This revision Oliphant seems to assign to Dekker (see 6); Greg, I believe rightly, sees the latter as merely the reviser of another author's original Scene VIII,[1] and that author can only have been Munday.

(d) Addition V, lines 1–26, was an insertion partly (18 lines) written on a piece of paper pasted over deleted lines 844–76 on the lower portion of folio 14a, pp. 29–30, and intended to precede Heywood's scene (IX), commencing at line 878 of the original version, folio 14b, p. 30. Oliphant believes the author of this insertion was Munday.

5. D (Shakespeare): lines 123–270, Addition II, pp. 73–8. A cursive English (or Secretary) hand, found only in folios 8a, 8b and 9a, and indicating in the words of Maunde Thompson 'a skilful and experienced penman',[2] but one whose style was somewhat modified by speed or animation. He shows a disposition for curves and flourishes, especially at the end of a line or word terminating in *e*. The punctuation is of the lightest.

Shakespeare's supposed contribution is an entirely individual revision of Munday's Scene VI of the original version, lines 473–565, folio 10, pp. 17–20. But he is not thought to have had much knowledge of the play, as his speech-prefixes are vacillating, and in Greg's description he is a careless writer.[3] The Shakespearian revision may not be confined to the lines in D's hand-writing: there is the further passage noted in 4(b) above, which I believe with Bald to be the scribe C's transcription of Shakespeare's work, rather than Dekker's (see Chapter 6, p. 56).

6. E (Dekker): lines 212–42, Addition IV, pp. 87–8. This hand is a mixture of English and Italian script, characters in the two styles being distinct, but not carefully made. The punctuation is full, with a fondness for the colon, with occurs regularly after speech-prefixes, and occasionally at the end of speeches. The thirty-one lines, which appear on the bottom half of folio 13b, are an extension of the revision of Scene VIII (see 4 (c)). As the preceding 211 lines were a transcript by C of revised work, and the style is very like that of the extension, the odds are that the whole revision (lines 1–242) was Dekker's, and that the latter merely augmented in his own hand what C had just transcribed. Oliphant seems uncertain whether the lines 735–876 of the original version, which Dekker's revision superseded, were his or Munday's; but I am convinced they were the latter's.

---

[1] *Shakespeare's Hand in Sir Thomas More*, p. 47.
[2] *Shakespeare's Hand in Sir Thomas More*, p. 70.
[3] *Sir Thomas More*, M.S.R., p. XVIII.

Appendix V
The Orthographical Characteristics of Ralph Crane

Ralph Crane was a poor man of humble original talents, employed by the King's Men, Shakespeare's Company in the second decade of the seventeenth century, probably just before or after Shakespeare's retirement. His penmanship in a neat Italian hand was a model of calligraphy, and he is considered to have had an influence on the punctuation and other orthographical features of some of the plays in the First Folio. For this Folio he is generally thought to have provided some half-dozen transcripts: *The Two Gentlemen of Verona*, *2 Henry IV*, *The Merry Wives of Windsor*, *Measure for Measure*, *The Winter's Tale*, and *The Tempest*. These transcriptions, of course, are lost; but others by Crane exist, and include Ben Jonson's Masque *Pleasure Reconciled to Virtue*, *Sir John van Olden Barnavelt* (a play thought to be mainly Massinger's), Fletcher's *Demetrius and Enanthe* (for Sir Kenelm Digby) and Middleton's *Witch* and *A Game at Chess*. I have had the opportunity of examining the last three manuscripts, together with the holograph of Crane's own supposed compositions, *Divers Zealous Meditations* and *The Works of Mercy* (both in the Bodleian Library). Of *A Game at Chess* there are no less than six manuscripts extant, one in the hand of the author, and two in Crane's; the others are in unknown hands, but none gives the full text of the play.

Interest in Crane is partly to discover the degree of his adaptability to different authors. In making transcripts of plays he undoubtedly varied in his practice; but he always edited punctuation to conform more or less to his own ideas; and the same applies to his marks of elision. It is difficult to assess his changes of spelling in transcripts, but he shows his hand in the commoner forms such as *theis* and *I'll* (for *Ile*).

As regards the commoner grammatical forms (pronouns, auxiliary verbs etc.), he seems to retain the usage of the author, though it is possible that he substituted *hath* and *doth* when he thought of it, for *has* and *does*, believing the former to be the correct literary forms. If he did this, he may, like the printers in their books, have considered the rank and learning of the person or persons for whom the transcript was made. It is certain that in his own work he prefers *hath* and *doth*, also *I'll* to *Ile*, *ev'n* to *e'en*, *nev'r* to *ne'er* and so on. He is careful to mark elision in contracted forms, but indifferent (as were most printers) in using the apostrophe to mark syncope of past participle endings, e.g. *Demetrius and Enanthe* (M.S.R.) 19, *washd, curld, perfum'd*. He does not use the apostrophe for the possessive genitive. His capitals are often simply ornamental, and affect any part of speech. He inserts ^ over the exclamation O, but refrains from exclamation marks.

As regards punctuation generally, his fondness for hyphens and parentheses has frequently been noted. The double hyphen seems to come from the Continent. But it is doubtful whether his varieties of hyphenation and his tricks of parenthesis can be regarded as idiosyncratic; he merely used them to excess. They appear in the early quartos of Shakespeare's poems, and were cultivated by some of the printing-houses, notably the firms of Jaggard and Field. Crane's orthography was modelled on Jonson and the best printers; and capitalization is its most unruly feature. He frequently capitalizes pronouns and even the relative *that*. He also uses commas heavily, e.g. before a defining relative clause.

The high percentage of colons in *Demetrius and Enanthe* (M.S.R. Introd. p. ix) may be due to Crane's copy; they mark off the rhetorical units of the speeches. His own work reveals a nice sense of the logical value of a semicolon. I believe the symbol ⁊ was strictly intended for questions in the body of a sentence, i.e. where the period had not yet been reached.

The Jonsonian elisions in *Demetrius and Enanthe* are interesting, and probably inconsistent, because Fletcher's later verse is so prosaic in its rhythms that the metrical ictus was sometimes difficult for the scribe to determine. This type of elision Crane must have acquired from Jonson; but he also developed a characteristic shorthand, e.g. *'has* (= he has), *art'thou* (= artow) and *'believe' Sir*, where the apostrophe stands for omission or corruption of the colloquial pronominal forms, and not for metrical elision at all. Much of this is pedantic and literary, and intended to interpret the colloquial contractions of the stage for the gentlemanly reader. If natural speech rhythms meant the use of extra syllables at the end of a line, they also implied them within the line, and the Jonsonian elision ('the use of an apostrophe to indicate that a vowel is not to count metrically although it is retained graphically') may not have been so much a suppression of a syllable as a slurring or syncopation of it, ·as in colloquial speech.

Besides *I'll*, Crane uses the modern contractions *they're* and *they've* for the commoner combinations *th'are* and *th'have*. He is found to employ *'em, 'hem* and *them* for the accusative of the personal pronoun in unstressed positions, but *'hem* outweighs *'em*.

Scribes continued the mediaeval practice of writing *o* for *u* when the latter occurred next to m, n, v or w, because of the difficulty of distinguishing the minim strokes of individual letters. Printers took over the tradition, and preserved it sporadically. The *o* was pronounced *u*. Similarly, the spellings *floong*, *hoong*, *soong* are not peculiar to Crane, but occur commonly in Jonson and other Elizabethan and Jacobean writers; *oo* is the graphic representation of a sound of indeterminate value.

Appendix VI

'New Light on Seventeenth-Century Pronunciation from the English School of Lutenist Song-writers' by Evelyn H. Scholl, P.M.L.A. LIX. 2(1944)

The following is a summary of Miss Scholl's findings:

1. Nouns ending in conson.+*ion*, e.g. *affection, passion, opinion*: 177 such words occur; pronunciation of the ending is monosyllabic, probably [ʃən], as in Modern English. Only eleven instances of dissyllabic endings occur in the musical settings.

2. Nouns ending in conson. + *-eus* or *-ior*, and adjectives ending in conson. + *-ious* or *-eous*: 41 such words occur. Campïon makes the endings of *Morpheus, hideous, various, curious* and *glorious* dissyllabic. Except after *r*, however, and often with *r*, the endings are monosyllabic and pronounced [jəs]. The endings of words like *behavior* and *Savior* are monosyllabic.

3. Words ending in *-ient, -ience, -ier,* or *-iest* (superlatives): Twenty-seven such words occur, excluding the superlatives, and only four have dissyllabic endings, viz. *patience, conscience, orient* and *experience*. The superlative ending *-iest* is always monosyllabic.

4. Words ending in *-ial, -ian, -iance*, where the *i* is not long and stressed: Of the twenty-seven such words that occur, only four are dissyllabic in their endings (but not always), *memorial, dalliance, alliance, defiance*.

5. Words ending in *-ual*: Seven are found, and the endings are regularly dissyllabic, except in the case of *mutual* and *continual*.

6. Contiguous vowels, of which the first is long:

    (a) [uə] or [uI] in words such as *cruel* and *wooing*. Invariably two syllables. Only in one poem are *reneweth* and *pursueth* rhymed with *truth* and *youth*.

    (b) [iI] in words such as *seeing, deity*. Invariably two syllables, except in the case of *being*, where there were twelve dissyllabic, to eight monosyllabic, uses. Gill says *being* has two syllables.

    (c) [aII] in words like *dying, sighing, eyeing*. There is no syllabic reduction. *Envying* is generally stressed on the second syllable, and rhymes with *dying*.

(d) [aɪe], in words such as *quiet, trial* and *viol*, has no syllabic reduction, though *diamond* is sometimes a word of two syllables. *Violence* is once used in verse by Campion as a word of two syllables, but he gives it three notes in the musical setting. Where the combination [aɪe] occurs before a final *r* sound, as in *fire, briar*, the pronunciation may be either monosyllabic or dissyllabic, with a preference for the former, except in words like *higher* and *flyer*, in which *-er* is a suffix.

(e) Words in *-ower* or *-our*, of which the diphthong is not clearly determined, such as *power, hour*. Of the 115 such words found, only six had dissyllabic pronunciations; the tendency to increase a syllable is in the *-ower* group.

(f) The word *prayer* occurs fifteen times, but is only four times dissyllabic. *Note:* Of the words ending in an *r* sound (not yet silent in Elizabethan English), and preceded by the vowel combinations specified in (d), (e) and (f), nearly all had the option of use as monosyllables or dissyllables. The commonest ambivalent words of these groups found in Shakespeare and the verse citations of the *O.E.D.* are *fire, bower, flower, hour, prayer*, and *briar*, the last usually disssyllabic.

7. *Ever, never* and *over* are always dissyllabic, and respected as such in the music, even when they occasion metrically redundant syllables. In the latter case the reader or singer was not apparently expected to supply the doublet *e'er, ne'er*, or *o'er*, though all poets use the contractions frequently enough when they intend monosyllables. Shakespeare never wrote *whether* when he intended *wher*.

8. *I am* is never coalesced, and is always two syllables.

9. The negative *not* is never contracted. In Modern English, where *not* follows the verb 'to be', an auxiliary verb, or a verb of incomplete predication such as *can* or *must*, the negative of the combination is the element that is contracted colloquially. In Elizabethan and Jacobean English, it is the verb that is curtailed. All 106 examples of such combinations in the song-writers follow the latter principle, e.g. She's not, she'll not. The earliest of the modern combinations, *shan't* and *won't*, came just after the Restoration.

10. Poetical and colloquial contractions were used by all the songwriters. Aphæresis, mostly of the common prepositions (e.g. *'mongst, 'gainst*), occurs twenty-three times, and its object is the use of a preposition, noun or verb etc. with a syllable less than the normal form. Enclitic *it*, following a preposition or verb, occurs twice in a song set by Jones, the pronoun losing its syllabic value, viz. *Upon't* and *heal't*. Similarly *let's* (= let us) is commonly monosyllabic. But the kind of apocope, such as *th'* and *i'th'* before consonants, advocated by Van Dam and Stoffel to eliminate trisyllables, which is

frequent in the Shakespeare and Jonson First Folios, is not resorted to by the Lutenists. In the phrase *i'the cradle*, Jones gives *i'* and *the* separate notes; and in the extra-metrical feet of *Nor the wish of a thought*, Dowland attempts no contraction, but gives each word its full syllabic value. *The* is never contracted before a consonant.

11. *Spirit* and *sprite* are observed as dissyllable and monosyllable respectively, like *never* and *ne'er*.

12. *Heaven* or *heavenly* occurs 123, and *even* twenty-six times; of these 102 instances of *heaven* are monosyllabic, and twenty-five of *even* also. There were in use two reduced forms of *even, e'en* and *ev'n*, but they must have been pronounced differently, because the former is never rhymed with words like *heaven*. Of the other endings conson. + *-en, giv'n, forbidd'n, hidd'n, swoll'n* and *fall'n* are capable of reduction to monosyllables, even when the words are spelt in full. Words ending in *-ten, -ken, -sen* or *-zen* never have syncope of the final syllable. The monosyllabic equivalents of *often* and *taken* are *oft* and *ta'en*.

13. Words ending in *-est* may be either superlatives or the second person singular of verbs; in both cases the ending was capable of syncope.

(a) Superlatives, however, revealed only eight instances of syncopation in 114 examples. Two of those were in *highest*, which probably called for a glide sound similar to that in *higher* (see 6(d)); and three others were *unworthiest, happiest*, and *beautiest*, dealt with in 3. Miss Scholl suggests that the syncopated pronunciation of *happiest* was [hæpjəst].

(b) The reverse is true of the verb-endings in *-est*: the majority are syncopated. *Shouldst, wouldst, canst*, and *mayst* are invariably syncopated. But of fifty-eight other verbs, only eight fail to syncopate the ending. Spelling does not always indicate pronunciation; *mayest*, for example, is always monosyllabic. In Campion *joyest* and *playest* are monosyllabic, and in Dowland *freest* is dissyllabic. Though Jespersen claims that syncope of *e* is not common after *r*, it occurs in *retir'st, hear'st, wear'st*, and *dar'st*. Even where the stem of the verb ends in *-t*, the awkward-sounding syncope is permitted, e.g. *might'st, gett'st, let'st, bait'st, ought'st*. *Note:* Gill gives the full pronunciation to the *-est* ending in both verbs and superlatives. Shakespeare, on the other hand, follows the distinction of the Lutenists in 1500 examples cited in Bartlett's *Concordance*; but this, of course, depends, not on the spelling, but on the lines being counted for syllables.

14. (a) There are 134 notional verbs in the Lutenists whose third person singular present indicative ends in *-eth* or *-th*. Syncope of the *-eth* end-

ing rarely occurs, the orthography *chirp'th* in Cavendish being given two notes in the music; the genuine examples of syncope are *renew'th, pursu'th, lie'th, ow'th, grow'th* etc. There are 915 notional verbs with the ending -*s*.

(b) There are 152 uses of *hath*, 201 of *doth*, and 3 of *saith*, and no alternative -*s* endings for these verbs occur until 1632, when Porter has three examples of *has* and one of *does*.

(c) There is no justification for the view of Hart and Hodges that verbs ending in -*eth* and -*s* are similar in pronunciation, and can be rhymed. The verbs with -*s* endings are a syllable shorter.

15. Unstressed vowels a, e, i, o, u, y, when found between consonants, the second of which is *r*, *l*, or *n*, are frequently syncopated. In *every* the *e* was lost even in Chaucer's time.

(a) The most frequently sacrificed vowel is *e* before *r* and *l*, fifty-seven examples being syncopated and seventeen not. *Misery, memory* and *merrily* are never syncopated.

(b) Before *n* syncope of *e* takes place twelve times, as against two unsyncopated examples. Of the latter one is *countenance*, where the metre requires two syllables, but the music is given three notes. It is noteworthy that the -*ten* syllable said to be unsyncopated in twelve, does take syncope if a final -*ing* follows, e.g. *threatening*, which Campion and Jones treat as dissyllabic.

(c) In the case of vowels other than *e* in such syllables, syncopation is the exception rather than the rule. *Harmony* and *felony* are never syncopated. The *o*, *u* and *y* vowels were apparently not completely neutralized.

16. Unstressed *y* and a following vowel, whether in a single word like *pitying*, or as conjugate naked vowels of two words in *many a*, were, with a single exception, not merged by the Lutenists, but given separate notes. The pronunciation was [pɪtjɪŋ] and [mɛnjə], if coalescence took place in the verse; but the songwriters preferred not to observe it.

17. Synaloepha in combinations such as *th'other* involves most frequently apparent, and not real, elision. Theorists like Campion in his *Observations*, who point to actual loss of *e*, are influenced by classical rules, not English practice. Not even his own settings uniformly support genuine elision, since eleven out of twenty of Campion's instances show no contraction. In the other songwriters, forty-four out of fifty-seven examples are uncontracted. *The* is usually contracted before an unaccented syllable, e.g. *th'enchanter*, except in Jones and Campion. Milton elided the *e* chiefly before stressed vowels, and Pope before unstressed ones.

18. The preposition *to* before a vowel or mute *h* occurs eighty-six times in the Lutenists, thirty-eight being before verbs. Contraction of *to* occurs thirty-three times, sixteen before unaccented syllables and seventeen before accented ones.

(a) Among the prepositional infinitives, *to* is only five times contracted out of thirty-eight, and all before unaccented syllables.

(b) Before articles, adjectives, nouns and pronouns *to* is contracted only once in forty-three instances, viz. *t'her* in a setting by Campion, who elsewhere, however, gives *to her* two notes.

Note: Though the conditions under which *to* and *the* are contracted before vowels are similar, contraction of the preposition is less frequent.

Appendix VII
Shakespeare and *The Two Noble Kinsmen*

Few things offer greater testimony to Shakespeare's reputation in his day and the commercial acquisitiveness of the publishers, than the ascription to him on the title-pages, either wholly or in part, of plays in which he can hardly have added more than a passage or two. Of the apocryphal plays, excluding *Pericles* and *Henry VIII* (which are now admitted to the canon), only *The Two Noble Kinsmen* has been urged as his, or partly his, with any plausibility. No play has produced as much conflicting evidence, and left such vagueness in the minds of those who look for certainty, as *The Two Noble Kinsmen*. On one hand the play is regarded as pseudo-Gothic pastiche, on another as one of the finest things in Jacobean drama. That one of the participants in this obviously collaborated play was Fletcher is practically certain from both the internal evidence of the writing and the external evidence of the play's history. Shakespeare's name appears with Fletcher's as joint author, on the title-page of the first edition, the quarto of 1634, and both names appear again in *The Stationers' Register*. The subject of the play is more likely to have been Shakespeare's than Fletcher's; he would naturally have been attracted to the story in Chaucer's *The Knight's Tale*, on which the plot is based; but the planning of the play is unlike the practice of Shakespeare. Though the traditionalists will have nothing to do with it, there is some weight in the partial ascription to Shakespeare on the title-page, borne out by what follows in Act I. The opening song has been suggested as Shakespeare's:

> Roses their sharpe spines being gon,
> Not royall in their smels alone,
> But in their hew.
> Maiden Pinckes, of odour faint,
> Dazies smel-lesse, yet most quaint
> And sweet Time true.
>
> Prim-rose first borne child of Ver,
> Merry Spring times Herbinger,
> With her bels dimme.

Oxlips, in their Cradles growing,
Mary-golds, on death beds blowing,
Larkes-heeles trymme.

All deere natures children sweete,
Ly fore Bride and Bridegroomes feete,
Blessing their sence.
Not an angel of the aire,
Bird melodious, or bird faire,
Is absent hence.

The Crow, the slaundrous Cuckoe, nor
The boding Raven, nor Chough hore
Nor chattring Pie,
May on our Bridehouse pearch or sing,
Or with them any discord bring,
But from it fly.

Dr. J. S. Smart, Shakespearian scholar of the last generation, is said to have held that this is all Shakespeare contributed. The attempt to find the seams of the structural parts contributed to the play by three to five hands must once again be based on lingnistic evidence. My conclusions, thus far, are as follows: There was an old play *Palamon and Arcite* presented by Shakespeare's Company in 1594 and 1596. It is possible that Shakespeare set about revising this play about 1611, but did not get very far. The reworking was then taken in hand by Beaumont and Fletcher for a production known to have taken place in 1613, the same year as the production of *Henry VIII*. Fletcher did most of this work, but the play was finally retouched by another and unknown writer between 1624 and 1626, for a revival in the latter year. This is probably the version printed in the quarto of 1634.

Appendix VIII

The Historical Development of Punctuation Marks

I

Introductory

In the Introduction to Part II of his *Codices Latini Antiquiores* Professor E. A. Lowe remarks that punctuation is a chapter of palaeography that still remains to be written. To trace the history of punctuation in English, as in other modern European languages, it is necessary to go back to ancient times, to original manuscripts or facsimiles, and early printed books, especially those published before 1700.

A study of the history of punctuation must take into account two main functions (a) intelligent elucidation of the text, and (b) pauses necessary for breath. This involves a distinction, never clearly made, between logical and rhythmical, or, as some prefer to reword it, between syntactical and elocutionary punctuation. The early scribes and printers cared little for such distinctions, partly because they dealt with literary works of all kinds. Nevertheless, conventions arose, and were in use by scribes of the twelfth, and printers of the sixteenth century. Writers in the past had to take their cue from the professional scribes and printers, whose conventions were guided by two main considerations, economy of time, and the rules of the scriptorium or printing-house in which the work was produced.

The several theories of punctuation, at the present time, are based mainly on eighteenth- and nineteenth-century precept and practice. For an understanding of the punctuation of earlier periods, for example Shakespeare's, these have proved unsatisfactory. Neither the rhythm nor the syntax of speech is essentially logical, though parts of grammar may be. Punctuation is, in fact, a convention of mixed origin; but, as with other linguistic developments, its rise has a certain historical continuity.

II

The Use of Stops in Classical and Mediaeval Times

The word 'punctuation' is derived from Mediaeval Latin, and its first recorded use in the *Oxford English Dictionary* is in 1539. When the term originated, it was applied to Hebrew texts and Psalms; specifically, to the Masoretic texts which began to appear when Hebrew, as a spoken language, was replaced by Aramaic about the beginning of the first century B.C. Hebrew persisted as a scholar's language, and it became necessary to preserve, for literary and religious purposes, the traditions of pronunciation and intonation practised in the synagogues. The punctuation that the Masorites introduced included accents and other symbols to aid correct reading, but consisted mainly of the insertion of vowel sounds, absent in the older Hebrew writings, because an alphabet of consonants only was used. The system was not perfected until the sixth or seventh century A.D., by which time word separation was fully developed in Hebrew texts, a good deal earlier than in classical ones.

The practice of stopping, which is now called punctuation, had its origin with the Greeks. That there was anything approaching a system, however, is denied by palaeographical evidence. The Greek manuscripts of pre-Christian times show that, before the Alexandrian Age, which began about 300 B.C., there was no punctuation at all. The Greek reader of classical times was evidently an intelligent person; for he had not even the meagre assistance of word-separation. An occasional dot (or comma) might be introduced between words where there was possible ambiguity, but such instances were rare. Complete separation of words was never achieved in Greek and Roman times, and appears only in Latin manuscripts of the eleventh century.[1]

The only pause or break indicated by Aristotle, the *paragraph*,[2] was a short stroke placed immediately below the initial word of the line in which the sense is brought to a conclusion. Alternative to this stroke was the *diple* or wedge, like an English V placed horizontally. The paragraphing stroke was also used in the drama (for instance in the *Antiope* of Euripides) to mark changes of speakers, as their names did not appear before the words they were intended to utter. Finally, the stroke was used in strophic verse, e.g. in the British Museum papyrus of the Odes of *Bacchylides* (first century B.C.) to mark the end of strophe, antistrophe or epode. Maunde Thompson says that the paragraphing stroke eventually developed into a new symbol (*T*), employed by later Latin scribes specially to mark the head of a new paragraph, and that this was the source of the familiar symbol, like a reversed P with a double vertical stroke, employed by the early printers.[3] A symbol resembling this *T* is still used by John Bale in his manuscript improvements to *King Johan* (c. 1560), in order to indicate the stanzaic structure of the verse.

The first symbols used in Greek manuscripts were thus not stops or pauses in

[1] See Maunde Thompson, *Introduction to Greek and Latin Palaeography*, p. 57.
[2] See 'Rhetoric', III.8.
[3] See Maunde Thompson, op. cit., p. 59.

the modern sense. But an academic interest in punctuation, as we know it, arose in the succeeding age, one of great scholarship, which centred round the libraries founded by the Ptolemies at Alexandria. According to Sandys,[1] Aristophanes of Byzantium, who was appointed Librarian of the great Alexandrian Library about 195 B.C., first systematized, if he did not invent, the use of stops for the purpose of editing texts. He is also credited with the provision of the symbols for quantity (makron and mikron), and for accent (acute, grave, and circumflex), the latter to preserve pronunciation, which, Sandys explains, 'was being corrupted by the mixed populations of the Greek world'. The population of Egyptian cities such as Alexandria, except for an intellectual minority, was not essentially Greek in character; and the need for punctuation marks, as an aid to intelligibility, probably arose when Greek became the educational and cultural medium throughout the Eastern Mediterranean world.

The most useful stops introduced by Aristophanes of Byzantium were those that correspond to our semicolon (*hypostigme*), comma (*mese stigme*) and full-stop (*teleia stigme*). The symbols consisted of a dot placed respectively at the foot, in the middle and at the top[2] of the lettering or *grammata*, as it was called. But the system of Aristophanes was devised for the textual work of scholars, and does not seem to have been generally accepted by scribes; for it does not appear in extant documents, the high point (full-stop) being the only one of these stops regularly used before Christ, for example in the *Bacchylides* papyrus (first century B.C.).

In the Christian era, to which the majority of manuscripts belong, the scribes of Latin manuscripts attempted to follow the Greek symbols, though uncertain of the value of the stops placed in certain positions. They translated the Greek names as *subdistinctio*, *distinctio media* and *distinctio finalis* respectively. By the seventh century A.D. they seem to have abandoned any fixed value for the point in the body of a sentence, and inserted it simply to indicate a break or pause of some sort. The first of the modern stops to appear was the semicolon, with its present form, in the seventh century; it was followed by the comma (a symbol derived in form from a small medial virgule), and the mark of interrogation in the ninth century. But at this time the full-stop was still an uncertain symbol.

In addition to its ordinary function, the semicolon (;) was used from the eighth century as a mark of *interrogation* in Greek Script. The origin and function

---

[1] *History of Classical Scholarship*, Ch. VIII.

[2] Different interpretations of these positions are given by Sandys op. cit., and Maunde Thompson, *Introduction to Greek and Latin Palaeography*, p. 60. I have accepted the account of the latter; Sandys regards *hypostigme* as the comma, and *mese stigme*, the middle dot, as the colon.

of the inverted semicolon, which also appeared in the eighth century, is not satisfactorily explained; it is often represented by a dot surmounted by a schoolmaster's tick, and Maunde Thompson suggests that its value might have been between our comma and semicolon.[1] There is some probability that, in other than Greek texts, the inverted semicolon gave rise, in the ninth century, to the modern mark of interrogation already referred to. The symbol (tick above point) is used to mark questions in the manuscript of John Bale's *King Johan* (*c.* 1560), and unmistakable inverted semicolons for a question mark occur in the quartos of *The Troublesome Reign of King John* (Black-letter or Gothic type, 1591) and *King Lear* (1608).

The word *virgule* has been used, and needs some explanation. It is a French word from the Latin *virgula*, meaning 'a small twig or rod', and the symbol for it appears originally to have been the Greek *koronis*, resembling our figure seven (7). In mediaeval manuscripts it was simplified to a thin sloping or upright stroke, with the value roughly of the modern comma. In manuscripts of Chaucer and other poets, the virgule was also used to mark the caesura, or medial pause of the verse line.

III

Other Readers' Symbols

There are other symbols, generally regarded as punctuation marks, which are not really stops or pauses, but signs to the reader; for instance, the apostrophe or mark of elision, the hyphen, and marks of quotation, deletion and isolation. Most of the following seem to have been in use by Aristophanes of Byzantium:

(a) *Apostrophe* (through French and Latin, from Greek *apostrophos*, meaning 'the turning away or rejection of a letter'). The symbol for this was a curve, a straight accent or a dot. In Greek the symbol had other functions; for example, (i) placed after a name, to mark its foreign origin, (ii) to separate double consonants, and (iii) to distinguish concurrent identical vowels. The last survived in Elizabethan and Jacobean printed plays.

(b) *Hyphen* (from the Greek noun *hyphen* derived from the adverb of the same form, meaning 'together'). This was a curved or straight short line placed under letters to indicate compounding. It occurs as a straight line in the Harris Homer (first century A.D.).[2] The use of a symbol to denote word-division at the end of a line came much later, and was at first a

---

[1] See *Introduction to Greek and Latin Palaeography*, pp. 60–1.
[2] This was a papyrus of the eighteenth book of the *Iliad*, recovered 1849–50, and was first owned by A. C. Harris of Alexandria.

N

simple point. In the eleventh century the modern line appeared sporadically, and was systematically used in the twelfth century.[1] Some of the early
printers, notably Gutenberg in his Bible, used the double stroke for end-
of-the-line word-division.

(c) *Marks of quotation.* Either a wedge, cross, horizontal stroke or waved
stroke was inserted in the margin of Greek manuscripts to draw attention
to a quotation. A less frequent practice was indentation or extension into
the margin.

(d) *Marks of deletion.* Inverted commas, dots and even accents were used in
Greek manuscripts to mark off deleted words or passages, one at the
beginning and one at the end. A line drawn through the offending words is
also found.

(e) *Marks of isolation.* Where a modern printer would use italics to isolate a
word from the rest of the text, the Greek scribe usually drew a line above
it. The British Museum papyrus of a grammatical work of Tryphon
(c. 300 B.C.) is a unique document in that it contains such markings as well
as partial separation of words.

IV

Time and Elocutionary Value of Stops

It can be assumed, then, that by the ninth century A.D. scribes were punctua-
tion-conscious, though palaeographers are not entirely sure of the significance
of the symbols they employed. Punctuation, starting as marks of separation,
next became an instrument of textual and syntactical elucidation, and finally
added the function of breathing pauses, to which had been arbitrarily given a
certain value in time. At what stage did the time-pause concept assume importance? It needs little imagination to suggest that it may have developed with the
language of drama, poetry, oratory, or song, and that it came into being in the
late Middle Ages or the European Renaissance.

Words are like coins; they have their obverse and reverse in sense and sound;
and sounds are not only spoken and heard, but require for their continued production breath and attention. In the use of words (speech), the one side of the
coin gives us *science* (intelligibility), the other side *art* (admiration). Style arises
when proper attention is given to both these functions. When natural speech
is converted to writing, however, intonation disappears; and punctuation is a
partial attempt to replace it by the use of recognized symbols.

In Greek rhetoric there had also been developed a system of dividing texts
into periods, or sense-groups, which came to be known as *Colometry.* This

[1] See Maunde Thompson, *Introduction to Greek and Latin Palaeography,* p. 58.

system was employed for such literature as was intended to be read in public, for instance, speeches, scriptural texts and the like. The poetical books of the Bible, such as the Psalms and the books of King Solomon, were marked off in this way, and the Greeks called them *bibloi stichereis*. St. Jerome followed this system (which he had also found in the manuscripts of Cicero and Demosthenes) throughout his Latin version of the Bible, the *Vulgate*, and his famous phrase 'per cola et commata', in the preface to *Isaiah*, records the ancestry of two of our punctuation symbols, the *colon* and the *comma*. A *comma* was apparently a clause of less than eight syllables, and a *colon* (or limb) one of from eight to seventeen syllables.[1]

Many of the colons in *The Authorized Version of the Bible* (1611) are probably traceable to Hebrew and Greek colometry, for example in Psalm 73.

2. But as for mee, my feete were almost gone: my steps had wellnigh slipt
12. Behold, these are the ungodly: who prosper in the world, they increase in riches.

Here the colons mark pauses; they are not syntactical, but rhythmical. A study of poetical pauses will no doubt show that they sometimes coincide with syntactical stopping; but as frequently they do not, because speech, as art, is not to be dominated by the logical bias to which syntax tends to lean. The dual purpose of punctuation has thus been the cause of·much misunderstanding.

But if ancient colometry helps to explain the rhythmical pause, it does not explain the relative value given to the pauses concerned, such as, 1 for the comma, 2 for the colon or the semicolon, and 3 for the period. The date of emergence of the time concept is uncertain, but it is generally supposed to be as late as the sixteenth century. The principle is stated in England by George Puttenham in his *Arte of English Poesie* (1589) Book II, Ch. 5, and by Simeon Daines, more precisely, in his *Orthoepia Anglicana* of 1640.[2] The actual time-value must, of necessity, be arbitrary; and I can only suggest that the theory is a legacy of the song and hymn-writers of the age of syllabic verse, commencing with the Ambrosian hymns in the latter half of the fourth century. But the matter needs detailed investigation, particularly in the Romance and Germanic literatures of Western Europe; no account appears to exist. As applied to literature in general, and even to poetry in particular, the system was probably fallacious, but it persisted for many hundreds of years, and even now dies hard.

[1] See Maunde Thompson, *Introduction to Greek and Latin Palaeography*, p. 70.
[2] See edition by M. Rösler and R. Brotanek (Halle, Max Niemeyer, 1908), p. 70. Daines calls the semicolon *Comma-colon*, and gives it a pause-value of 2, the colon a value of 3, and the period 6, though he admits the value of this final stop varies according to place and circumstance.

V

Summary of uses in the Scribal Period

It may be concluded that punctuation in the scribal era flourished only in periods of scholarship. The purpose of scholars was to elucidate, and they were able to use punctuation best to this end when the syntax of their language became more or less settled by literary usage. At the same time, increased attention to punctuation was usually given when ancient traditions of literature were in danger of disintegration, for example, in Greek in the Alexandrian Age, in Hebrew at the time of the Masorites, and in the Latin of Western European scribes at the end of the sixth century, when the Roman Empire was in decline. By the ninth century every scribe worthy of the name was using punctuation marks of some sort, but his system, like his spelling, was a matter of individual taste. In many manuscripts some of the punctuation is the work of a later hand. During the three centuries (seventh–ninth), the most persistent users of punctuation were the Irish and Anglo-Saxon scribes, to whom Latin was an alien tongue. In their use of Latin they had nonetheless some guidance from traditional scholarship; but when punctuation was applied to the rising vernacular literatures of Western Europe, it was inevitably simpler. After the twelfth century the scribes contented themselves with the use of the colon and the period, reserving the semicolon for abbreviated words. The colon was simply an intermediate stop, often replaced by the inverted semicolon (usually a dot superseded by a tick), or what is now the exclamation mark (!). This last symbol was not, however, used for true exclamations. In cursive writing no punctuation was usually deemed necessary at all.

VI

The Age of Printing

Punctuation, as we have come to know it, is an invention of the age of printing; but its development was tardy. The tradition that the printers inherited from the scribes was a slight one, actuated by no clear conception of the purpose of stops. Consequently the early printers, like the scribes, were conservative.

In Coster's *Doctrinale*, printed in Haarlem about 1458, and sometimes claimed as the first printed book, there is no punctuation at all. Gutenberg, Fust and Schoeffer in Germany apparently used only the point and the colon; Sweynheym, Pannartz and Jenson in Italy did likewise, but the two former added the semicolon as a mark of abbreviation. In Italy and France the early printers took the liveliest interest in punctuation. In Italy the virgule, mark of interrogation, comma and round brackets were already in use in the last quarter of the fifteenth century;[1] and it is possible that earlier dates can be found for their employment in the work of the fifteenth-century printers of Paris. Crosses were frequently introduced by the Italian printers instead of round dots for the colon and period. The printer in Italy who had most foresight in the use of punctuation was Aldus Manutius (1450–1515). This great man, who devoted his life to scholarship, made his colleagues in the printing-house speak Greek, and founded his types on the best handwriting of his amanuenses. He also made a study of punctuation and determined the future use of the comma, semicolon, colon and period. His refinements can be seen in the reproductions from his *Hypnerotomachia Poliphili* (1499), and the beautiful editions in italic of Vergil's *Bucolics* (1501) and the works of Petrarch (1501).[2]

In England the press of Caxton (1420–91), the first printer in Europe to confine his attention to the productions of his own tongue, employed three punctuation symbols, the virgule, the colon and the final point or period. His virgule is an angular line of separation between words, and this was for several decades preferred to the comma in black-letter printing. The first use of the comma noticed in black-letter is in Copland's *Devout treatyse called the tree and twelve frutes of the holy goost* (1534).[3] Very few incunabula produced anywhere in Europe were printed in Roman type; but after 1500 this type came increasingly into use. John Siberch, the first Cambridge printer, in 1521 printed an *Oration* of Archbishop Bullock in a fine Roman type; and Wynkyn de Worde, who acquired Caxton's press at his death, in 1528 printed the *Dialogues of Lucian* in italic. In these works are found the earliest uses of the comma to replace the virgule.[4]

VII

English Names for Symbols

The second quarter of the sixteenth century marked the appearance in English of many names for stops, whose etymology and history are of interest. My information is largely dependent on citations in the *Oxford English Dictionary*. As might have been expected, the symbols themselves were in use by printers considerably before their names appear in writing.

1. *Distinction.* This was the usual name given to pointing in England in the

---

[1] See W. Dana Orcutt, *The Book in Italy*, plates 64a, 87, 76 and 69.
[2] Ibid., plates 36, 38, 39.
[3] See F. S. Isaac, *English and Scottish Printing Types*, Fig. 46.
[4] Ibid., Figs. 49 (b) and 10 (b).

sixteenth century. The first use recorded in the *O.E.D.* is dated 1552, and the last in Ben Jonson's *Grammar* (1640). Jonson seems to have got the term from Richard Mulcaster's *Elementarie* (1582), and the latter owed it probably to the Latin grammarian Pierre de la Ramée, whose *Grammatica* appeared in 1572.

2. *Virgule.* The first use in English cited by the *O.E.D.* is as *virgulers* in 1610 by Marcellini. Hoffman in his *Beginnings of Writing* (1895) says that 'according to Orozco y Berra these virgules or commas represent the verb to blow or to hum'. This is an amusingly conjectural derivation, comparable to Alexander Hume's statement that the comma 'is pronounced in reading with a short sob',[1] the word 'sob' in Scots meaning 'a puff or breath of air'.

3. *Comma* (from Greek *komma*, a piece cut off, a short clause). The first use in English noted by the *O.E.D.* is from Palsgrave. Even as late as the seventeenth century the name was used for 'a group of words in a sentence', as well as for the pause itself. In Greek rhetoric and prosody the pause must originally have been intended to enable the phrase to be mentally digested. The term 'inverted commas' does not appear in English, according to the *O.E.D.*, until 1838 (*Hallam's History of Literature*).

4. *Colon* (from Greek *kolon*, clause, sentence, or portion of a strophe). The first use in English noted by the *O.E.D.* in 1589 is from Puttenham; but, strangely enough, Jonson in his *Grammar* (1640) calls the symbol (:) simply a 'pause'. In Greek rhetoric and prosody the colon's general function was to mark off a rhythmical period. The term *semicolon*, originally intended for a shorter division of the sentence, apparently did not occur in English until 1692, in the text of Ben Jonson's *Grammar* found in the third folio. In the version of the second follio (1640), probably set up from Jonson's own notes, the symbol (;) is called *subdistinction*,[2] and Simon Daines in his *Orthoepia Anglicana* of the same date calls it *comma-colon*.

5. *Period* (from Greek *periodos*, a way round, a rounded or completed sentence). The first use recorded in the *O.E.D.* in 1533 is by Sir Thomas More. In Greek the term was applied to the full grammatical sentence, with the parts properly related according to the principles of rhetoric. The phrase 'full-stop' is a comparatively new coinage, dating apparently from Mason's *English Grammar* (1886).

6. *Apostrophe* (in the sixteenth century *apostrophus*). The first recorded use in

---

[1] See *Of the Orthographie and Congruitie of the Britan Tongue* (1617), Ch. 13.

[2] Jonson in his *Grammar*, Bk. 2, Ch. IX, suggests that the comma indicates a longer pause than the sub-distinction (semicolon). This is surely erroneous. He himself uses the semicolon as a logical, rather than a temporal, pause.

the *O.E.D.* in the sense of 'a rejected letter', is from Shakespeare's *Love's Labour's Lost* (1594), Act IV.2.126.

7. *Hyphen.* The first use cited in the *O.E.D.* is by A. Hume (1617). Mulcaster in his *Elementarie* (1582) calls the double hyphen, for syllable division at the end of a line, a 'breaker'.

8. *Point of Interrogation.* In Spanish this was placed, inverted, before the question also. The first use recorded in the *O.E.D.* is from Florio's *Dictionary* (1598).

9. *Note of Exclamation.* The first use noted in the *O.E.D.* is by J. Smith (1657), with illustrative symbol. Not much reliance need be placed on the suggestion that the symbol is derived from the Latin exclamation of joy *Io*, the first letter being superimposed above the last.

10. *Brackets* (the singular apparently from Spanish *Bragueta*, diminutive of *braga*, Lat. *bracae*, breeches). Square brackets were originally called *crotchets* (1676), and round brackets parentheses (1715). The first English use of the word *brackets* is noted by the *O.E.D.* in G. Fisher's *Instructor* (1750); yet the symbol was in use by English printers in the latter half of the sixteenth century, and round brackets were employed by Alexander Minutianus in Milan as early as 1498.[1]

11. *Dash* (from the Middle English verb *daschen* or *dassen*, probably from an unrecorded Old Norse form *daska*). In the *O.E.D.* the first authenticated use of the word for the punctuation mark occurs in Swift, *On Poetry* (1733):

> In modern wit all printed trash is
> Set off with num'rous breaks - - and dashes —

12. *Quotation Marks.* These were at first placed only before sententious sayings and proverbs, the commas being at the foot of the line. They were originally called quotation *quadrats*, and this term is first recorded in the *O.E.D.* from Moxon's *Mechanic Exercises* (1683). The first use of the term 'quotation marks' cited in the *O.E.D.* is dated 1897.

VIII

Aldus Manutius on the Use of Symbols

The author of *Interpungendi Ratio* (1561) was not Aldus Manutius, printer of the classics, who died in 1515, but his grandson, son of Paul, who inherited his father's printing establishment. The treatise is only part of a greater work *Orthographiae Ratio*, and consists of seven pages commencing on page 791. Manutius inherited the tradition of textual integrity of his grandfather, and his

---

[1] See W. D. Orcutt, *The Book in Italy*, plate 69.

notes are concerned wholly with the logical and syntactical function of stops. He discusses only such symbols as writers and printers used before and during his own time: the comma, semicolon, colon, period, mark of interrogation and parentheses (or round brackets), though he does not always give them these names. Their practice had, in the main, been demonstrated in the texts printed by his grandfather.

Manutius starts by saying that complex ideas, if separated, become more intelligible. The comma is to separate words that differ only slightly from each other, but separation without purpose is an excess that clogs instead of advancing the meaning. Yet he himself uses it, as did Ben Jonson later, to separate co-ordinates; for example, 'public, and private affairs'.

The semicolon, on the other hand (says Manutius), is employed to separate words opposed in meaning to each other, or to mark off by a pause of inter-mediate value a dependent statement; for example, 'Our good sense teaches us that, if our lot be ill, we must not grieve too much; if good, we must rejoice with moderation.'

The colon, next stop in length, effects a stronger break in the sentence; and in a long sentence has often to be repeated, thereby breaking the sentence up into its integral parts.

The full-stop is used after the completion of a sentence; but in some writers, who prefer short sentences, has a kind of intermediate function like a colon; in which case it is not followed by a capital letter. If an altogether different subject is introduced, then the full-stop must be supplemented by a space. Manutius seems to have in mind modern paragraph indentation.

Manutius has no exclamation symbol, but advises the use of a single point. When a question is prominent at the beginning, and the sentence then con-tinues for some length, a question mark should not bring up the rear, but a single point should be employed. Manutius is against the use of brackets for interpolated phrases and clauses, and suggests that the latter should be marked off by commas and semicolons. Parentheses are for words that do not form part of a sentence, and do not depend on any word either preceding or following.

IX

Conclusion

It is a safe generalization that, in the last quarter of the sixteenth century, if not earlier, composition was heard by a sort of internal ear, and not planned, until Ben Jonson demonstrated it in his first folio, for the perusal of a silent reader. The arguments in Donne's *Sermons* and Hooker's *Laws of Ecclesiastical Polity* (works contemporary with Jonson's) were couched in complex terms of eloquent persuasion, and not of logical reasoning, which favours a shorter and more manageable structure of sentence.

The evolution of modern punctuation is bound up with the rise of prose of plain-statement in Jonson, Bacon, Dryden, Hobbes, Addison and Swift. For nearly a century the structure of prose adumbrated in the works of Ben Jonson, and punctuated by him to mark its logical and syntactical features, co-existed with the older cadenced sentences, modelled on Cicero, in prose of longer flight and periodic structure. Modifications in the method of punctuation necessarily accompanied changes in the method of exposition, and the different uses to which prose could be put. The result was that the eighteenth century editors of Elizabethan plays inherited a totally different system; hence A. W. Pollard's statement: 'By (Dr.) Johnson's day the punctuation which we find in Elizabethan books, more esxpecially in plays, may be correctly described as a lost art. Dr. Johnson might do what he pleased with colons and commas. He could make them help to show how a sentence of Shakespeare's should be parsed; but he could not make them show how it would be delivered by a great actor—because that might have interfered with the parsing.'[1]

In the seventeenth century, along with changes in sentence structure, and the rejection of what Thomas Sprat calls 'the amplifications, digressions and swellings of style',[2] went certain modifications in the value and function of the stops themselves. Though the comma was, and is, the most individual of all stops in use, by 1700 writers and printers had become far more economical in their employment of it than Ben Jonson. By the beginning of the twentieth century Fowler could, indeed, regard the excessive use of commas as a spot-plague.

During the period from Ben Jonson to Dr. Johnson the semicolon, while retaining its temporal function, became also a point of balance and precise distinction, but one used only when longer clauses or sentences had to be separated. It is thus at one and the same time a breathing stop and a mark of logical separation.

But the most revolutionary change came in the use of the colon; and it took a long time to effect, not being complete until the nineteenth century. This was the complete rejection of the colon as a time-pause, whose value originally lay between a semicolon and full-stop. The old colon was a long pause, and frequently necessitated the capital letter after it that Ben Jonson had been careful, in the appropriate place, to give. By the eighteenth century it was being used as a logical stop, alongside of its old temporal function. In the nineteenth century logical function alone remained, being confined, except for individual

---

[1] *Shakespeare's Fight with the Pirates*, p. 89.
[2] See 'History of the Royal Society' in Craik's *English Prose Selections* (Vol. III), p. 272.

foible, to use before lists, and to mark off statements that expand or explain what has already been adumbrated.

By the Restoration in England the battle for reformed punctuation, based in intention, if not always in practice, on the syntactical relations of the parts of the sentence, had been won. To illustrate some aspects of this transformation, I append a passage from pages 205–6 of James Harrington's *Commonwealth of Oceana*, printed by D. Pakeman in 1656:

> These things among us are sure enough to be censured, but by such only as doe not know the nature of a Commonwealth; for to tell men that they are free, and yet to curb the genious of a People in a lawfull Recreation unto which they are naturally inclined, is to tell a tale of a Tub. I have heard the Protestant Ministers in *France*, by men that were wise, and of their own profession, much blamed in that they forbad Dancing, a Recreation to which the genious of that aire is so enclining, that they lost many who would not loose that; nor doe they lesse then blame the former determination of rashnesse, who now gently connive at that which they had so roughly forbidden. These sports in *Oceana* are so Governed, that they are pleasing for private diversion, and profitable unto the Publique: For the Theaters soon defrayed their own Charge, and now bring in a good Revenue. All this so far from the Detriment of virtue, that it is to the improvement of it, seeing Women that heretofore made havock of their Honours, that they might have their pleasures, are now incapable of their pleasures, if they loose their Honours.

But for the old temporal colon after 'Publique', and the use of capitals to mark substantives, the punctuation is modern. It is to be noted that the first letters of all nouns are not capitalized. The capital to mark the verb 'Governed' may indicate that the capitalized words are those that bear the major emphasis in reading. But it is just possible that the capital letter is here a relic, like the finale -*e* in Elizabethan spelling.

In punctuation, little progress has really been made since the late seventeenth century. The ambivalence of our code leaves plenty of room for individuality, and it is certain that standardization in the use of stops is neither practical nor desirable. In one branch of orthography a great freedom was sacrificed, when spelling became fixed in the eighteenth century. In pointing, it is to be hoped that this individualism will be preserved, even if it leads to the eccentricity of a recent poet who revolutionized his system by the simple device of putting a full-stop after every word.

Index